OXFORD READINGS IN FEMINISM

CONTEMPORARY FRENCH

OXFORD READINGS IN FEMINISM

Contemporary French Feminism

Edited by

Kelly Oliver

and

Lisa Walsh

UNIVERSITY PRESS

OXFORD
UNIVERSITY PRESS

Great Clarendon Street, Oxford OX2 6DP

Oxford University Press is a department of the University of Oxford.
It furthers the University's objective of excellence in research, scholarship,
and education by publishing worldwide in

Oxford New York

Auckland Bangkok Buenos Aires Cape Town Chennai
Dar es Salaam Delhi Hong Kong Istanbul Karachi Kolkata
Kuala Lumpur Madrid Melbourne Mexico City Mumbai Nairobi
São Paulo Shanghai Taipei Tokyo Toronto

Oxford is a registered trade mark of Oxford University Press
in the UK and in certain other countries

Published in the United States
by Oxford University Press Inc., New York

Introduction, Notes, and Selection © Kelly Oliver and
Lisa Walsh 2004

The moral rights of the authors have been asserted

Database right Oxford University Press (maker)

First Published 2004

British Library Cataloguing in Publication Data

Data available

Library of Congress Cataloging in Publication Data

(Data applied for)

ISBN 0–19–9248346

1 3 5 7 9 10 8 6 4 2

Typeset in Minion
by RefineCatch Limited, Bungay, Suffolk
Printed in Great Britain by
Ashford Colour Press Limited, Gosport, Hampshire

Contents

CONTENTS

Notes on Contributors

Sylviane Agacinski is a professor of philosophy at the École des Hautes Études in Paris, where she is responsible for the research seminars in the social sciences. From 1986 to 1992 she was director of Collège International de Philosophie, in Paris. She is the author of several books, including. *Mimesis des Articulations, Qui a peur de la Philosophie?, Aparté: Conceptions and Deaths of Søren Kierkegaard, Volume: Philosophie et Politique de l'architecture, Critique de l'égocentrisme: l'événement de l'autre, Le Passeur de temps: Modernité et nostalgie, Parity of the Sexes*, and *Politique des sexes [précedé de] Mise au point sur la mixité.*

Alain Badiou. Philosopher, writer, and social critic, Alain Badiou was born in 1937 in Rabat, Morocco. He completed his *Agrégation de philosophie* after being a student at the École Normale Supérieure and the Université de Paris IV, Sorbonne. He taught philosophy at the Lycée de Reims between 1963 and 1965 and at the Université de Reims from 1965 until 1992. Badiou is currently a professor of philosophy at the École des Arts, Philosophie, et Esthétique (The School of Arts, Philosophy and Aesthetics) at the Université de Paris VIII, Vincennes-Saint-Denis, where he leads a research group on the topic of 'Lieux et transformations de la philosophie' ('Place and Transformations of Philosophy'). He also holds a professorship at the École Normale Supérieure at Paris. He is the author of several books, including *L'Être et l'événement, manifeste pour la philosophie, Le Nombre et les nombres, D'un désastre obscur, L'Éthique, Deleuze, Saint Paul. La Fondation de l'universalisme, Court traité d'ontologie transitoire, Abrégé de métapolitique*, and *Petit manuel d'inesthétique.*

Françoise Collin was born in Belgium and holds a doctorate in philosophy from the University of Louvain. She started her career teaching in Brussels and currently leads seminars at the Centre parisien d'études critiques (The Centre for Critical Studies) and lives in Paris. She is the author of several books, including *Maurice Blanchot et la question de l'écriture, Le Rendez-vous, Le Sexe des sciences, Emmanuel Levinas, Le Différend des sexes, de Platon à la parité, L'Homme est-il devenu superflu? Hannah Arendt, Je partirais d'un mot: le champ symbolique, L'Imagination politique des femmes*, and *Les Femmes de Platon à Derrida: Anthologie critique.*

Monique David-Ménard was born in Lyon in 1947. She completed a masters degree in philosophy with Paul Ricœur (Université de Nanterre, 1968), a doctorate in clinical psychopathology and psychoanalysis with Pierre Fédida (Université Paris VII, 1978), and a doctorate in philosophy with Jean-Marie Beysade (Université Paris V, Sorbonne-nouvelle, 1990). She is currently

Professeur de Chaire Supérieure and a director of research at the Université Paris VII, Denis Diderot. She is a practising psychoanalyst, and presently serves as the Secretary of the Scientific Commission of the Société de Psychanalyse Freudienne. She is the author of several books, including *L'Hystérique entre Freud et Lacan: Corps et langage en psychanalyse*, *La Folie dans la raison pure: Kant lecteur de Swedenborg*, and *Tout le plaisir est pour moi*.

GENEVIÈVE FRAISSE is a research associate at the National Centre for Scientific Research (CNRS), where she produces a distinctive blend of philosophical, historical, and feminist analyses. In 1974, Fraisse helped to found the Centre for Research on the Ideologies of Revolt at the University of Paris VIII, Vincennes, from which *Révoltes logiques* (Logical Revolts) was launched in 1975. She is the author of several books, including *Clémence Royer, philosophe et femme de sciences*, *Muse de la raison: démocratie et exclusion des femmes en France*, *Opinions des femmes: de la veille au lendemain de la Révolution française*, *L'Exercice du savoir et la différence des sexes*, *La Différence des sexes*, *Les Femmes et leur histoire*, and *La Controverse des sexes*.

GISÈLE HALIMI. Born on 27 July 1927 in French colonial Tunisia (La Goulette), Gisèle (Zoïza) Halimi first travelled to France to study law and philosophy at the Institute of Political Studies in Paris. She became a lawyer in 1948, and practised law in Tunisia until 1958, when she was called to become a member of the Paris Bar Association. Halimi served as the French ambassador to UNESCO from 1984 to 1986, when she retired back into private practice. She is the author of several books, including *Djamila Boupacha* (with Simone de Beauvoir), *Le Procès de Burgos*, *La Cause des femmes*, *Le Programme commun des femmes*, *Viol: le procès d'Aix-en-Provence*, *Le Lait de l'oranger*, *Embellie perdue*, *La Nouvelle Cause des femmes*, *Fritna*, and *L'Autre Moitié de l'humanité*.

FRANÇOISE HÉRITIER was born in France in the 1930s. She studied with Claude Lévi-Strauss at the Collège de France in the late 1950s, and in the early 1960s began ethnographic fieldwork in sub-Sarahan West Africa, primarily with the Samo, Pana, and Mossi peoples in the Upper Volta. Héritier currently teaches at the Collège de France and serves as director of studies at l'École des Hautes Études en Sciences Sociales. She is the author of several books, including *L'Exercice de la parenté*, *Les Deux Sœurs et leur mère: Anthropologie de l'inceste*, *De la violence: Séminaire de Françoise Héritier*, and *Contraception: contrainte ou liberté?*.

JULIA KRISTEVA was born in 1941 in Bulgaria. She was educated by French nuns, studied literature, and worked as a journalist before going to Paris in 1966 to do graduate work with Lucien Goldmann and Roland Barthes. While in Paris she finished her doctorate in French literature, was appointed to the faculty of the Department of Texts and Documents at the University of Paris VI, Denis Diderot and began psychoanalytic training. Currently, Kristeva is director of the Department of Science of Texts and Documents at the University of Paris VII, where she teaches in the Department of Literature and Humanities. She is the author of several books, including *La Révolution du langage poétique, Pouvoirs de l'horreur, Histoires d'amour, Soleil noir: Dépression et melancolie, Les Nouvelles Maladies de l'âme, Sens et non-sens de la révolte: Pouvoirs et limites de la psychanalyse I, La Révolte intime: Pouvoirs et limites de la psychanalyse II,* and *Le Génie féminin, vol. i, Hannah Arendt* (Paris: Fayard).

MICHÈLE LE DŒUFF was born in 1948 in France. She completed her doctorate degree in philosophy in 1980 and has subsequently taught in the women's studies department at the University of Geneva and in the philosophy department at her alma mater, the *École Normale Supérieure* at Fontaney, where she also held the position of conference director. Le Dœuff is currently research director at the *Centre National de la Recherche Scientifique* (CNRS/ National Centre for Scientific Research). She is the author of several books, including *L'Imaginaire philosophique, L'Étude et le rouet,* and *Des femmes, de la philosophie, etc. Le Sexe du savoir.*

CLAIRE NAHON is a clinical psychologist currently completing her doctorate in Fundamental Psychopathology and Psychoanalysis. Her research focuses on the notion of trans-sexuality, as opposed to transexuality. She is the author of several articles, including 'Granoff, le freudisme et la puissance animique', 'Les transsexuels: d'une certaine vision de la différence', and 'L'envers du miroir ou la psychanalyse à l'épreuve de l'homosexualité'.

KELLY OLIVER is W. Alton Jones Chair of Philosophy at Vanderbilt University. She is the author of seven books: *The Colonization of Psychic Space: A Psychoanalytic Social Theory of Oppression, Noir Anxiety* (co-authored with B. Trigo), *Witnessing: Beyond Recognition, Subjectivity Without Subjects: From Abject Fathers to Desiring Mothers, Family Values: Subjects Between Nature and Culture, Womanizing Nietzsche: Philosophy's Relation to 'the Feminine',* and *Reading Kristeva: Unraveling the Double-Bind.* She has edited several books, including *The Portable Kristeva, The French Feminism Reader,* and *Between the Psyche and the Social.* She has also edited special issues of *Hypatia: A Journal for Feminist Philosophy* and *Studies in Practical Philosophy: A Journal of Ethical and Political Philosophy.*

SABINE PROKHORIS trained at the École Normale Supérieure. Currently she is a professor of philosophy, and a practising psychoanalyst in Paris. She is also an editor of the journal *Les Temps modernes.* She is the author of several books, including *Le Drame de Faust dans l'œuvre de Freud: Travail de la citation et élaboration métapsychologique,* and *Le Sexe prescrit: La Différence sexuelle en question.*

MONIQUE SCHNEIDER was born in 1935 in Mirecourt, a village in Lorraine, France. After graduate work at l'École Normale Supérieure, she taught in

Grenoble until 1970, when she was appointed director of research at the Centre Nationale de la Recherche Scientifique (National Centre for Scientific Research), Paris. Schneider has been a practising psychoanalyst since the 1980s, and is affiliated with l'École de la Cause Freudienne (School of the Freudian Cause). Now director of research emerita at the CNRS, Schneider practises psychoanalysis in Paris. She is the author of several books, including *De l'excorcisme à la psychanalyse: le féminin expurgé, Freud et le plaisir, La Parole et l'inceste: de l'enclos linguistique à la liturgie psychanalytique, Le Trauma et la filiation paradoxale. De Freud à Ferenczi, La Part de l'ombre. Approche d'un trauma féminin, Don Juan et le procès de la séduction, Généalogie du masculin.*

Lisa Walsh received her Ph.D. in 1998 and is now a lecturer in French Studies at the University of Nottingham. Her first book, *Subjects of Love and Desire: Readings in Maternity and Ethics* is forthcoming with Rowman & Littlefield Press. She recently published a translation of Sylviane Agacinski's *Parity of the Sexes* as well as several articles, such as 'Paternal Perversion, the Imaginary Father and the Promise of Love', and 'From Paternity to Maternity: Lévinas, Irigaray and the Shifting of Ethical Paradigm'. She is also an editor at *Nottingham French Studies.*

Acknowledgements

We would like to thank Teresa Brennan for supporting this project. For researching and writing the biographical introductions, we would like to thank Doris Rita Alfonso for Chapters 2 and 7, Cynthia Paccacerqua for Chapters 1, 5, and 11, Steve Edwin for Chapters 4, 8, and 12, and Lysanne Fauvel for Chapters 3 and 10.

We would like to thank Katherine Roberts for translations, which were funded by Florida Atlanta University.

We would also like to thank the following people for their permission to allow the reproduction of their work in this anthology: Sylviane Agacinski, Alain Badiou, Françoise Collin, Monique David-Ménard, Geneviève Fraisse, Gisèle Halimi, Françoise Héritier, Julia Kristeva, Michèle Le Dœuff, Claire Nahon, Sabine Prokhoris, Monique Schneider.

Introduction
The Swell of the Third Wave

Lisa Walsh

On ne naît pas femme: on le devient.
(Simone de Beauvoir)

Simone de Beauvoir's famous dictum, literally translated: 'One is not born woman, one becomes this', quite aptly encapsulates the theoretical bulwark of what has come to be known as 'first wave' feminism in France.[1] Although many French women had fought for varying degrees of equal status under the law prior to the late nineteenth century, the first wave of French feminism is generally considered to have begun with the suffragettes' turn of the century struggles for the right to vote and to have concluded with existentialist feminism's call for equal recognition for women at all levels of the social and symbolic orders. De Beauvoir's groundbreaking opus, *The Second Sex*, dissects the inner and outer workings of a historical, patriarchal oppression of women—in such diverse domains as biology, politics, philosophy, and literature—as a means to demonstrating the undeniable veracity of the above dictum. Expanding existentialism's claim that 'existence precedes essence' to include the essence of the 'fairer sex', de Beauvoir sets herself the monumental task of a thoroughgoing examination of the ways in which femininity, and even femaleness, are cultural constructs which may or may not be taken up by any given individual. And here the rather awkward literal translation proves useful. The French pronoun 'on', like its English equivalent 'one' is not gender specific: 'one', in other words, is born free of gender definition and only later becomes 'woman'—pronominalized here with a masculine/neuter pronoun best translated as 'this'. One does not become 'her' (in which case the feminine pronoun 'la' would have been chosen) but rather 'this'—a social category called 'woman'.

First wave feminism, then, as most rigorously theorized by de

1

Beauvoir in its existentialist incarnation, argues that if women are inferior to men, it is not because they were born that way, but rather because they became that way through an insidious form of cultural indoctrination most often cleverly disguised as biological determinism. In order to throw off their shackles, women must first recognize the intense network of symbolic underpinnings inherent in the oppressive construction of the masculine/feminine hierarchy as equivalent to the male/female distinction. Once the necessary connection between female and feminine, male and masculine has been revealed as not so necessary after all, an individual might then, theoretically at least, be born of the female sex (here figured as gender neutral), and yet still reject any or all of those negative qualities associated with femininity—passivity, irrationality, masochism, and so on ad nauseum—qualities traditionally used to justify her unequal status within the public sphere as well as her relegation to the private one. In other words, once the now rather standard sex/gender, nature/nurture divide is recognized as such, individuals of the female sex might hope to *become* more than 'this'.[2] Since, as de Beauvoir argues, it is this *becoming woman* that has kept the 'second sex' in its place throughout the history of civilization, if female subjects can avoid this unenviable fate, their socio-cultural status as inferior beings will no longer be justifiable, and patriarchy will lose its strongest symbolic foothold. Women (as opposed to 'woman') can and should reject the negative pole of the masculine/feminine binary; only then will they be able to lay claim to the same status as that afforded to men. The end goal, it is important to note here, is the Enlightenment ideal of Equality.

The socio-political revolutions constitutive of May 1968 inaugurated a 'second wave' of feminism in France, one characterized by a turn away from a valorization of Equality and a move towards an affirmation of Difference.[3] Fuelled by a profound mistrust of politics as well as the notion of the individual inherent therein, this new generation of feminists seeks to effect what they see as a far more profound change in the patriarchal order not by challenging an unequal status of women with regard to men, or femininity with regard to masculinity, but rather by turning the very concept of Equality as a tool of phallocentric mastery on its head. Working (loosely) within and against the theoretical paradigms of socialism, psychoanalysis, and phenomenology, these feminists attack the dichotomous denigration of woman in relation to man by refusing the binary structure as such. They argue that by positing one term as positive and its other as a mirror negative, all sense of true difference becomes impossible. In other words, woman within the current symbolic framework is not so much unequal to man as she is his opposite, and consequently nothing other than the inverted mirror image of the Same. The oppression of women stems not from a denial of equal access to the positive terms of the binary, but rather from the symbolic division of the entire social and sub- jective fields into a violently oppositional systematics of Sameness that makes any sort of real difference—especially the fundamental difference(s) between man and woman—altogether impossible.[4]

Second wave feminism in France, then, might be seen as, in certain key respects, a direct response to and against first wave feminism. Refuting many of the most basic theoretical premises of de Beauvoir's analysis, second wave feminists approach the problematics of mascu- line domination from what has often been seen as a more abstract, less pragmatic position as they attempt to unravel the most profound symbolic manifestations of an other femininity. In particular, they seek to rethink those psychically grounded sexual differences related to the intricate dynamics of meaning, power, and language. To this end, many second wave feminists turn to aesthetics and psychoanalysis as means of unearthing the heretofore repressed truly other to—as opposed to the mirror opposite of—a hegemenous masculine order. For these women writers, once feminine subjectivity finds a certain figuration or expression outside the constructs of masculine ideology, vast symbolic changes become not only possible, but inevitable. The masculine symbolic order, on this reading, has always depended upon an absolute exclusion of 'true' femininity to maintain its logical illu- sion of universal coherence. Regardless, however, on closer inspection, this masculine pretension to all-inclusiveness cannot completely erase all traces of the feminine voice, and this is most especially evidenced within the domains of literature (in particular avant-garde literature) and psychoanalysis (in particular certain strains of post-Freudian thought). Consequently, whereas first wave feminism rejects psycho- analysis as yet another patriarchal means of explaining away women's inferiority, second wave feminists tend to view Freud's discovery of the mysteries of the unconscious as an invaluable tool in the struggle against patriarchy's denials of femininity.

While a solid explication of the particularities of the development of psychoanalysis in France would be impossible to present in this context, it is important to understand the uniquely French return to Freud in the years prior to May 1968 in order to approach the contri- butions of second wave French feminisms as well as many of the texts included in this collection. To put it rather roughly, then, Freud's simplistic and confused remarks on the nature of femininity caused a comprehensive, and comprehensible, rejection of psychoanalysis on the part of first wave feminists, a rejection that for the most part subsists in Anglo-American feminisms to this day. In France, however, Jacques Lacan's reinterpretation of Freud, whereby a biologistic determination of sexual difference gives way to a linguistic or symbolic one, proves fruitful as a theoretical framework within which one might begin to question not only the social and political functionings of patriarchy, but also the most profound mechanisms of the conscious and unconscious constructions of masculine and feminine subjectivities.[5] Lacan's work, then, becomes one of the main interlocutors within French feminist thought in the movements of the second wave. Lacan's linking of the unconscious to the symbolic order, to the extent that the unconscious is said to be structured like a language, holds out hope that even if feminine subjectivity has been refused and buried throughout the reign of patriarchy, it cannot have been thoroughly erased, and can therefore be excavated (just as is the unconscious in the course of the analytic process)—for the most part through recourse to aesthetic production.

As Geneviève Fraisse points out in her contribution to this collection, psychoanalysis and literature have proven the chosen sites of engagement as discourses concerning the relations between the sexes, and for this reason, second wave French feminists turn to these two sources as a means to delving into both historical and contemporary outbursts of an other femininity. During this period, one finds a renaissance in the production of feminine literature,[6] a revaluation of literary texts of the past that demonstrate qualities rendered invisible in their femininity, and a turn to psychoanalysis and post-structuralist philosophy as theoretical touchstones. The central proponents of second wave feminism, Hélène Cixous, Luce Irigaray, and Julia Kristeva (at least within the Anglo-American context—I will return to this rather sticky problematic),[7] despite their heterogeneity as thinkers, hold in common the contention that philosophy has always figured subjectivity on a masculine model of identity which insistently refuses to acknowledge that which lies outside the parameters of a unified, thoroughly self-conscious subject. In order to maintain this psychic model, then, sexual difference—as true *difference*—is denied as a logical impossibility within a theoretical field of sameness wherein no form(s) of otherness can be tolerated.

Psychoanalysis, and again, in particular Lacanian psychoanalysis, becomes useful here in its positing of an otherness inherent to each speaking subject: the unconscious, in its complete inaccessibility to the symbolic mechanisms of the conscious mind, creates a psychic structure whereby the subject is necessarily split or alienated from herself. To put it quite simply, one can never claim to *know* oneself according to traditional conceptions of knowledge. Furthermore, the question of sexual difference lies at the very heart of the subject's strangeness to herself, for it is through castration, instantiated with the last moment of the Oedipus complex, that the subject becomes fully subject *to* the symbolic order (as a subject *of* language). Not coincidentally, it is also at this moment that the subject takes up a position with regard to sexual identity. The girl, or feminine subject, enters into a *different* relation to the symbolic order than does the boy, or masculine subject. Though, needless to say, all this is quite complicated as well as contentious, suffice it to say that on Lacan's theorization (which is in many respects—and in particular in his valorization of the phallus as point of reference for all signification—controversial from a feminist point of view), masculine and feminine ego identities (i.e what it *means* to be a man or a woman within any given culture) differ distinctly from biological bodies (cf. Freud) and unconscious functionings—all of which maintain a substantial stake in the ways in which sexual difference plays out in the individual and collective psyches. So, whereas traditional philosophical understandings of subjectivity had considered the subject a neuter (read masculine!) being, femininity begins to play a pivotal role within a psychoanalytic understanding of subjectivity.

While second wave French feminism's psychoanalytic turn lends itself to criticism on many fronts—aside from the above-mentioned reservations as to the wisdom of a feminist adoption of psychoanalysis, a patriarchal discourse—the most recurrent point of contention between these feminists and feminists working from certain other conflicting theoretical points of view has been the question of essentialism. It has been argued that with the notion that subjects take up *either* a feminine position *or* a masculine one, and even if the feminine position is said to be privileged in some sense, one is returning to a pre-Beauvoirian notion of an essential woman that might potentially undermine women's ability to determine their own individual essences free from the constraints of gender identity.[8] In other words, women are once again forcibly defined in relation to Woman. In addition, it has been argued that the primacy given to sexual difference as before and beyond all other sites of difference—for example race, sexual orientation, and ethnicity—tends to negate or minimize the importance of these differences in both the social and psychic fields. And while these critiques are quite prevalent amongst other feminists writing in France, they are perhaps most interesting for our purposes here in understanding the Anglo-American receptions, both positive and negative, of 'French feminism' as mapped out through the texts of this second wave.

Before, then, turning to the third wave and the texts collected here, I would like to take into brief account second wave feminism's trans-atlantic (and to a lesser extent, trans-channel) impact. With the arrival of the second wave in many anglophone countries (the United States, England, and Australia most notably), 'French feminism', unlike let's say Italian Marxism, has most often found itself punctuated by inverted commas, an indication that the term should not be entirely understood as corresponding to some commonly understood or proper meaning, as the literal sum of its two terms. From the 1970s forward (i.e. with the onset of its second wave), 'French feminism' comes most commonly to refer to a variety of feminism qualified not only by its national origins, but also by *something else*—a certain sup-plement that somehow loosely traces the reception of these diverse, psychoanalytically informed theories of sexual difference within a more or less foreign Anglo-American context. And whereas feminisms did develop in France according to a certain logic internal to nation-ally defined intellectual and cultural climates, 'French feminism', it has been argued, did not exist *as such* prior to its transatlantic export. Do the inverted commas then serve to vitiate 'French feminism's' nationalizing first term?

Christine Delphy, a well-known French materialist feminist, answers in the affirmative arguing that in a colonizing move, American feminists have focused exclusively on those veins of feminism in France concerned with these questions of difference.[9] Accusing psy-choanalytically and/or phenomenologically informed feminisms of essentialism, she believes that American feminists have embraced, and indeed *created* the second wave as exclusive of, among other things, equality and materialist feminisms, for political reasons that have nothing to do with the historical, intellectual reality in France. Because, for Delphy, American feminists dare not hold such danger-ous positions as their own, they champion certain views as trendy European imports. In this way, the supposed national exteriority of these affirmations of difference relieve them of both intellectual and political responsibility while simultaneously allowing them, under the guise of feminism, to espouse anti-feminist doctrine. To this extent, Delphy ironically reiterates the traditionally Anglo-American feminist critique of feminisms of difference, but also attributes the flourishing of these feminisms to an Anglo-American colonialist enterprise designed to undermine materialist feminisms both within the United States and abroad. Yet while Delphy is quite correct in her reading of the powerful theoretical transatlantic connections that have developed in and around 'French feminism', I would argue that these connections have far more to do with the unique philosophical contributions made by feminisms of difference, contributions that are unarguably *French* in their debts to *French* philosophy and psychoanalytic theory. The importations of these theories of difference have provided many Anglo-American feminists with highly useful tools with which to think their political projects in terms other than those proffered by an Anglo-American philosophical tradition—even in those frequent cases when 'French feminism' itself is under explicit attack.[10] This is not, of course, to say that these were or are the *only* feminisms thriving in France. Nor is it to say that they are the only ones of any 'universal' relevance. Rather, it is to affirm that these so-called feminisms of difference have held, and continue to hold, particular interest in their diversions from radically Anglo-American notions of individual equality and identity.

With this in mind, for the present volume we have chosen texts that address primarily questions of difference, singularity and universality in order to begin to embark upon the process of thinking through the constitutional implications of a generational 'third wave' of feminisms in France. As we have seen, first wave French feminisms are categorizable (albeit a bit too neatly) as belonging to an intellectual climate roughly figured as modernity, stretching from the beginning of the twentieth century through the 1960s. Similarly, second wave feminisms have been quite justifiably linked to the era of postmodernity, in part due to their engagements with theories of post-structuralism. Now, although most of the questions posed by 'post'-philosophies appear to have been rather well digested by the academic corpus, a turn-of-the-millennial post post generation of ideas and thinkers has yet to be christened with any sort of *nom propre* (proper name). This said, however, there has been for some time a great deal of speculation as to whether we have entered into a historical moment of 'postfeminism', a moment characterized by the fact that most, if not all, of the goals feminism set out to achieve have been achieved.[11] On this view, then, feminism has become a moot political ideology and should either be abandoned in favour of more timely and progressive ideas or analysed in its effects as a historical movement. This volume presents a timely and convincing refutation of these attempts to tack the depoliticization of the post prefix onto an intellectual movement that continues to make strong contributions towards a rethinking of women as subjects within an increasingly confusing world context. In an age, however, when women have made so very many strides at all levels of the social and political, in large part as a result of the brilliant and rigorous work of several generations of feminists, what, one might ask, are we fighting for? And in particular, what does the current generation of French feminists, the third wave, offer to the furtherance of the cause of women at both the national and the global levels?

Indeed, within a political climate heated by the manifold spectres of globalization, one might wonder as to whether nationalizing adjectives still hold any intrinsic meaning or value, or whether universality has collapsed into the global logic of Capital and now holds sway over the intellectual as well as the political and economic domains. In her influential essay 'Women's Time',[12] Julia Kristeva argues that first wave French feminisms attempted to stake a certain claim to universal Woman's place in historical, linear time. Within a socio-political national context, French women sought to assert a certain identity to men in terms of concrete rights and status. Second wave feminism, on Kristeva's reading, with its emphases on Freudianism and Socialism, situated itself within a trans-European context which lay in direct opposition to the competing terms of ego psychology and consumer capitalism which determined, to a large extent, the social conscience of the United States. However, feminism now rejected the notion of linear time in addition to patriarchal models of the social and the historical, and therefore no longer sought to eke out a position therein. In correspondence (if not always solidarity) with other marginal movements of this cyclical moment of 'rupture', second wave feminism rejected universalism: 'we recognize an irreducible and self-sufficient singularity that is multifaceted, flowing, and in some ways non-identical'.[13] To put it succinctly, feminism no longer demanded certain rights that were beneficial to *all women*, but rather, affirmed the radical particularity of each woman as a unique feminine subject. A nationalist global position, then, has given way to a trans-European marginal one.

In a Hegelian turn, Kristeva goes on to make predictions as to a supercessive moment, a third generation of modern feminism wherein the negation of the first wave by the second produces a third moment that ultimately transcends the first two. The second wave, for Kristeva, has paved the way for a possible transition into a post-chronological spiritualism whereby the symbolic contract would no longer sit out-side the particularity of the individual subject (and therefore in a position of alienation to her). In other words, we have 'an *interioriza-tion of the fundamental separation of the sociosymbolic contract*'.[14] Within this context, the second wave's privileging of psychoanalysis and aesthetics takes on an added moral dimension at the level of an imaginary, utopian ethics. Kristeva argues that so long as anthropo-morphism reigns and man and woman remain self-identical, femi-nism will continue to be a necessary moment in the struggle towards a sense of subjectivity incorporative of both same and other—whether that other be figured as belonging to another sex, race, nation....

In reading through the vast productions of French feminist thinkers writing at this turn of the millennium, it does indeed appear that those who have sought to sound the death knell of feminism have been more than a little premature. Perhaps, however, Kristeva may have been correct in wondering as to whether a third wave feminist project as ethical spiritualization of the social contract might ultimately be no more than a utopian fantasy. The following twelve texts reveal that many feminists writing in France today are still struggling with some of the same issues as their forebears of the first and second waves. For although women in France have gained significant legal rights through the struggles of twentieth-century feminists, they have wielded tan-gential (if any) political power as a result of record levels of under-representation in elected governmental bodies. Consequently, until quite recently many feminists have put their energies toward passing what is commonly known as the 'parity law', a 1999 law guaranteeing women equal representation on the voting ballot. The long struggle to enact this law both galvanized and divided feminists in France, for once again the question was raised as to whether women should seek a status of equality or one of difference. Although this collection does not specifically focus on the parity question, it is important to acknow-ledge that these often rather abstract notions have had a substantial impact on the French political scene.

Keeping in mind that even the above descriptions of first and sec-ond wave feminisms cannot possibly pretend to include the immense diversity in feminist thought over the last century, it is important to note that the equality/difference distinction, reductive though it may be at many levels, does hold historical relevance in terms of a certain trajectory in the thinking of the position of women in a male-dominated society. Hindsight, though far from twenty/twenty, does afford a clearer field of vision than does foresight, and the ways in which this current generation of feminisms will ultimately continue to unfold remains to be seen. With this caveat in mind, we present the following texts to an English-speaking audience in hopes of giving the reader a sense of the ways in which nationally contextualized, globally relevant (more and more each day it would seem) theories of feminine difference are being deployed in contemporary French philosophy across the disciplines. These innovative, and often surprising, engagements with the most recent debates in feminist theory in France will provide the reader with a basic overview of the ways in which notions of masculinity and femininity continue to be problematized within the framework of a larger feminist political agenda. This volume constitutes a small contribution to an immemorial struggle. May the dialogue continue and flourish in ever new and exciting ways.

Notes

1. *The Second Sex*, trans. H. M. Parshley (New York: Random House, 1989).
2. On the sex/gender distinction see: Christine Delphy, 'Rethinking Sex and Gender' in *French Feminism Reader*, ed. Kelly Oliver (New York: Rowman & Littlefield, 2000), 63–76; Judith Butler, *Gender Trouble: Feminism and the Subversion of Identity* (New York: Routledge, 1991); Moira Gatens, *Feminism and Philosophy: Perspectives on Equality and Difference* (Bloomington: Indiana University Press, 1991); Tina Chanter, *The Ethics of Eros* (New York: Routledge, 1994).
3. Obviously there are many other feminisms in play in post-1968 France. I am referring here only to those feminisms that have come to be termed 'second wave'.
4. It is important to note that these feminists are championing difference within a philosophical climate in which a self-identical notion of the subject is under heavy attack. Theories of difference are, so to speak, in the air. Most famous, perhaps is Jacques Derrida's elaboration of 'deconstruction' in his 1967 *De la grammatologie; Of Grammatology*, trans. Gayatri Spivak (Baltimore: Johns Hopkins University Press, 1976).
5. See Jacques Lacan, *Écrits*, trans. Alan Sheridan (New York: Norton, 1977); and *The Four Fundamental Concepts of Psychoanalysis*, trans. Alan Sheridan (New York: Norton, 1981).
6. In her rousing manifesto calling women to write their bodies, ' "The Laugh of the Medusa" ', Hélène Cixous famously dubs this form of feminine discourse 'l' écriture féminine'. See *French Feminism Reader*, ed. Oliver 257–75.
7. In her influential overview of French feminisms, *Sexual/Textual Politics*, Toril Moi terms Cixous, Irigaray, and Kristeva 'the Holy Trinity'. Toril Moi, *Sexual/Textual Politics: Feminist Literary Theory* (London: Methuen, 1985). See also Kelly Oliver's *Reading Kristeva: Unraveling the Double-Bind*, ch. 7 'Importing "The French Feminists" '. (Bloomington: Indiana University Press, 1993).
8. One also finds numerous accusations of biological essentialism levelled against these theorists to the extent that they often have recourse to metaphors

culled from the female body in attempting to refigure a theory of feminine subjectivity completely divorced from masculine frames of reference. Ann Rosalind Jones's article 'Writing the Body: Toward an Understanding of *L'Écriture Féminine*', published in *Feminist Studies* (Summer 1981) was one of the first and most influential articles to attack the French Feminists all together. Like Stanton before her, Jones also condenses some of their differences in order to dismiss Kristeva, Irigaray, and Cixous as proponents of an essentialist notion of 'l'écriture féminine'. See also Monique Plaza ' "Phallomorphic Power", and the Psychology of "Woman" ', *Ideology and Consciousness*, 4 (1978); Dorothy Leland, 'Lacanian Psychoanalysis and French Feminism: Toward an Adequate Political Psychology', *Hypatia* (Winter 1989); Domna Stanton, 'Difference on Trial. A Critique of the Maternal Metaphor in Cixous, Irigaray, and Kristeva', in Jeffner Allen and Irish Young (eds.), *The Thinking Muse. Feminism and Modern French Philosophy* (Bloomington: Indiana University Press, 1989); Susan Suleiman, 'Writing and Motherhood', in Garner et al. (eds.), *The (M)other Tongue: Essays in Feminist Psychoanalytic Interpretation* (1985). For a related criticism of the universalist or imperialistic tendencies of Kristeva, Irigaray, and Cixous, see Gayatri Spivak's 'French Feminism in an International Frame', *Yale French Studies*, 62, (1981).

9. See 'L'Invention du "French Feminism": une démarche essentielle', in Christine Delphy, *L'Énnemi principal 2: penser le genre* (Paris: Éditions Syllepse, 2001). 'The Invention of French Feminism: An Essential Move', *Yale French Studies*, 87(2001), 190–221.

10. See e.g. Judith Butler's criticisms and appropriations of Cixous, Kristeva, and Wittig in *Gender Trouble*.

11. For example, theorists like Camile Paglia and Christine Hoff Summers argue against feminism by arguing for 'post feminism'. For an analysis of similar arguments see Rhonda Hammer's *Antifeminism and Family Terrorism: A Critical Feminist Perspective*, (Landham, Md.: Rowman & Littlefield, 2001).

12. Julia Kristeva, *The Portable Kristeva*, ed. Kelly Oliver (New York: Columbia University Press, 1998), 349–69.

13. Ibid. 355.

14. Ibid. 367 original emphasis.

1 Difference/Indifference between the Sexes

Françoise Collin*

Françoise Collin was born in Belgium and holds a doctorate in philosophy from the University of Louvain. She started her career teaching in Brussels and currently leads seminars at the Centre parisien d'études critiques (The Centre for Critical Studies) and lives in Paris. In 1971 she published her first book entitled *Maurice Blanchot et la question de l'éscriture* (Maurice Blanchot and the Question of Writing), one of the earliest major studies on Blanchot. She is best known as the director of the interdisciplinary independent journal *Les Cahiers du GRIF* (*GRIF-Group de Recherche et d'Information Feministe*/Group of Feminist Research and Information) that she founded in 1973. It was the first feminist journal in the French language and one of the most widely recognized theoretical and political venues for European feminist dialogues. Her numerous books, articles, and lectures reflect the diversity of influences from which her philosophical position is nourished; their topics extend from Borges, Burroughs, and Blanchot, to Arendt, Beauvoir, and the history of philosophy. Her fascination with words is evidenced in her writing, which brings together art, literature, and philosophy. For Collin words can link dispersion and rationality in non-totalizing pluralistic narratives: 'thinking and writing emerge fundamentally from the same rigor and the same sense of fiction'.[1]

Belonging to the generation of 1968 and the feminist movement, Collin avoids the duality of 'difference' and 'universalism' that have traditionally divided feminists. Instead her feminism stems from the idea that gender is the outcome of specific historical junctions and thus must be constantly theoretically and politically reworked and redefined. In Collin's view, there is no one true embodiment of gender, but a material reality that is structured in every society by the effects of the roles, images, and power structures to which one gender is subjected by another. The category of 'women' is a historical product of marginalizing institutions that operated under the name of universality.

In 'Difference/Indifference between the Sexes', Françoise Collin argues against a Marxist interpretation of the feminist movement as synonymous with the class

* 'Difference/indifférence des sexes' in *Actuel Marx* (30:2), *Les Rapports sociaux des sexes*, 2001 (pp. 189–99). Reprinted by permission of Presses Universitaires de France.

13

struggle as theoretically situated within traditional notions of universalism. While she agrees with the materialist proposition that sexual relations are socially constructed, she locates the feminist problematic not in the difference between the sexes, but rather in the hierarchical dissymetry that has cross-culturally placed women in a position of subordination with regard to men. The goal of feminism, then, should not be an erasure of sexual difference but rather a deconstruction of masculine domination. On Collin's reading, it is impossible to envision or foresee what a feminist future might look like as there exists no historical precedent for this new kind of postmodern, post-metaphysical revolution—a 'permanent' revolution that, unlike its predecessors, does not seek to replace an existing order with an *alter* order.

Although the French ideals of democracy and republicanism may indeed assume a homogenous society of 'citizens' stripped of all individual difference, a distinct gap remains between metaphysical and political realities and, for Collin, an assumption of sexual indifference is both dangerous and unrealistic. A feminism grounded in deconstruction as theorized by Foucault, Deleuze, and Derrida represents a unique and challenging critical model that constantly reactivates the question of the social construction of the sexes, even, and especially, in the face of shifting forms of kinship and sexualities. Theory, for Collin, is never quite up to the complexity of political actions, and a true transformation of the social relations of the sexes must be thought within the context of an ever-changing history with no fixed 'end' or defining 'Idea'. Feminism as informed by deconstruction, then, becomes a politics of displacement, free from all norms, one which disseminates the alterity of the other of the One and enlarges rather than destroys the symbolic domain.

In this article I will concentrate on a critical analysis of the notion of the 'social relationships of sex' and the way it confronts the notion of 'difference between the sexes'. I will also concentrate on the more recent notion of 'indifference between the sexes', and on how these ideas relate to the question of domination, tracing the notion of naturalism through to its form of 'fully developed naturalism'.

This return to the notion of social relationships of sex or of the social construction of sex, which is now replaced by the American notion of 'gender', is to be distinguished from any 'naturalist' conception of the status of the sexes which would conceal the notion of 'difference between the sexes', held in suspicion by naturalists. No one, and certainly no feminist, whether she terms herself differentialist or univeralist,[2] would challenge the social nature of the sexual order, or the necessity, as well of the possibility, of transforming it. Rather, the question is to determine how, and in view of what, this transformation should occur. Every answer to this question, whether it involves retaining but reformulating the notion of difference between the sexes, or adopting the notion of indifference between the sexes, is haunted by the spectre of naturalism. For, if the first answer presupposes an irreducible 'nature' of difference, which may not necessarily be translated as duality, since difference and duality are not synonymous, the second is based upon the hypothesis of what Marx, referring to the class system, termed 'fully developed naturalism'—in other words, a state where conflict in relationships is resolved.

Reaching such a state is in fact the aim of the traditional notion of universalism, and of the more current idea of indifference between the sexes, which, despite its apparent novelty, could well be a reworking of that earlier notion. It is a state where sex would not only cease to be a factor of discrimination, but where sex would no longer describe an individual, would no longer be relevant, would even, thanks ultimately to a good deal of work in the right direction, cease to relate to techno-science. If universalism presupposes an erosion of differences for the good of the individual, 'indifference' presupposes rather the individual's capacity to play with all these differences. In either case identity is not constituted by any determining factor: the subject transcends differences and claims to be in some way master of them.

However, like the notion of difference between the sexes, the notions of social relationships of sex and of the social construction of sex do not take into account or identify, and even help to cover up, the specific target of the feminist movement, which is the hierarchical form of these relationships defined in terms of power. For the political problem with the idea of social relationships of sex is not so much the specific characteristic of the relationships—the fact that they are 'social'—but the fact that they are articulated in terms of domination. The notion of 'social relationships of sex' or of 'social construction of sex' thus borrows from the honourable mantle of scientific validity a politically unacceptable plan of action. We would not express exploitation as 'social relationships of class', or racism as 'social relationships of race'. So why do we make this slip of the tongue in attempting to align the 'struggle of the sexes' with the 'class struggle'? The fact is that the 'struggle' in the matter that concerns us cannot be conceived in terms of the same dual model as the 'class struggle', because the two constituents—partner (sexual or social) and adversary—are too closely bound up with each other.

Thus, in any debate relating to gender, there is always a risk that the ontological question—what are, fundamentally, the relationships between the sexes and what are gender identities?—will replace the political question: how do we want to transform these relationships, in what direction shall we push them from their present position? Is there an ideal conceptual form of relationships between the sexes— either in their traditional or an eroded form, or are we in fact working with these relationships as we find them in our current circumstances, here and now, and not as they are represented in such a way as to guarantee the *unanimity* of all concerned? While all feminists, and to a certain extent, all women, are agreed in challenging domination and hierarchy, there is less agreement on how domination should be over- come. This has been evident in France regarding the attempt to achieve equality in political institutions, and can also be witnessed in the development of new techniques of procreation and parenthood.

But disagreement, if it is well founded and a source of dialogue, is fertile. It is *unanimity* that should make us suspicious. There are two possible standpoints which can be summarized as follows: does equality among human beings require their sameness—their in- difference—or is equality, as Beauvoir saw it, an 'equality in difference', allowing 'differences in equality'[3] to exist even if these differences do not exhaust the humanity of each in the *mitsein*,[4] that is to say in the whole of being, in the shared world.

....

SOCIAL RELATIONSHIPS OR RELATIONSHIPS OF DOMINATION
....

The social nature of the relationships between the sexes—the fact that they are produced or constructed—is attested to in the variations of these relationships both throughout history and across different cul- tures. Scholars of history, sociology, and ethnology have deployed their talents of intelligence and curiosity to identify the modalities of the relationships between the sexes particular to each era, each back- ground, each culture, and each micro-society. No one today denies the wealth of these historical and cultural variations which could be ana- lysed endlessly. The relationships between the sexes are indeed social relationships, constructed and modulated into both new and repeated configurations by different societies through their respective practices and symbolic orders. Human inventiveness is infinite in weaving the fabric of domination, but so is our inventiveness in resistance, in unpicking the stitches.

Feminism, however, in the 'wild thought' of its early days, below or beyond historical and cultural analysis, beyond the produced or constructed variations in the social relationships between the sexes, aimed at the invariable aspect of these relationships: in other words, the fact that underneath all the different forms of these relationships lies a repeated, persistent asymmetrical or hierarchical structure, which is translated into the domination of women by men, of woman by man. This constant has been testified to by ethnological studies showing that the law of the exchange of women between men dictates all modes of social organization.

It is this constant which is being re-examined. It is not simply a matter of stating that relationships between the sexes are 'social', a fact that even the most conservative observer can grasp; it must be stated that these relationships are constructed asymmetrically in the schema of domination, and therefore that they can and should be deconstructed. It is not a question of contesting a historical or ethnological truth believed in the past—as though the past dictated the future—but of contesting the unshakeable nature of this truth by developing a transforming plan of action which would undermine it. It has always been a question of proving through action the invalidity of a universally established fact.

Simone de Beauvoir well understood the untimeliness of any transforming action which, having no historical precedent, must be invented on the basis of the idea that action must be used to confront universal truths, and which can only be justified through its own results. For me, it can be qualified as a 'politics of the unrepresentable' since it follows no model either in reality, because there is no moment that escapes from history, or in representation. It is a highly critical voice, creating its truth as it advances, cutting its path through circumstances as the obstacles it overcomes allow, and at every turn making the risky decision of how to proceed. No Idea guarantees action, and no Heaven determines the form of action. From the 'it is so' based on the 'it has always been so' can be articulated an 'it will no longer be so', which is the essence of all practical politics freed from any metaphysical or naturalist tether.

It is therefore necessary to talk about revolution, even if it is a new kind of revolution—one without physical violence, without the putting to death of a tyrant, without destruction of the status quo with a view to building the future on a *tabula rasa*. Rather, it is a task of constant undermining, a widespread whittling away of the boundaries between public and private through an irrepressible and

17

unstoppable movement—a 'permanent revolution' rather than a completed revolution—a revolution carried out with the industrious gnawing of termites. Those involved in this revolution should have a clearer agreement on what should be abandoned than on what should be brought into being.

To affirm, once the fantasy sketched out in a moment by the matriarchy of early feminism has dissipated, that which was everywhere and always will no longer be, such is the impertinence and daring insolence of the current feminist movement when it questions the knots that have bound the relationships between the sexes for centuries. This belief in change to come has, to a certain extent, been borne out as it has been affirmed. For thirty years now circumstances have gone some way to proving the feminist movement right.

THERE IS ONLY ONE SEX

The notion of the construction of sex or of social relationships of sex, like that of the difference between the sexes, conceals rather than reveals one other fundamental fact: that in these relationships there has never in reality been more than one sex, and that is the female sex, since according to men, humankind is embodied by men, in relation to which women constitute a kind of special case or anomaly. The gendered and sexual character of the male has in effect been identified as human, and for centuries has been confused with the specific character of the human. In the history of the explicit or implicit thinking of different cultures, there are not two sexes to which specific functions are devolved and which would share out the social arena between them. Rather, there is a specificity and a particularity of the female sex (*tota mulier in utero*) in relation to the generality of humanity incarnated by men, a 'natural' vocation as opposed to a cultural vocation based on a symbolic operator—unreason as opposed to reason, body as opposed to mind, a biological life as opposed to a symbolic life.[5]

The identification of woman with the sex organ—or with her biology—as a distinctive characteristic is clear not only in forms of popular language. The history of science and ideas constantly repeats that the construction of the sexes occurs in a relationship where woman is the sex organ, material at the disposal of and function of the species.

In woman, 'the essence of the sex is not limited to a single organ but is spread out in different degrees of sensitivity, so that woman is not

18

woman in one place, but actually in every place in which she can be imagined'.[6] In confronting the question of the sex, all the philosophers of history identify it with women. Thus the small creature born from a woman's womb is a prey to the species, and only becomes a human being, in other words only enters into the function of language, through the ritual branding of the paternal function. Because the mother is a 'certainty' for the child, her function is reduced and artificial, since it is the father who relates to the process of naming. This asymmetry is also evident in psychoanalysis which, while it sexualizes the sexes, seeing them both as bound to castration, renews the confusion by elevating the particularity of one sex, through various theoretical contortions, to the level of the Signifier, the phallic signifier which is certainly not the same as the penis, but does relate to it. That the Name takes over the body is the very expression of the child's entry into the symbolic order, and of the importance of this in law. The problem is that the Name is that of one, which is one of the two, but is posing as a Third, and that the Third becomes identified with power.

Simone de Beauvoir notes this in her nevertheless anti-establishment thinking in *The Second Sex* when she indicates that the man (masculine) is the bearer of the universal and that as a result the liberation of women would depend upon them gaining access to the masculine position. It is for this reason that the statement 'there are two sexes'[7] was initially, in the climate of that time, seen as subversive. It was the response of the oppressed to the oppressor on equal terms: you too are a specific sex, and not the incarnation of Man.

So, having agreed with Beauvoir that 'one is not born a woman, one becomes one', it is logically necessary to add what she omitted, that 'one is not born a man, one becomes one' both psychically and socially. The relationship is constructed, the two entities confronting each other in the relationship are constructed, and the inequality between them is constructed.

....

CLASS AND SEX
....

In France and in Europe generally, the analysis of relationships of sex developed by feminism in the 1970s was inspired by systems of thought based on class relationships, which at that time still dominated the prevailing left-wing political horizon and could not be ignored. But the stance of theoretical and practical autonomy assumed by feminism and the feminists in relation to Marxism and the Marxists also attests to the impossibility of matching up one method of analysis with the other. In other words, it is impossible firstly to consider the relationships of sex as a sub-section of class relationships, and secondly to think of them in the same terms.

In fact class relationships relate to a particular level of social relationships: the relationships of production which link together capital and work and are seen as the determining factor in all other relationships. Marxism argues that there is one isolatable cause of domination defined as exploitation, and that is the economic order. This applies even when the perspective becomes global and claims to allow a complete overturning of society. On the other hand, relationships of sex relate to a complex structure which is at once political, social, economic, sexual, and cultural, and the ramifications of which are felt both in public and private spheres. There is no possibility of isolating the particular level of the structure that causes domination, and therefore no possibility that a specific change will lead *ipso facto* to a transformation of the whole.

On the other hand, the relationships of capitalist production which Marx attacks are specific to a certain point in history and to Western culture. Even though capitalism originated before the industrial era, it constitutes a specific state of work relationships at a given point in time, and not their unique form throughout history and in all cultures. Capitalism essentially pertains to advanced Western industrial society, and this has been used by some to justify the failure of communism in countries such as Russia which were in a state of post-feudalism at the beginning of the century. Consequently it may be conceived that a specific historical state is followed by another historical state which would correspond with its ideal state—the state of 'fully developed naturalism'—representing the 'end of history' which undoubtedly constitutes the influence of Hegel in Marx's thought. In Marx's words, communism is 'the real appropriation of the human essence by and for man . . . a fully developed naturalism . . . a humanism . . . the genuine resolution of the conflict between man and nature and between man and man . . . the riddle of history solved':[8] nothing less. Thus there is an essence of human relationships, a state in which, freed from the constructions—from the social relationships—which alter them, they recover the natural state which communism claims to offer as an entry into earthly paradise.

Hand in hand with the objective of the dissolution of class relationships comes the project or the fantasy of an 'undifferentiated' society, a society free from fixed places, in which functions would be perpetually interchangeable: 'In communist society . . . nobody has one exclusive sphere of activity but each can become accomplished in any branch he wishes . . . to do one thing today and another tomorrow, to hunt in the morning, fish in the afternoon, rear cattle in the evening, criticise after dinner, just as I have in mind, without ever becoming hunter, fisherman, herdsman or critic.'[9] It is now known that this fantasy of perfect indifferentiation actually concealed a fixity of roles, and that as a result any possibility of contesting this fixity was stifled, and also that the dissolution of the State actually proved to be the augmentation of the State. Marx's examples of the worker in relation to the indifferentiation of his occupations do not directly touch on the status of his identity, which is reduced by Marx to the spontaneity of his 'wants'—today we might say of his 'desire'. The growth in specialization has besides given the lie to this seductive variety of roles whose claim to reduce working time—which includes both work and leisure—does not seem to be realized either.

FROM UNIVERSALISM TO INDIFFERENCE BETWEEN THE SEXES

It seems that the objective of the dissolution of the classes as a means to resolving the conflict between them is a principle sometimes echoed in another objective which is occasionally articulated—that of the dissolution of the sexes, or of the dissolution of the differences between the sexes. While for some domination must be dissolved in order to maintain a different difference involving no hierarchy, for others, it is difference itself which must be abolished in order to achieve indifferentiation, just as the classes had to be, or should have been, abolished. This difficulty aside, the hypothesis of the dissolution of the classes depends on the disappearance of their material foundation, that is the capital/work relationship, while the idea of the dissolution of the sexes leaves intact the material foundation of bodily form in the sexual and reproductive relationship. Can we, should we, like good materialists, logically consider this material foundation to be non-existent and do away with the idea of the bodily incarnation of gender?

The universalist position characteristic of French political thought and of republicanism in general sees democracy only as a relationship between individuals which transcends their national, regional, linguistic, and gender differences, and their particular path in life. Citizenship erodes and neutralizes all these factors in the name of a supposedly homogenous public arena. But we know—and this fact was fully denounced by Marx—that this founding ambition of democracy has hidden and continues to hide discrimination and that it produces a common world which hides more than it helps to dissolve its own asymmetry and glaring inequalities to the ends of a centralism determined by those in power. The founding universality of democracy and 'universal suffrage' have in any case marginalized one half of the nation on the grounds of gender, giving rise to lame pretences at parity which are as much use as a plaster cast on a wooden leg. This universality has marginalized and continues to marginalize numerous other social and economic categories. It is worth asking whether stating indifference between the sexes does not risk assuring the continuation of universality rather than correcting it, by cloaking factual differences and inequalities. The effect of stating indifference between the classes and between people of different origins is that a world of identical individuals is postulated, in which all forms of 'affirmative action'—so badly expressed by the term 'positive discrimination'—are stigmatized.

Like the ideology of universalism, that of indifference between the sexes risks hiding, confirming, and even strengthening the privileged status of one section of the community. There is a gulf between metaphysical truth and political truth. In order to radicalize the historical position, to be more Marxist than Marx on this count, historicity must on the one hand be taken as a concept which it is impossible to overcome, and on the other it must be linked to action and understood as a political concept. The metaphysical dream of fully developed naturalism and any other 'fully developed' ideology must be renounced. In this sense feminism is related to the postmodern or the post-metaphysical, whereas Marxism is still related to the modern. Feminism is a critical voice, and follows no ideological model of thought whether it is designated as Idea or Nature.

....

TWO CASE STUDIES: HOMOSEXUALITY AND REPRODUCTION
....

The question of social construction of gender has been recently reactivated in the context of two important debates: the new forms of family relationships and the recognition of homosexuality, there being some overlap between the two. In these two contexts the idea of a 'de-dualization', even of an interchangeability of gender positions, has developed. In both debates, it is as though a path to equality of the sexes through their progressive indifferentiation has been laid—an appeasement not only of the domination of one sex by the other, but also of the specificity of each sex. 'There will no longer be man or woman' said Saint-Paul, father of the 'universal',[10] masking in this way his male chauvinism.

The movement for homosexual recognition seems to relate to the same key point as feminism—that is, to gender—and some would even like to assimilate the two, even to frame the women's movement within the homosexual movement. However, while both movements relate to the question of gender, they do not view it in the same way. The issue of sexuality and the issue of sex may well overlap, but they cannot be reduced to the same thing. In the case of the homosexual movement it is a question of preference of desire, or the form of sexuality; in the case of feminism it is a question of the status of the social category of biologically defined women, whatever their sexual preference, at least in the first instance. Monique Wittig once wrote 'a lesbian is not a woman': however, a lesbian certainly shares the social and economic conditions of other women.

Contrary to what is sometimes stated, the emergence of the public recognition of homosexuality far from confirming the indifference between the sexes seems, at least initially, to highlight even further their disunion. The same is true when ancient Greece is used to illustrate the homosexual cause, since it is also an illustration of sexism, women being excluded from the City. Further, the sexual, cultural and even fantasy practices of gays and lesbians today are not interchangeable, a fact highlighted by Marie-Jo Bonnet, who can certainly not be accused of homophobia, when she observes a 'phenomenon of normalization of the masculine model in the gay movement'.[11] This phenomenon of normalization absorbs rather than actualizes the symbolic value of the relationship of one woman with another woman, which is denied by masculine society, patriarchal society or the 'society of brothers'.[12]

Thus heterosexuality introduces the relationship of forces between the sexes right into the heart of the intimacy between them. Homosexuality is exempt from this particular form of confrontation, but it still brings into action the social stakes of gender and the stakes of sexuality, which are always in a dual and hierarchical form. One can quote the hypothesis that this persistent masculine or virilocentric hallmark is a throwback to the heterosexual world which is bound to disappear, but there is no evidence to date that this is anything more than a speculative hypothesis. Despite the fact that gay men have been and still are penalized because of their sexual orientation, they still benefit from the same social, economic and cultural status as other men.[13] The masculine viewpoint is still misogynist even when it is not heterosexual. The fantasy representation and the appropriation of feminine images on the carnival floats at gay pride parades, for example Hollywood stars such as Judy Garland and Greta Garbo,[14] adds to the catalogue of caricatures of femininity. The section of the gay movement in favour of marriage (Pacs in France provides them with a marriage substitute) is by its own admission more concerned to appropriate the traditional social family structure than to explode it. The problem of the relationships of sex can in no way be confused with the problem of the relationships of sexualities.

The erosion of difference is no more obvious in the relationships of sexualities than it is in the relationships of sex. If homosexuals have to fight so hard for recognition, that is precisely because they do not see their form of sexuality as 'indifferent'; it is because their sexuality is directed towards an absolutely determined object, and when that object is forbidden or not recognized, they suffer unjustly. With very few exceptions, gay men and women are tied to their preference for the same sex just as heterosexuals are tied to the opposite sex, even if in both cases this preference concludes and includes the complex development of a polymorphous psychological foundation. This is highlighted in a recent book by Sabine Prokhoris which draws on Freud: 'the love object is not chosen primarily or directly because it is a "man" or a "woman". But whether it is a man or a woman will feature in some way, because that is how these signifiers of gender function. The intensity of loves linked to an "umbilicus" of desire come to be replaced by figures which will find themselves to be "masculine" or "feminine" as much by chance as because of the meanders and the layers of oedipal loves'.[15] The complexity of the development of the choice of object does however reveal one limitation which it is impossible to avoid: the 'confinement to one or other defined state of desire'. For while it is thought that the limiting choice of heterosexuality is 'constructed', even imposed, by social laws, the no less limiting homosexual choice which in our society has led to a painful need for secrecy can only be understood in this way with difficulty, and all the more so because it does not constitute a political choice, but only becomes a political motive after the event. In either case, indifference about the choice of object is rare.

So, from the point of view of sexuality as much as from the point of view of different cultures or political practices, homosexuality provides evidence of difference rather than indifference between the sexes. When deconstructed, the social construction of normative heterosexuality does not to date reveal a lack of differentiation in the social relationships of sex. And neither does it reveal lack of differentiation in sexual acts: rape, prostitution, not to mention incest and pederasty, form a deviant and minority, but almost institutional (at least in the case of prostitution) constituent of masculine sexuality, whether hetero or homosexual.

Is the erosion of difference any more evident in the new scientific and legislative procedures of reproduction? The social construction of sex can and equally should be confronted with the new issues facing familial relationships, which little by little are overturning the process of reproduction on one hand and the traditional structures of Western familial ties on the other, apparently eroding the asymmetry of the paternal and maternal, masculine and feminine roles which are involved.

Women's claim to the freedom to decide in the matter of sexual reproduction has been through many developments since the 1970s. Today it is possible to see these developments in the same spirit as the initial intention or to argue that they are working against it.

The demand for 'a child if I want and when I want', which originally meant 'no child if I don't want one' has been made possible. Science has now made it possible to provide sterile individuals and couples with the child they desire, and even heightens this desire by manipulating it. Science suggests to these people: not only can you have a child if you want and when you want, you can also have the child that you want, or that someone else wants for you and through you—the perfect child. Heterosexual intercourse is no longer necessary to achieve this:[16] it is all carried out in a laboratory by injecting sperm into an ovum. It is thus perfectly possible for lesbians to become parents, but not for gay men since there does not yet exist an artificial womb. Even if such a thing does not lie in the distant future men and women whether hetero or homosexual are still not interchangeable and remain 'different' in terms of reproduction, even if paternity has become biologically identifiable. Only adoption seems to erode the difference between mother and father, man and woman, by according them potentially the same legal position in the child's upbringing. However this position is becoming less and less exempt from reference to the so-called biological relationship, to which the suppression of the anonymity of the biological parents lends force in France.[17]

So, while a woman can become a mother without a man, using sperm deposited in a 'bank' by an anonymous donor, a man cannot become a father without a womb, which may be obtained through goodwill or money. Cloning threatens to accentuate this asymmetry since it would mean that just a cell and an ovum would need to be joined, opening up the possibility of purely feminine reproduction. So, at the moment at which paternity, which for centuries was a legal or symbolic status (a man was declared the father if he was the husband of the mother, or if she named him the father) has become biological, its role becomes potentially superfluous from this point of view. Science (but who is science?) opens up numerous possibilities for reproduction but seems at the same time to dictate the order of these possibilities and to shape the desire to have a child into demand.

Whatever the forms of filiation, or family relationships, which these advances will introduce into the social and legal order, they at least attest to a resistance to an 'indifferentiation' between sexes and even accentuate it in the matter of reproduction. A couple of men are absolutely compelled to seek the help of a woman either from goodwill or for money in order to have a child which is biologically linked to them, while a couple of women can make do with some anonymous sperm, or even with a so-called superfluous embryo abandoned in a laboratory.

Has this asymmetry in the matter of reproduction, which puts women in a privileged position, been the motive of the domination to which women have been subjected in the patriarchal structure as some theorists, both men and women, have stated? Does the idea of 'social construction of sex' under the empire of masculinity come to ratify the idea of feminine weakness or does it, following the 'ancient project of matricide',[18] reinsure an architecture of ancestral power through new techniques? Does law determine reality or does it come to cover reality with 'fiction' as has been demonstrated in the artificialist tradition of Roman law by Yan Thomas,[19] among others? These big theoretical questions serve as a horizon, but only as a horizon, to a transforming action arising out of certain conditions, here and now, in which decisions must be made which have no guaranteed long-term effects. How can an egalitarian notion of social construction of sex replace an unequal notion of social construction of sex? This is the question put by women in the light of feminism and which must be dealt with in the present set of circumstances and the choices which are available within it. The social and political advances made by women in the course of the last thirty years cannot be contested. However, they are not sufficient to overturn the still virilocentric framework within which they were achieved, even in the West. Women are still making their way, between the disdain and the praise of motherhood, through a world of men which was constituted centuries ago. They are still coming forward 'through word and action' in a world of men. Scientific advances leave them with the same political problematic.

BETWEEN DIFFERENCE AND INDIFFERENCE: DECONSTRUCTION

The transformation of the social construction of sex or of social relationships of sex is not carried out on an empty stage, but on a specific, although complex and evolving, historical stage. The politics of the sexes is not a speculative politics which can be based upon a representation of its aim—on an Idea—or which can build a new world from nothing. The transforming action operates upon a particular set of circumstances at a given point in time. It is not a matter of completely substituting one world for another, but of chipping away at this given world in many different ways, which are usually lateral and always adventurous. No concept is actually free of ambiguity, and no concept can express the true complexity of any situation. Theory is always simultaneously expression and mask, fixing what is in actuality: theory necessarily lacks the force and the complexity of the stakes it has raised, even if it is absolutely necessary to those stakes. This is the first commandment of true 'materialism', which does not conceive politics as the application of a principle, that like a conjuring trick, can pull a rabbit out of a hat. 'We always theorize too soon. Let's not make our achievements an illustration of our theories,' Genevieve Pastre has written recently.

As Foucault showed at a time when the idea prevailed of head-on struggles based upon the supposed identification of the dominant force, power cannot be localized in one person or in one determined point, the destruction of which would suffice to bring down the whole structure. It is always a question of a complex whole where gains and losses are inextricably mixed. Thus the notion of deconstruction illuminates better than that of destruction the tasks of negation and

27

positioning which are the driving force behind the political work undertaken by women.

Post-metaphysical or postmodern politics is defined by deconstruction, which takes as its starting point the social relationships of sex in which each of us is caught, and violates them and changes their forms without claiming to offer a normative solution which would define their right form. It is a politics of displacement which undermines the agreed demarcations of place. It is a politics belonging to women— and to men—in the public and the private sphere, and on the artificial boundary between the two. It is a politics whose truth is being continually created and which undermines the age-old network of the workings of sexism without identifying a unique cause for it. Deconstruction does not substitute one construction for another on the basis of new foundations, as a revolution completed in a moment would claim to do. Beginning with the ancient 'two' which preserves the uniqueness of the One in order better to position the other as Other to the One, deconstruction strengthens the other in order to transform alienation to otherness, at the same time disseminating this otherness. Deconstruction decentres and de-numerizes: it is not concerned with the victory of the one, or of the two, nor with difference or indifference, but with the precarious relationship between them. Deconstruction is a movement, a turbulent force. And so it is appropriate to name the feminist revolution the women's 'movement', for it is also a turbulent force, and it should also be, whether they like it or not, the men's movement.

We are indebted to the philosophers of the second half of the twentieth century—to Foucault, Derrida and Deleuze—for having, through many developments, put into theoretical terms this method of revolution which does not involve a radical annihilation of the current set of circumstances in order to institute a new set of circumstances, but which translates the current situation by working on it from within, and through outbursts and advances which have always to be rethought and rectified. This is a plan of attack based on contamination rather than confrontation.

The revolution of the sexes, the revolution of gender, is a revolution based on gaining ground, not through head-on opposition but through guerrilla incursions, the outcomes of which can never be predicted. The confrontation in this revolution is hand-to-hand combat. There is no fast track, no key to all the doors, but instead multiplicities of advances in the form of networks, of gathering strengths. It is hard to predict exactly what is at stake in this historic overturning.

But for the first time in history something has begun to shift in the relationships of sex and reproduction, and this fact deserves to be highlighted as a major event of the twentieth century, full of promise, but also of risk. The transformation of the 'social relationships of sex', between difference and indifference, is undertaken at the price of risk. And naturalism, as a metaphysical ideology, is the contrary of a materialism based on action.

Notes

1. Editor's note: Françoise Collin, 'Comme si un livre de philosophie avait quelque chose à voir avec écrire', *Revue des sciences humaines*, 1 (1982), 9.
2. Differentialist thought affirms a certain duality of the sexes, even though it criticizes the way in which this duality is translated into the social order. Universalist thought absolutely denies the existence of this duality. On this topic I recommend the articles 'Difference des sexes' (F. Collin) and 'Patriarcat' (C. Delphy) in *Dictionnaire critique du féminisme* (Paris: PUF, 2000). But it is also important to note that the notion of difference cannot be reduced to the idea of duality.
3. Simone de Beauvoir, *The Second Sex* (New York: Vintage, 1997), 740.
4. The term is borrowed by Beauvoir from Heidegger.
5. See F. Collin, *Le Différend des sexes* (Paris: Pleins Feux, 1999), and F. Collin, E. Pisier, E. Varikas, *Les Femmes, de Platon à Derrida: Anthologie critique* (Paris: Plon, 2000).
6. Roussel, quoted by Geneviève Fraisse in a study on doctor-philosophers in the 1800s: 'L'Homme générique et le sexe reproducteur', in *Vivants et mortels, Psychanalyse et techno-sciences, Revue du College de Psychanalystes*, special issue (1988).
7. This is the title of a book by Antoinette Fouque but the phrase could point for example to Luce Irigaray. It must not be forgotten that these two pupils of Lacan were reacting against the affirmation of the phallus as the unique signifier for both sexes.
8. Karl Marx, *Economic and Philosophical Manuscripts of 1844*, 'Private property and communism' [Online]. **www.marxists.org/archive/marx/works/1844/manuscripts/comm.htm**.
9. Karl Marx, *The German Ideology, Idealism and Materialism* [Online]. **www.marxists.org/archive/marx/works/german-ideology/ch01a.htm**.
10. This is the theory of Alain Badiou in *Saint Paul, la fondation de l'universalisme* (Paris: PUF, 1997).
11. Marie-Jo Bonnet, 'La Relation entre femmes, un lien impensable?', *Esprit* (Mar./Apr. 2001).
12. Resulting from what Carole Pateman terms the 'social contract between brothers', who sees in this democratic contract a recasting and not the abolition of the old patriarchy.
13. Because of the continuing difference in men and women's salaries, a couple of gay men is richer and a couple of lesbians is poorer than a heterosexual couple.

FRANÇOISE COLLIN

14. D. Halperin recently highlighed in a talk at the HESS the interest of carrying out an analysis of the cultural figures that the gay movement chooses to borrow from straight culture.
15. Sabine Prokhoris, *Le Sexe prescrit* (Paris: Aubier, 2001), 293.
16. The feminist demand of the 1970s for the right to a sex life without pregnancy through contraception and abortion has become a demand for the right to pregnancy without intercourse. Is this a logical development or a perversion of the original demand?
17. Is the possibility for an adopted child to find its birth parents, or at least the mother, an acknowledgement of the importance of biology or of the importance of completing what is known of one's history with what happened before? Both interpretations are possible if one maintains that no maternity or familial bond is purely biological.
18. The phrase in Monique Scheider's: 'L'Enfant de la science', in *Psychanalystes: vivants et mortels; psychanalyse et technosciences, Revue du college de psychanalystes* (Oct. 1988), 74.
19. 'L'Union des sexes: le difficile passage de la nature au droit, Entretien avec Yan Thomas', in *Le Banquet,* 1st and 2nd semester (1998), nos. 12 and 13. The author opposes the Roman law of fiction with the Christian law based on 'nature'. It will be noted that for the subject that concerns us, that is the social relationships between men and women, recourse to fiction or nature produce the same hierarchical effects.

2 A Deceptive Universalism

Gisèle Halimi*

Born on 27 July 1927 in French colonial Tunisia (La Goulette), Gisèle (Zoïza) Halimi first travelled to France to study law and philosophy at the Institute of Political Studies in Paris. She became a lawyer in 1948, and practised law in Tunisia until 1958, when she was called to become a member of the Paris Bar Association. Halimi has made her reputation by defending leftist causes (the Basque Liberation Front, the Algerian Liberation Front, and the prosecuted Algerian activist Djamila Boupacha), and celebrity figures such as Simone de Beauvoir and Jean-Paul Sartre.

Halimi is the co-founder (with Simone de Beauvoir) of *Choisir, la cause des femmes* (Choice, Women's Cause). *Choisir* began as a defence for the signers of the infamous 'Un Appel de 343 femmes' (The Call of 343 Women), a full-page ad appearing in *Le Nouvel Observateur* on 5 April 1971. Signed by 343 well-known women admitting to having had abortions (then illegal in France), the call immediately provoked a national debate on abortion rights—quite a feat since a 1920 law forbade any public discussion on the topic.

Guided by Halimi's strong vision, *Choisir* decided to take the arcane abortion laws to trial. In 1972, Halimi defended the test case for abortion rights at Bobigny, a great success that lead (two years later, in 1974) to the passage of liberal abortion and contraceptive rights (drafted by the then Minister of Health, Simone Veil). Riding on the momentum, *Choisir* proceeded collectively to author 'The Common Programme for Women', documenting the needs of women in the fields of law, politics, medicine, and education, and proposing ways of addressing these needs. Published during the legislative elections of 1978, it was meant to serve as an informed voter's guide to the issues and candidates of the day. Halimi unsuccessfully ran a campaign for the office of deputy that year, but was later elected to the French National Assembly as an independent socialist (1981). Halimi served as the French ambassador to UNESCO from 1984 to 1986, when she retired back into private practice.

'Un universalisme trompeur' (A Deceptive Universalism) appears in *La Nouvelle*

---

* 'Un universalisme trompeur', in *La Nouvelle Cause des femmes*. (Paris: Seuil, 1997), 87–106. Reprinted by permission of Seuil.

Cause des femmes (The New Women's Cause). In this essay, Halimi argues that the *Declaration of the Rights of Man and the Citizen*, which serves as foundation for the modern French Republic, is deceptive in its claim to universality. The bedrock of universal rights is a concept of equality according to which all individuals are 'equally equal'—or interchangeable regardless of skin colour, religion, ethnicity, social status, or sex. However, such an equality is both false and illusory. Through a careful reading of the document, Halimi shows that the letter of the law in fact assumes a masculine subject.

Ironically, the French Revolution by which white, bourgeois men wrested citizenship from the nobles and clergy that oppressed them also represented a great political defeat for women. From 1789 to 1944, the rights to vote, to public assembly and speech, and to private property were denied to women. First in abstract terms, the denial was made concrete with the passage of the Napoleonic Code of 1804, that rendered women minors by law, and required their obedience to their fathers and husbands. Women did not recover until after the Second World War, when they fought and gained the right to vote.

Halimi concludes that such a denial of women's humanity is a violation of the principles of equality upheld by the *Declaration of the Rights of Man and the Citizen*. The falsehood of this universalism needs to be countered by a truly democratic and republican equality that is inclusive in its universalism, and which recognizes the multiplicity of human differences.

It is widely acknowledged that the Declaration of the Rights of Man and of the Citizen (26 August 1789) and the founding texts of the Republic—among the most important of which are our Constitutions referring in 1791, 1946, and 1958 to the Declaration—created the universalist theory of public law.

First Article of the Declaration: 'Men are born and remain free and equal in their rights'.

Article 6: 'All citizens ... have equal right to all public dignities, places and jobs ...'.

All the Constitutions of the Republic establish in forceful terms the principles of equality among citizens and of the unity and indivisibility of the French people.

The notion of universalism is rigged up on the scaffolding of equality. However, it would be a mistake to see universalism as a notion applicable to everybody. It is true that the castes, elites, or social and political classes of the *ancien régime* no longer exist. They have been replaced and their functions taken over by citizens on equal terms.

However, in order to become universalist, an equality of this kind must be taken to its absolute limit. The consequence of this kind of equality is the *interchangeability* of all individuals seen as *equally equal* in the nation.

The citizen born of universalism is, according to our current Constitution, an individual whose colour, religion, ethnicity, social situation and, I would stress, sex (we will come back to this later), are suppressed. The individual is undifferentiated, willingly abstract. The individual is just a sketch of a human being designed to support the rights and duties of the Republic. This sketch is neither white nor black, rich nor poor, man nor woman.

We should acknowledge the enormous progress for France and for the world brought about by enshrining the citizen in the Constitution. The intention in doing so is marked with the intelligence of the Enlightenment and the generosity of the Republic in sweeping away the privileges which, from birth, created an unequal and oppressive society. No more serf or nobleman, no more bourgeoisie or third estate; instead, a sovereign people, indivisible, united, and whose constituent citizens come together in absolute equality to decide their future.

So much for the theory.

Liberated from absolute monarchy, individuals gained a political identity in becoming citizens. It is therefore clear that the rights of Man cannot be criticized to the extent that they are universal—that is, to the extent that they apply to the whole of humanity.

What therefore, you may ask, is my problem with the enlightened philosophy which inspired the foundations of our Constitution? What is wrong with these texts that created an admirable voluntarist humanism? In sum, what is there to criticize in the victory over medieval obscurantism and over all forms of apartheid?

Woman. *Cherchez la femme.*[1] Is a *citoyenne* the same as a *citoyen*? Does she have the same rights, same dignity, same power? Alas not ... Until 1944, republican universalism excluded women from citizenship, in the same way that the insane, minors, and the poor were excluded (although the poor, as long as they were male, benefited from the so-called universal suffrage established in 1848). The real trouble is the definitive and irreversible nature of the exclusion of women. Women are born and remain women. The madman, however, can recover his reason, the minor will get older and achieve majority, the poor can hope to get rich ...

It is precisely because the universalism of the French Revolution, through generalization and abstraction, reduced the universal subject of human rights to a masculine subject, that there is deception in the realization of these rights.

33

The sociologist Christine Delphy, director of the journal *Nouvelles questions feministes*, stated to the Observatoire de la parité[2] that: 'This model is in reality a false universalism', for 'it has raised the dominant gender to the status of paradigm—easily done since it was the only model; secondly, the dominated gender's appeal for inclusion met with the reply: "Come in, and do as I do"; the model of universalism demanded of the dominated that they should conform to the model, be like the model. This is clearly impossible, since men are only men to the extent that they exploit women, so women cannot behave like the model because: (i) they have nobody to exploit; (ii) they would have to cease being exploited themselves in order to have equality with men; and (iii) if men had no more women to exploit they would no longer be men or at least not the same. So, by definition, women cannot be equal to men today, because "as they are today" presupposes the subordination of women. This is why the fear of certain differentialist feminists that equality signifies the alignment of women with the masculine model is unfounded.'

The discrepancy between theory and practice results principally from the negation of sexual difference.

Certain progressive historians, angered by the irrationality and the injustice of exclusion maintain that the rights of Man = the rights of man and of woman. They maintain that the citizen, mentioned in all these sacred texts, is also the woman citizen, but that the circumstances and the state of society have not allowed women to affirm themselves the equals of men. This is nonsense. In rereading the texts it is clear that the citizen is masculine.

To take two brief examples:

Article 4 of the Constitutional Act of 1793 entitled 'On the State of Citizens' states: 'A citizen is any *man* born and resident in France, of age etc., or owning property . . . or *married to a French woman*'! Do we really imagine that 'any man' can mean 'any woman' or that the criterion of 'married to a French woman' is open to a woman? The vicious irrationality of this measure is clear; a French woman can, through marriage, bestow a right upon someone (necessarily a man): the right of citizenship from which she herself is excluded. I take my hat off to this masterpiece of misogyny.

As a second example, in article 4 of the Constitution of 22 August 1795, under the heading 'Duties' is written: 'No one is a good citizen unless he is a good *son*, a good *brother*, a good *friend*, a good *husband* . . .'. This is the final nail in the coffin. The astonishing naivety of this statement aside, how could a woman fulfil these demands? Son, father, etc.: the exclusion is quite explicit.

The Declaration of the Rights of Man, a wonderful philosophical and political leap towards the brotherhood of men, unique (except for the United States) in the history of the nineteenth century, kicked the *citoyenne* out of the universalist *citoyen*. Our Revolution proclaimed itself universalist, while in reality it proved to be gendered—a masculine revolution. The result was the exclusion of women *in law* for almost two centuries, and in modern times, the exclusion of women *in fact*. The real irony is that the Revolution promoted women to the title of 'citoyenne', at the same time refusing them the rights of public citizenship: the right to vote, to stand for election, to speak at political meetings etc.

Let's be quite clear: from 1789 to 1946, either deliberately or by omission, each Constitution of the Republic refused women their civil rights.

Women were deprived of their civil rights in this way for a long time. According to the Napoleonic Code of 1804 a woman is a perpetual minor who, to quote the pleasant phrase of the preamble, 'like the fruit tree, belongs to the gardener', and 'owes obedience to her husband' (article 213). This smacks of the religious commandments handed down by our ancestors. Generosity, fraternity, universalism, and revolution are not consonant with equal rights for women.

As early as 1795 the women's clubs were shut down by decree of the Convention. Women were forbidden to make speeches and to demonstrate in the streets, and were confined to the home. They were no longer allowed to attend political meetings (and were forced to dress up as men to gain access to them), or to wear the revolutionary tricolour *cocarde*[3] which had to remain 'a respectable institution'.

A radical misogyny, bordering on a kind of racism, settled on the Revolution. The heroes—Marat, Babeuf, Robespierre—expelled women from the progression of History. The old demons born of the religious and sexual taboos returned to transform the women who fought for the Revolution into threatening monsters in the eyes of these patriotic leaders. Invective rooted in the very past that had supposedly been swept away by the Revolution became the currency of political language. The 'tricoteuses'[4] of the Revolution became nearly a century later the 'petroleuses' of the Commune, to give way at the beginning of the twentieth century to the 'suffragettes'.

Olympe de Gouges, the author of the Declaration of the Rights of Woman, died on the guillotine, a 'tricoteuse'. Louise Michel, a leader of the fight for freedom during the Commune was imprisoned, a 'petroleuse'.[5] Remember Mary Wollstonecraft or Emily Davison who, like others in England, was prepared to throw herself under the horses of the Guard to demand the right for women to vote: a 'suffragette' (as we might say 'majorette', or today 'jupette').[6]

The French Revolution coincided with the greatest political defeat of women. Man is not the representative of humankind, the abstract bearer of equal rights: Man is only man, the male. *Exit* the woman citizen in a country where citizenship confers to the individual (male, of course) freedom and responsibility.

Amongst this chorus of almost pathological anti-feminism, I should mention the happily discordant and stubborn voice of Condorcet, the revolutionary marquis, philosopher, and scholar. In various writings, of which the most famous is his article published in 1789 'On the admission of women to the right of citizenship', he demanded civil and political rights for women. For Condorcet, reason is either a universal capacity or does not exist at all. He contests the supremacy of men, either as soldiers or as husbands. In the name of Reason, shared equally by the sexes, and also in the name of a strict application of universalism, the Man of the Declaration is for Condorcet both man *and* woman. For him, the legislating assembly had 'by excluding women from citizenship, violated the principle of equality of rights by calmly denying half of humankind the right to participate in law-making'. Condorcet pleaded his cause with skill but was ignored by his peers in the assembly. Finally, having refused, on principle, to vote for the death of King Louis XVI, he was prosecuted by Robespierre, arrested by decree in July 1794, condemned to death in his absence having dared to reaffirm the sacred right of everyone to their property, and died mysteriously in his cell. The cause of this death—suicide, accident, illness?—is still unknown.

The weaknesses of universalism became associated with syllogisms whose apparent coherence led to scorn and repression. For, if each man is identical, interchangeable with any other man in the world, the system results in the negation of the multicultural, in the suppression of difference.

It was in the name of the *homo universalis* that the colonial expeditions of the nineteenth century were decided, in order to bring to different peoples the humanist ideals of the Revolution. It was, in sum, so that these faraway 'others'—these savages, good or bad, these lazy children—could benefit from the progress of the Enlightenment and of civilization (universal in nature, civilization could only be white and Western) that their claims to their own identity were crushed in blood and scorn. Not to mention that other monumental weakness of the universalist system—the fact that the Constituents of 1789 were able to maintain slavery (which was only definitively abolished by the Constitution of 1848!).

To a large extent, the brand of universalism termed 'extensive' by the philosopher Étienne Balibar, was responsible for building empires and justifying the great hegemonies.

In the end, the 'legislators of the human race', as Michelet named them with exaggeration, created a strangely limited, 'situated' citizen... 'Behind the abstract man of the Declaration lies the bourgeois man of 1789'—Sartre was quite right. And the History of France, which teaches us that the great political changes, the revolutions and the progress of the eighteenth and nineteenth centuries were the work of a third masculine estate (the bourgeoisie) oppressed by the aristocracy and the clergy, is right too.

To sum up: the universal citizen is a man (and not a woman), white (and of no other colour), and bourgeois (not working class or colonized).

From this dubious universalism was born the lasting exclusion of women. The abstract nature of this universalism was used to justify a concrete inequality. We know the consequences. I have given several incontestable statistics to illustrate the participation/exclusion of women. Women had to wait until the end of the Second World War to obtain the right to vote.

The issue seems to be understood, even by the uncontested defenders of the system. For example, the constitutionalist Olivier Duhamel, in a hearing of the Observatoire de la parité, conceded that 'Certainly, for 150 years that article [the 1st article: "Men are born free and equal in rights"] had no real value, or, more exactly, Men were only men and not the whole of humankind, since women remained excluded from citizenship'. The preachers of universalism are certainly stubborn. Almost to a person they recognize, regret, and deplore the exclusion of women and yet for some strange reason they refuse to submit universalism to objective examination. Perhaps they are afraid that such an examination would establish the link between the theory of universalism and the practical consequences that this theory has had for almost two centuries.

I have dealt elsewhere with the universalist fervour of some women who clash swords with the feminists fighting for true political equality (parity). I have read in various places the accusation that we are endangering republican and democratic principles by denouncing them. This accusation is as grotesque as it is simplistic. The critical analysis of theories which, while generous in word led to the exclusion of women from public life, is a duty—a republican duty. And this would not be the first task accomplished; for we will have first not only rid our obscure texts of intellectuals, but also have taken up arms against any attack on the Republic and its values. For this is what is at stake.

What is the value of a republican power denied to women republicans? And what mysterious fear inhabits those who are against parity? In what way would a truly equal parliament threaten the Republic? I know that for some, to modify the Constitution by introducing the obligation for parity smacks of the crime of lèse-universalism...[7] But we will come back to this point later.

In the meantime, universalist theory leaves women in search of equality and completely disempowered. Do women claim this equality at the same time that they proclaim themselves women, and not that asexual being called 'Man'? Do they stress the misdeeds of 'gender', the division of social roles and places on the basis of sex? Are they trying to establish that in politics more than any other sphere of life, the Man of the Declaration of Man, is in fact man, the masculine sex, and not the neutral prototype he has been compared to? That the citizen is a purely masculine construct with not the slightest feminine element?

Universalism will refer these women back to ... universalism. This is the denial: an entire humanity reduced to and identified with the masculine. A refusal to take into account sexual difference, which is in fact primary and imprescriptible.

Will women succeed in making understood, through statistics and their lived experience, the discrimination they suffer because they are women, and only because of that? There will be a refusal to hear them. The abstract and total assimilation of one sex with another, the feminine with the masculine, will prevent them. The specific inequality which strikes the woman citizen will not be recognized. This is the denegation: the refusal to take into account the existence of injustice, although it is real, concrete, and proven.[8]

Disoriented, diminished in their difference, pilloried by the impalpable universalist theory, women are swept away beyond their control. The *real* confinement of women is exacerbated by the fact of being confined within the *abstract* principles used to oppose that confinement.

In this way universalism acts as a gag. The sub-citizen accused—still accused!—of anti-republicanism for having justly claimed the right to serve the Republic better must turn back to herself. It is too difficult, too complicated, men won't let go... So unfortunately she lets go, along with many others!

To regain a shred of energy and a voice with which to speak, women need to oppose this deceptive universalism with another universalism, still republican, but truly universal. A universalism in which women refuse the erasure of their identity as women and build our humanity together with men. A universalism which recognizes its own diversity.

Notes

1. Translator's note: This phrase was first used by Alexandre Dumas *père* in his novel *Les Mohicans de Paris*. Its implication is that the key to a mystery is a woman, and she has only to be found for the mystery to be solved (*Oxford English Dictionary* (*OED*)). Halimi uses the phrase to imply that women are missing from universalism, and that including women in republicanism would solve many of its problems.
2. Translator's note: The Observatoire de la parité entre les homes et les femmes ('Watchdog for equality between men and women') is a French government agency established in 1995 to deal with issues of sexual equality. Cf. www-.observatoire-parite.gouv.fr/
3. Translator's note: The red, white, and blue rosettes worn as party badges during the Revolution.
4. Translator's note: *Tricoteuse*, meaning a woman who knits, was applied to women in the French Revolution who knitted during meetings of the Convention and at guillotinings (*OED*).
5. Translator's note: Petroleuses were women who used petroleum to burn down buildings during the Commune in May 1871 (*OED*).
6. Translator's note: The word means 'mini-skirt', but is also a slang word for a woman politician.
7. Translator's note: Here Halimi is playing on the term *lèse-majesté*, meaning the crime of treason in a monarchy, to express the idea of the betrayal of the principles of universalism in a republic.
8. The terms 'denial' and 'denegation' are borrowed from psychoanalysis and were used by E. G. Sliedewski, author of a masterly report, *Sur les idéaux démocratiques et les droits des femmes*, in a seminar of the Counsel of Europe (1989), in 'La Démocratie paritaire: 40 years of activity of the Counsel of Europe'.

3 Versions of Difference

Sylviane Agacinski*

Sylviane Agacinski is a professor of philosophy at the École des Hautes Études in Paris, where she is responsible for research seminars in the social sciences. From 1986 to 1992 she was Director of the Collège International de Philosophie, in Paris. She has written extensively on philosophy and politics, as well as other topics, including architecture. She is also active in the French political scene, including in the Feminist Parity Movement and in the debates surrounding the right of same-sex parents to adopt children. Intellectually engaged in current affairs generally, Agacinski writes regularly for several newspapers. Her husband, Lionel Jospin (Socialist Party), was the current Prime Minister of France.

Compared to her previous four books, Agacinski's recently translated *Parity of the Sexes* (originally published in 1998 as *Politique des sexes*, with a second edition in 2001 expanded to include an essay elaborating her concept of 'mixity'), extends her philosophical enquiry much more directly than before into explicitly political terrain. As she explains in the preface to the English edition, her intervention was spurred on by the French debate about sexual and political parity. Agacinski's contribution to this debate is to be found in her book's third and last main part, entitled 'Politics'. Focusing on the realm of political power, she addresses the issue of the relationship between equality and parity by producing a model in which parity does not entail an ideal of equality between the sexes but rather calls for an equal number of females and males to be representatives in every arena of political power. It is partly due to this rearticulation of the theory of parity that the French law requiring each political party to put 50 per cent women on its slate for each election was passed in May 2000.

It was said of Cézanne that he was "imaginative *in front of* things."[1] I suppose that, in general, human imagination works that way: it imagines the real. This is at least one possible way of conceiving these cultural *folds* of which I spoke earlier.

* 'Versions of Difference', in *Parity of the Sexes*, trans. Lisa Walsh (New York: Columbia University Press, 2001), 21–39. Reprinted by permission of Columbia University Press.

Thus the natural difference of the sexes is only the enigmatic "starting point" for the infinite deployment of meanings that the difference of *genders* takes on in all aspects of social life. Nature gives the *two*; cultures invent a multiplicity of possible variations of this duality. Humans are very imaginative in front of the sexes. The very multiplicity of these *versions of difference* indicates that they are the fruit of original creations.

Consequently, one must not confuse *reference* to the natural reality of the sexes with *submission* to a natural order. Nature inspires us, but the abundance of symbolic forms and social structures of the duality of kinds demonstrates a diversity of translations we'd have to call free, since no one translation is any more accurate than another. There are only versions of difference, with no original version. Versions, translations, interpretations: all of these words express an action giving meaning and value, a gesture without which sexual difference would remain meaningless.

Many versions or *expressions* of difference exist: political expressions related to the distribution of power, aesthetic expressions treating the *figuration* of the sexes and the representations of masculine and feminine, economic expressions implying a sexual division of labor. And still others. The multiplicity of these expressions and their great variety through space and time permits us to think they express nothing immutable, if not difference itself and its relation to birth and death. Like all sexed beings, the human individual is destined to die and survives as a species only by "reproducing" itself (as we so wrongly put it, since individuals are not all identical). Beyond the psychological, sociological, or political questions, sexual difference comes back to only one issue, the one linking birth and death. I am speaking here of death as biological fate, the death biologists link to sexual reproduction—both of them belong to the same "logic of the living." This is why we cannot separate the meaning and value of sexual difference from the question of generation, even if expressions of difference lead us well beyond the domain of reproduction, toward politics.

Natural difference, in its essential connection with birth, says nothing to us about the way in which relations between men and women find themselves concretely regulated. These relations are conventional; they result simultaneously from power struggles and negotiations, and they are thus political. Although very real, natural differences never directly engender social or cultural norms. The norm is always moral, political, and aesthetic.

Thus there is always a *politics of the sexes*, that is, a necessity for each

41

of the sexes to advance a politics, consciously or not, because there is no *truth of the sexes*, no absolute knowledge of sexual difference, and thus no correct or obvious way to give it a definitive status. At best, there is *play* and there are *stakes*, difficult relations to negotiate, which involve power struggles and from which no one is exempt. There is no position of advantage, no possibility for arbitration. All of us, men and women, are thus committed to strategies that take into account, as do all strategies, the other's calculations, the other's desires and interests.

Unless one of the two sexes wished to and could survive without the other—which perhaps the mastery of cloning will permit—the game is programmed, inevitable. Each sex can only measure its strengths, endlessly negotiate its positions, determine its politics as best it can.

However, the political nature of this relationship has only really appeared quite recently, because the natural givens and the power struggles have, until now, favored Kate Millett's "Politics of the Male."[2]

To speak of a politics of the sexes, in the plural, is, rather, to emphasize the need for both sexes to become conscious of a certain closure to the scene where male/female relations are played out and also of the fact that this game seems to have no end.

The political nature of the male/female relation does not open up the prospect of an ultimate emancipation or peace. Rather, this politicization marks the *inevitability (fatalité) of eternal discord*. Without this originary discord, human relations would be deprived of their first enigma, their first doubt about the identity of the other and the problem forever posed by coexistence with him—or her. Uncertainty and misunderstanding are the motivating forces in relations between the sexes, for the first anthropoids, no doubt, as for Marivaux's characters. There had to be a breach, there had to be a *game*, in order to invent rules, ruses, compromises.

Now the game does not derive solely from a natural difference but from conflicts of interest and mutual dependence. Men and women depend on each other for the satisfaction of their desires as well as for procreation. Many other disputes follow. We aren't likely to ever get beyond them, and we shouldn't complain about them.

In certain respects, it might be considered that the ideal of the reduction of difference or, as it's called, the "*disappearance of genders*," would constitute a totalitarian fantasy in aiming for a uniformization of individuals. There is nothing worse than the dream of a society of like individuals liberated from conflicts by their very likeness. What is often called "the end of ideologies"—and that is more precisely only the end of ideologies *of the end*—signifies that we have ceased to believe that struggles and conflicts—indeed wars—could and should have an end, and that, if this end is attained, they would stop. We have ceased to hope for permanent peace with justice realized and freedom achieved. We no longer believe in the final liberation of men or women nor in the lasting resolution of the conflicts between them. In this sense *we are departing from the feminism* that subscribed to modern theories of liberation. But we can only depart from it because this feminism has prevailed with regard to the essentials, at least in Western civilization, since women have become conscious of the fact that they are responsible for their own destinies, that they must think about and fulfill them.

Conscious that we can transcend *neither* differences *nor* disputes, we must now develop a way to think about universality that doesn't lean to one side or the other but allows humanity its mixity and thus its internal alterity.

By *versions of difference*, I do not mean simply institutional forms that relations between the sexes have historically taken on but also the mythological and theoretical forms that have provided diverse interpretations of sexual difference through representations or conceptual systems.

Theories of difference, just like myths, have always been political theories, that is, instruments of politics—conservative or transformative as the case may be.

The "subjection of women," according to the formulation of John Stuart Mill,[3] has no doubt been as universal as sexual difference. All over, and in a variety of forms, relations between the sexes appear as distinctly hierarchized, and men have established their power—at the same time as they legitimize it—on mythological, religious, ideological, or scientific grounds. The foundations of power in general were hardly called into question before the Enlightenment, much less the foundations of masculine power. Thus it is not astonishing that women have so rarely sought to determine for themselves their place and status. They have shaped themselves to the familial, economic, political, and religious orders instituted by those who have held the monopoly on power. An ancestral patriarchy has continually sustained the real power of men based on the idea of a supposedly *natural* subordination of women. Naturalist theories have always contributed to the establishment and founding of the political order. But, as we well know, the "natural" order is always permeated with the *political use* we wish to put it to. What we are given, and this is no small thing, is immediately interpreted and evaluated.

Aristotle thus elaborated a *hierarchical* theory of natural sexual difference running through all areas where this difference is expressed—in particular the "biological," with the roles of masculine and feminine in generation, and the political, with the place of men and women in the *polis*. He affirms, for example, that the male alone plays an active role in generation because he alone provides the semen, that is, the generative principle, while the female only provides the material for the future embryo.[4] In his *Politics*, he bases the institution of the family on the "natural" superiority of man, the dominant element, and on the inferiority of woman, the subordinate element, declaring that "every family is governed in monarchistic form by the eldest male."[5] To speak of "monarchistic" form with regard to the family seems metaphorical, since Aristotle normally reserves this term to describe a type of political structure in the strictest sense. Nevertheless, and the place of the family at the very beginning of Aristotle's text proves this, Aristotelian politics could exclude neither the family nor women, in so far as, within the family, both authority and law are at stake. The family is a small monarchistic community entirely commanded by the father. As is often the case in Aristotle, the poet's words comes to pronounce a truth lost in the mists of time, and here, it is Homer who provides the principle: "Each one dictates the law to his children and to his wives."[6]

Such is the knot tying the natural to the political. The "natural" superiority of the male requires him to "dictate the law," that is, to institute a political order. If we continue reading these famous pages where Aristotle writes that "man is by nature a political animal," we realize that the aptitude for political life is given to human beings *with the word*. Indeed, it is because they can say "the useful and the harmful," because they can say "the just and the unjust" that humans, as opposed to animals, share the sense of good and evil and create families and city-states.[7] This beautiful remark on the word as condition for the possibility of politics awakens a suspicion on the part of the reader, and even more so on the part of the female reader, who asks herself if the human, in its feminine version, truly has the capacity to "speak." Because if indeed she does, she should be equally capable of saying the just and the unjust, and it no longer makes sense that men have the right to "dictate the law" to women.

Thus we must admit that, in some way, woman *cannot speak*. Either by nature, or because, according to men's laws, it is not right for her to speak, to say the law. By positing women and children as the primary objects of the law, Aristotle seems to found the familial hierarchy on a natural hierarchy. But, as woman is perfectly capable of speaking, and elsewhere Aristotle affirms that man and woman are both free, we might suspect that woman's silence is far less natural than political.

Indeed, men's governments respond more to political demand than to natural necessity. It is the master/slave relationship that explicitly refers to a difference between "he whose nature is to command and he whose nature is to be commanded."[8] While the interests of the familial community require that it be governed by only one person, Aristotle was so sure that male authority was not absolutely self-evident that he invoked a hierarchical principle more obvious and more natural than sexual difference: age difference. If the male serves as a guide for the female, it is also because the husband is traditionally older than his wife: "The older and fully developed being is destined to command the younger and imperfect being."[9] The "permanent inequality" at the heart of the conjugal community depends less upon woman's essential inferiority than upon the familial institution itself, which unites a mature, adult man with a young, inexperienced woman. Thus Aristotle logically considers the husband's authority over his wife to be a political power, different from the master/slave relationship that, according to him, is grounded entirely in nature.

In the history of theory on sexual difference, we nearly always encounter the family as the structure within which the subordination of women is established. Aristotle's merit is to have understood and demonstrated the political nature of that institution. The institutional order takes advantage of nature more than it follows from it in linking the husband's authority over his wife with the age difference between them. The places and roles of men and women are not defined by nature but institutionalized according to the functions each must carry out in order to ensure the survival and continuation of the family. Thus Aristotle is much less a naturalist than is often believed and much more political.

It seems quite tricky to decide if the definition according to which "man is by nature a political animal" should only be *understood* in the masculine version of *anthropos*. In this case, the male would by nature have a monopoly over the word and power and woman would naturally obey. But if, generally, all humans are political animals, and if, as Aristotle reminds us, man and woman are both free beings, the silence and obedience of the woman in marriage might already be the effect of political consent on her part. I am inclined toward this

SYLVIANE AGACINSKI

second interpretation, conforming to the idea of the family as the
first political community, site of the emergence of the law and
institutionalized power relationships.

This Aristotelian conception of the family, despite its eminently
phallocratic character, and in so far as it admits the political nature of
the man/woman relation in marriage, is more open than it might
seem, in that it allows for the possibility of transforming the institution. If woman is by nature free, and if she is also a political animal,
nothing prevents the possibility that one day she too will be able to
find the voice to "say the just and the unjust" rather than just listening
to the law dictated to her.

This is, in fact, what she has done. Thus the law is no longer only the
affair of men. And one may predict that, in the future, women and
men will together treat the affairs of the city-state.

Let us draw from this analysis of the family that nature is not the
basis for political order but that a political strategy always "works on"
a theory of nature. This strategy is not only at work in the field of
political theory but already in the fields of the natural and social
sciences. Concern with the hierarchization of the two sexes was also
expressed by Aristotle in his *Histoire des animaux* and in his treatise
De la Génération des animaux.[10] Furthermore, this hierarchy is applied,
by analogy, to the fundamental concepts of metaphysics, as when the
philosopher announces that "matter aspires to the Form just as the
female desires the male."

Thus sexual difference never seems to present itself directly, in its
crude state, as it were. It always manifests itself through an interpretation that has already inscribed the masculine/feminine couple into a
hierarchy. This appears even more clearly in comparing the Aristotelian
version of sexual difference and a theoretical version very far removed
from it, such as Freud's—as far removed in time as in point of view,
since it is a question of natural history in one instance and psychology
in the other.

We should note, however, and this is what interests me, that even
while relying upon totally different "facts," *these two versions arise
from the same logic*: the binary logic that opposes one to zero, presence
to absence, and the masculine sex organ to its privation—feminine
castration. In both cases, it is obvious that woman *lacks* something
man has, and, in both cases, the theoretician acts as if this lack is a
matter of a simple empirical assertion.

The following, however, must be considered. For Aristotle, woman
(and females in general) is deprived of the heat that would give her the

46

capacity to procreate. She is incapable of producing a seed, and through a sort of cooking process, of making it "take Form." Only the male can be considered as fertile because he produces the seed that will transmit the essence of the species to the embryo. Aeschylus had already written: "It is not the mother who gives birth to what we call her child: she only nurses the germ sown in her. The one who gives birth is the man who impregnates her."[11] We see that Jean-Pierre Vernant was not forcing an interpretation when he wrote that the "dream of a purely paternal heredity never stopped haunting the Greek imagination."[12] This dream was even more profound and more potent than the Platonic contempt for procreation.

By relying solely on the role of each sex in reproduction and opposing man's procreative power to woman's lack thereof, the Aristotelian theory of sexual difference leads to a thinking of femininity as *privation* and a generalized description of the female as a *mutilated male*.

A comparison with the Freudian theory of sexual difference reveals a similar logic. While the Aristotelian feminine mutilation was due to a lack of heat, and thus of semen, Freudian castration is due, for the child who has made the discovery, to the lack of a penis among girls. Beginning from a completely different choice of criteria, the emission of semen in one case, the anatomy of genital organs in the other, the same structuring of difference within the *presence/absence* opposition appears. We must stress that the choice of differential elements, which are not at all of the same order, seems to go without saying in both cases, while one might just as well point to other criteria, such as breasts or the ability to carry children. It's rather strange to suppose that children discover sexual difference through the anatomy of other children, as if the anatomy of adults were not immediately much more visible (a woman's breasts in particular) or as if a multitude of other attributes had not already placed this difference before the child's gaze. It is manifestly arbitrary to reduce the perception that children might initially have of sexual difference to the sight of the genital organs. From the point of view of ordinary experience, for children as for adults, the perception of genders—masculine or feminine—and of the distinction between men and women always precedes the sight of the anatomical sex. "Secondary" sexual characteristics—general morphology and even vocal quality—are perceived as signifying sexual difference well before the discovery of the genital organs.

If we pursue this comparison between these two theories, we notice that both fail to question the choice of differential elements. Everything takes place as if these elements were obvious, immediate givens.

47

It is true that psychoanalysis, with anatomical difference, relies on visible elements, while Aristotle speaks of more hidden things. In fact, the penis is visible. It is even, according to Freud, particularly apparent to the gaze of the child, who sees nothing *in the place of the penis* in the little girl. As for the Greek philosopher, he must develop a complex argumentation, and for good reason, in order to make apparent the exact location of woman's lack. But the result of the two "descriptions" is the same: the differentiation of the species into two sexes is substituted either for a unique masculine model from which woman more or less deviates and which she cannot transmit, or for a sole visible sex organ, the penis, and a sole sexual signifier, the phallus. Lacan, who knows quite well that these anatomical considerations are rather secondary in relation to the androcentric order, nonetheless justifies the choice of the phallus as privileged signifier because it is "the most salient of what can be captured in the real of sexual copulation." He also invokes the turgidity of the masculine sex, the "image of vital flux" that passes in reproduction, to legitimate the primacy of the phallus, while simultaneously distancing himself from the Freudian scene.[13]

Beginning from the child's gaze at the only sexual organ considered visible, the boy and the girl will thus be confronted, according to Freud, with, for one, the anguishing possibility of castration, and for the other, the "discovery" of her own castration.

There is, of course, no question of assimilating the theories of Aristotle and Freud since their fields and objects are not the same. The *Generation of Animals*, deals with the biological question of procreation, while the famous article "Several Psychic Consequences of the Anatomical Differences of the Sexes"[14] treats the relationship between anatomy and the psyche. But beginning from profoundly different historical and scientific contexts, the structure of masculine/feminine difference is still interpreted through the opposition between a thing's presence and its absence. The choice of differential traits seems relatively secondary in relation to the general meaning given to difference. What is essential, in each instance, is the primacy of the masculine and the definition of the feminine as lack, privation, and impotence.

Might one not see in the persistence of this structure the proof of its universality? And isn't sexual difference to be understood as an essential dissymmetry? But neither difference nor dissymmetry need necessarily be interpreted as a logic of lack. In its substitution of *one* for *two* (*l'un aux deux*), this logic is metaphysical. In its placement of the masculine at the center, it is political.

The hierarchization of difference is not merely the effect of its inscription in a binary system. If the sexual alternative places us well within a *binary* logic (*either* masculine *or* feminine), this logic is not necessarily a *logic of lack*, opposing one term to its absence. To the contrary, the binary structure formulated via the disjunction "a" *or* "not-a," or again, "one" *or* "zero," poses a hierarchy between positive and negative, presence and absence. "Phallocentrism" is a product of this structure in opposing the phallus to its lack and phallic virility to castrated femininity. This logic of lack must be replaced with a logic of difference, but a difference without hierarchy that I will term a *logic of the mixed*.

The mixed structure also poses an alternative, but it does not hierarchize this alternative. Sexual difference is indeed a dichotomy, and it also logically resembles a disjunction, since every individual is masculine *or* feminine—"a" *or* "b." But this disjunction only signifies that *either* "a" *or* "b" is true, and thus that "a" *and* "b" cannot both be true at the same time. This does not mean that one of the terms is positive and the other negative, that one is simply the negation of the other. More precisely, there is indeed, logically, a double negation: feminine is not masculine, and masculine is not feminine. But, if only one of the two negations is retained, the alternative is centered on one of the two terms. For example: woman is not a man. This is how androcentric logic functions. If one placed women at the center or at the summit of humanity, one would say: men are not women, designating the masculine as lack.

The logic of the mixed posits that the human is necessarily masculine *or* feminine, that there is a double version of "man," without one version being inferior to the other. This logic posits that a woman *is not a man* (which has always been said), but, in addition, that a man is this individual *who is not a woman* (which has been said far less often). Thus, the sexual alternative is not played out between that which is *present* or *absent*, unless in the sense that the lack is double. Each of the two is deprived of that which the other has or is.

According to this perspective, there is, so to speak, no unilateral castration, if you could call it that. In one sense, sexual difference leaves behind the logic of lack. In another, it suggests the idea of a double castration. Neither man nor woman constitutes "the whole human."

Taking into account, however, the fact that the sexual alternative applies to everyone, one might situate lack on the side of the metaphysical subject who denies the alternative. The *neuter subject*, in some

SYLVIANE AGACINSKI

sense angelic and beyond sex, a prelapsarian being, this figure attests to a dream of "purity," philosophical as much as religious. Because it cannot overcome the division of the human, this dream—or in other words, the anguish of mixity—will always remain rooted in a fantasy of a single, and not a double, humanity. But since this dream of simplicity has no model, it can only be represented by *one of the two sexes*. The misapprehension of mixity always replaces the two with *one* of the two.

Freud's theoretical superiority does not lie in his presentation of lack as an objective reality but, rather, in his thinking of lack as the effect of an unconscious interpretation of anatomical difference. Freud knows quite well that one is always, inevitably, engaged in interpretation. Nevertheless, from the moment this interpretation is given as universal, it becomes a rule and even a norm that Freud fails to call into question. For Freud, women must accept their difference and renounce their envy of the penis they lack.

Now, and it is here that theory reveals its political stakes, for Freud, "penis envy" is expressed in women through the desire to act *like men* and to have the same social ambitions as men! This transference of penis envy onto ambition suggests a necessary and natural relation between sexual difference and individuals' social and professional functions. We had to wait for Karen Horney[15] and Melanie Klein for psychoanalysis to pose the question of knowing whether the place and the status of men in the social and cultural order might not provoke women's desire to be men as much as, if not more than, the unique fact of having a penis. Freud finds it inherently natural that one must be a man, and thus have a penis, to exercise certain social functions. Ambition, for him, is normally masculine. Freud remains very conservative on this point because he still believes in an immutable social destiny for women. Ambition in women remains for him the expression of her desire to be a man—and thus of her "penis envy"—but he is unable to suppose that, inversely, a woman's ambition, in society such as it is (and even more as it was at the beginning of the twentieth century), provokes her desire to be a man. And provokes *in addition*, I might add, penis envy. . . . On this point, Simone de Beauvoir was right on the mark: "The covetous desire on the girl's part, when it appears, results from a preexisting valorization of virility: Freud takes it for granted when it must be accounted for."[16]

But the *political* dimension of Freud is limited neither to its traditionalism in terms of the distribution of roles in social life nor even to the psychoanalytic interpretation of anatomical difference. As we have just seen, the political dimension begins with the anatomical description itself, with the choice of the penis as the *sole signifier of sex*. From the outset, in order to "describe" difference, this theory chooses the trait *woman lacks*. The rest follows: castration, penis envy, child as *substitute* for the penis, etc.

However, the critiques of phallocentrism devoted to asserting early knowledge of the vagina, contesting penis envy and demonstrating the representation of the feminine sex from childhood on, have perhaps been misguided. This point of view subscribed to the very logic it contested in seeking a "feminine equivalent" of the penis—that is, in accepting the anatomy of genital organs as the primary criterion for the representation of the sexes (with the conscious and unconscious consequences this entails). The debate opposing the visibility of the penis and the invisibility of the vagina was already a trap. From the moment when *the locus of the sexual signifier* had been situated in the penis (or in any masculine feature), feminine *lack* followed. We must go much further toward a recognition of difference and, thus, dissymmetry. It is not *from one* that we must describe *the other*, or we privilege one of the two terms; we immediately hierarchize difference and remain within the logic of lack. On the contrary, we must locate a set of differential elements, including fecundity and the role of procreation, which are no less important than anatomy for the representation of the sexes and its conscious and unconscious psychic effects. That dolls, so well-loved by girls *in general*, and no matter what might be said, appear as penis substitutes rather than baby or child substitutes is an example of a kind of theoretical acrobatics that must be questioned and that bears witness to the androcentrism of the psychoanalytic order.

Here again, it is not simply the theoretician's sex that must be challenged but a philosophical difficulty in conceiving and defining difference *as such*. Because a difference is never itself seen, is not *presented* in *one of the two*, difference signifies the in-between and the gap. There is no *place*, no assigned placement for difference, only a way, for each of the two sexes for example, to be *otherwise* than the other one. If difference is nowhere, we cannot think about it by beginning from one element but, rather, by considering the play of elements, their relationships.

The androcentric, or phallocentric, structure, is always associated with other conceptual couples, also hierarchized, that qualify and reinforce the masculine/feminine opposition. This is the case, for example, with the active/passive couple: no matter which differential traits are retained to describe sexual difference, the masculine is always "active," while the "passive" qualifies the feminine—at least in the Western tradition. Thus, in Aristotle, for example, the male generative principle is *active* and the nourishing matter *passive*. In the Freudian field, it is the sexual energy of the drives that is active, because this energy prompts action in order to satisfy the drives (*les pulsions*). The libido is by nature male, and this renders feminine desire very enigmatic.

Would it be less apt to consider the desire to bear children and feminine fecundity determinant elements of sexuality and thus to wonder if men do not also define themselves through their incapacity to give birth? Couldn't this impotence create in him an over-estimation of his sex and penis worship as a substitute for the child he cannot carry? The theory of lack can always be inverted, and a primary way of deconstructing the traditional hierarchy consists in operating this inversion of negative and positive definitions. This is Antoinette Fouque's move when she writes: "To be born man is in large part to feel oneself excluded from giving birth."[17]

In this way one might oppose the absolute value of feminine fecundity to phallocentrism and completely reverse the traditional oppositions. It would be tempting to think that the Greek dream of a purely "paternal heredity" constitutes a symptom of the masculine *envy* of fecundity. It has been proposed, for example, that the Greek myths of *autochthony* that would have Athenian citizens born from the very ground of the fatherland (*auto-chtôn*) have as their effect, as Nicole Loraux demonstrates, the supplanting of the parental couple and the effacement of Mother Earth to the profit of *fathers' earth*.[18]

The question of difference and the androcentric response always bring us back to the mystery of birth. One might recognize in the Christian myth of the incarnation a way of establishing a purely paternal, direct, and mysterious filiation between God the Father and his Son. But the role of the Virgin Mary intervenes both to permit and prevent this filiation. She permits it, since, as a virgin, she gives birth outside any sexual relation, thus without a father. The Father, who "sends" a son to Mary, engenders without a woman. The incarnation thus takes place outside the relation between two sexes: on one side, a father/son relation without woman; on the other, a mother/son relation without man. The Christian myth of the incarnation, with Mary's maternity, thus establishes a strange compromise. Christ is indeed born of a father and a mother, but without there having been any relation between them. The mystery of filiation, of birth, intersects with the mystery of the relation—or nonrelation—between the sexes. As Hubert Damisch says with regard to the *Madonna del Parto*, the superb and enigmatic image of the pregnant Virgin, the figure of Mary is at the transitional moment between "Holy History and individual experience."[19]

But reversals of perspective do not necessarily result in a "gynocentric" position—the very word is barbarous—that is, a position that displaces humanity's *center* toward the feminine side. One would then remain in the same metaphysical logic—the logic of the same: the occultation of the two (*du deux*) to the benefit of the *one* (*l'un*): negation of difference to the benefit of the oppositions of presence/absence, activity/passivity, visible/invisible, etc.; a forgetting of the mixed structure to the benefit of a hierarchy. The reversal of the hierarchy vindicates women and shows that lack is also on the other side—so many actions with political and theoretical utility must still be pursued.

This is neither sufficient nor satisfactory philosophically. Binary logic and the hierarchies it institutes cannot be truly overcome unless we renounce the center in general, the desire for a center, and the desire that there be the *one* before the *two*, the single before the double. The thinking of sexual duality requires us to remain within difference, that is, in the in-between. It requires us to think about alterity without wanting it to return to the same—or to a single—identity. Thus: a renunciation of the logic of the center and the metaphysics of presence so that we might dare to affront this irreducible difference mixity suggests.[20]

Indeed, mixity designates a purely differential structure in which neither of the two terms is derived from the other. The *two* never derives from the *one* but, rather, the *one* always derives from the *two* of those who engendered the individual. However, this individual does not in any way exceed or "supersede" the originary sexual difference, he renews it in himself in being either *the male one of the two*—or *the female one of the two*—and not the unification of the two. The individual himself is traversed by difference, always avoiding aspirations to a single unity.

Nevertheless, everything leads to the realization that a nostalgia for the *one* haunts us and, without deciding whether this nostalgia is of a biological or metaphysical order, I will say that it is expressed through an anguish with regard to division and consequently an *anguish with regard to mixity*. Because if humanity is mixed, and not single, all individuals are confronted with their own insufficiency and cannot fully claim to be full human beings.

Each sex is thus "mutilated," or insufficient, and each sex knows the castration of not being the other. There is indeed a *lack essential to every human being*, which is neither the lack of a penis nor some other attribute of men, or women, but stems from being only male or only female. The consciousness of this originary privation has nothing to do with the myth of a lost completeness—each one being half of an initially full and total being—because this myth also refers back to a primary undifferentiated identity. To the contrary, such a consciousness implies the recognition of an originary division.

Most theories of sexual difference have attempted to reduce the mixity of the species through the subordination of the other to the one, the suppression of the dizziness brought on by the *two* through reference to a unique center. We can do no more than to propose a new theoretical version of difference, one which is both philosophical and political in its attempt to break with the nostalgia of the one.

Notes

1. André Masson, *Le Rebelle du surréalisme: Ecrits* (Paris: Hermann, 1976), p. 135.
2. *La Politique du mâle* (The Politics of the Male) is the French title of the American Kate Millett's book published by Stock in 1971. The original title was *Sexual Politics* (New York: Doubleday, 1969). It was essentially about denouncing patriarchal domination, which explains my choice of the French translation.
3. *The Subjection of Women* (1869) is translated by Marie-Françoise Cachin as "the subservience (*asservissement*)" of women" (Paris: Petite Bibliothèque Payot, 1975), but it is the idea of subjection, it seems to me, that is important here.
4. I explored this Aristotelian theory of generation in "Le tout premier écart," in *Les Fins de l'homme* (Colloque de Cérisy, Paris: Galilée, 1981).
5. Aristotle, *Politique* 1.5.1252b.
6. *L'Odysée* 9.114. [*Tr.*: I have translated the French translation of the Greek. The English translation of the Greek is as follows: "Each one rules his wives and children as he pleases." See Homer, *The Odyssey* 9.138–139, trans. William Cullen Bryant (Boston: Houghton, Mifflin, 1871), pp. 180–181.]
7. *Politique* 1.5.1253a.
8. Ibid. 1.1.1252a.
9. Ibid. 1.13.1259b.
10. Aristotle, *Histoire des animaux* (Paris: Les Belles Lettres, 1968); *De la Génération des animaux* (Paris: Les Belles Lettres, 1961).
11. Aeschylus, *Les Euménides*, 658–661, cited by Jean-Pierre Vernant in *Mythe et pensée chez les Grecs* (Paris: François Maspero, 1980), 1:133. [*Tr.*: Again, I

have translated from the French translation of the Greek to maintain continuity in the author's argument. The English translation (one among many of course) reads: "The mother to the child that men call hers is no true life-begetter, but a nurse of live seed. 'Tis the sower of the seed alone begetteth." See Aeschylus, *The Eumenides*, trans. Gilbert Murray (New York: Oxford University Press, 1925), p. 33.]

12. Vernant, *Mythe et pensée chez les Grecs*.
13. Jacques Lacan, *Ecrits* (Paris: Editions du Seuil, 1966), p. 692; Jacques Lacan, *Ecrits: A Selection*, trans. Alan Sheridan (London: Tavistock, 1977), p. 287 (translation modified).
14. Freud's article is from 1925. It is translated into French in *La Vie sexuelle* (Paris: PUF, 1973), p. 123 ff.
15. Beginning in 1926, Karen Horney contests the infantile ignorance of the vagina, poses the question of the social valorization of the penis, and hypothesizes the masculine repression of a desire for maternity. See *La Psychologie de la femme* (New York, W. W. Norton, 1967 and Paris: Payot, 1969).
16. Simone de Beauvoir, *Le Deuxième sexe* (Paris: Gallimard, 1978). The first edition appeared in 1949; Simone de Beauvoir, *The Second Sex*, trans. H. M. Parshley (New York: Vintage, 1989), p. 45 (translation modified).
17. Antoinette Fouque, "Il y a 2 sexes," *Le Débat* (Paris: Gallimard, 1995), p. 175.
18. See Nicole Loraux, *Les Enfants d'Athena* (Paris: François Maspero, 1981), p. 66 and *Points Essais* (Paris: Editions du Seuil, 1990.) See also *Né de la terre: Mythe et politique à Athènes* (Paris: Editions du Seuil, 1996).
19. Hubert Damisch, *Un Souvenir d'enfance par Piero della Francesca* (Paris: Editions du Seuil, 1997).
20. This is why the most fruitful research on the difference between the sexes has begun with the philosophical "deconstruction" of the "metaphysics of presence"—for example, the work of Jacques Derrida, most notably from *De la grammatologie* (Paris: Editions du Seuil, 1967), and *L'Ecriture et la différence* (Paris: Editions du Seuil, 1967) to *Glas* (Paris: Galilée, 1974).

4 Masculine/Feminine: The Thought of the Difference

Françoise Héritier*

Françoise Héritier was born in France in the 1930s. She studied with Claude Lévi-Strauss at the Collège de France in the late 1950s, and in the early 1960s began ethnographic fieldwork in sub-Sarahan West Africa, primarily with the Samo, Pana, and Mossi peoples in the Upper Volta. Héritier currently teaches at the Collège de France and serves as director of studies at l'École des Hautes Études en Sciences Sociales. At the Collège de France, she directs the laboratory of social anthropology formerly headed by Lévi-Strauss. Héritier has been actively involved in public debate on social and public health issues, including bioethics, HIV/AIDS, reproductive rights, and violence. From 1989 to 1994, she was President of the French Conseil national du sida (National Council on AIDS).

While Héritier has been closely associated with French structuralism as developed in contemporary kinship theory, her critical exploration of the links between systems of kinship and alliance and the social bases of gender links between systems of kinship and alliance and the social bases of gender hierarchy and masculine domination represents a significant development within that field. Héritier's concerns with questions of sexual difference and the status of universality in culture link her with other French feminists working to rethink universalism from the perspectives of those excluded by the false universalism of patriarchy. In 'La Valence différentielle des sexes au fondement de la societé?' and other works, Héritier uses ethnological and historical accounts to argue that biological differences between the sexes are at the foundation of all thought, generating a gamut of cognitive categories predicated upon the binary identity/difference. These categories based upon sexual differences constitute a universal 'alphabet' for diverse symbolic constructions, including culturally specific discourses of gender. The symbolic is anchored in the elemental differences between sexed bodies as they are perceived and lived in social groups, and these differences may be traced to

---

* 'La valence différentielle des sexes au fondement de la société?' and 'Le Sang du guerrier et le sang des femmes: Contrôle et appropriation de la fécondité' in *Masculin/féminin: La Pensée de la différence*. (Paris: Éditions Odile Jacob, 1996), 17–29 and 205–35 (abridged). Reprinted by permission of Éditions Odile Jacob.

binary differences of reproductive function. While historically and culturally encoded in diverse ways, binary sexual differences seem to be universally hierarchical and unequal. Women have been persistently devalued and dominated by men in both patrilineal and matrilineal societies, modern and ancient. In 'Le Sang du guerrier et le sang des femmes: Contrôle et appropriation de le fécondité' and other works, Héritier argues that discourses of fertility and sterility and bodily fluids are foundational in the symbolism of sexual difference and in kinship systems. She traces practices of male domination to the different bodily relations that men and women have to blood, fertility, and the material world. If the law of exogamy founds all societies, that law should be understood in its fullest historical and critical sense as the enactment of male domination through the control of female fertility and the exchange of women.

SOCIAL POWER AND ANTHROPOLOGY

The relationship between the sexes is an issue permanently at stake on a social level. It would be presumptuous to believe that the research of social scientists has a profound influence on legislators and decision-makers regarding this issue, or even that social scientists are heard and understood by the media. However, anthropologists are now consulted by and present at regional and national tribunals dealing with, for example, questions of bioethics or questions involving social relationships between the sexes. This allows a message to be heard which is often held by our colleagues to be unusual or even inappropriate. At any rate, a message is articulated—whether it is understood is another matter. The important point, without doubt, is that we are currently witnessing a greater openness on the part of the State and its constituent bodies to consider anthropologists as partners in decision-making on a legislative or any other level, and also that anthropologists are making greater efforts than in the past to make themselves publicly heard.

I also have in mind encounters with other colleagues whose daily work has the potential for action—the medical profession, for example. In 1991, I spoke at a conference on medical ethics about the attitudes of traditional societies towards epidemics.[1] From their reaction, it was obvious that at least some of the audience realized that underlying our rational understanding of epidemics is a system of representation little different from that of traditional societies, within which we all function, and that this system of representation must be taken into account when considering preventative health measures. While this example is not exactly related to the issue of the relationship between the sexes, the same kind of realization is needed regarding the relationship between the sexes: the existence and the depth of the symbolic moorings which go unnoticed by the groups of people who put them into practice must become understood.

It must be noted that relationships between men and women are often the subject of the tribunals mentioned previously. Although the relationship between the sexes is not generally the focus of anthropologists, we are nonetheless confronted with a double difficulty: social problems which are both real and urgent.

For example, we face issues such as medically assisted conception, the 'double work' of women both outside and inside the home, the situation of immigrant women, the consequences of longer life expectancy—especially for women—for pension schemes, and so on. These are concrete problems about which politicians need advice and guidance, but they are also problems which are pragmatic in nature and which need to be addressed immediately. The anthropological approach, which aims to illuminate the logic behind a situation, is not seen as relevant to these issues unless it can lead to people adopting a firm position, or guarantee in some way that ethical and technical decisions can be made. There is an attitude of selective deafness towards anthropologists. As a result it took me a long time to make even basic things understood in the Haut Conseil de la Population et de la Famille 'the High Council of the Population and the Family'— for example, that new methods of conception would have no effect on our system of filiation, that 'new' versions of filiation could not be invented except through cloning or by instituting a Platonic republic which suppresses the relationship between parents and children, and that it was therefore pointless to legislate as though this were the case.

The writings of anthropologists have a relatively small readership. Therefore we need to continue to strive to inform others in order to diminish as far as possible the selective deafness mentioned above and to reach a new level of communication which allows us to be fully heard by public authorities.

In other words, we need to overcome barriers in order to make it more widely understood that our work does not refer to totally exotic 'others', to strangers, to archaic mentalities, to ways of life now extinct, or to relics of any of these, but to ourselves, to our own society, to our own reactions, behaviours, and modes of representation.

To come back to my subject, the so-called anthropology of the sexes has never been for me an object of study in its own right as it is for some of my colleagues. I have deliberately never made it the focus of my research because I challenge the breaking down of the discipline of anthropology into autonomous sectors such as anthropology of health, of politics, of religion and so on. The focus and the methods are the same for all these sectors. Of course, researchers specialize in terms of ethnic groups, regions, and problematics. But anthropology is a single discipline, and dividing it into autonomous categories seems to me a mutilating and exclusory strategy.

SEXUAL DIFFERENCE, THE ULTIMATE BUFFER OF THOUGHT

That said, it seems to me that the observation of the difference between the sexes is the foundation of all thought, traditional as well as scientific. From its beginning, man's thought has inevitably focused on what was nearest to him: the body and its surroundings. The human body, as a site where various constants can be observed—such as organs, elementary functions, humours—presents one remarkable and indeed, scandalous, feature: sexual difference and the differing roles of the sexes in reproduction.

It appears to me that sexual difference is the ultimate buffer of thought upon which is founded an essential conceptual opposition: the opposition of the identical and the different. This is one of those archaic *themata* which is present in all scientific thought, ancient and modern, and in all systems of representation.

The relation between sameness and difference is the linchpin of all ideological systems which set up in opposition to each other pairs of abstract and concrete values (hot/cold, dry/wet, high/low, superior/ inferior, light/dark etc.)—the same contrasting values which are found in the codes used to classify the masculine and the feminine. Aristotelian discourse opposes masculine and feminine as hot and cold, animated and inert, air and matter respectively. But if we take the more recent example of the medical discourse of eighteenth- and nineteenth-century hygienist doctors, or of contemporary medical discourse, the explicit or implicit permanence of these systems of categorizing opposites becomes clear. In the 1984 edition of the *Encyclopedia Universalis*, the biologists responsible for the article on 'Fertilization' express the joining of sperm and egg—the precise mechanism of which remains unexplained—as the animation of an inert, vegetative material by an active agent, a source of life-giving energy. I see here not the remnants of the philosophical tradition from which we have inherited, but the spontaneous manifestation of an interpretative code, valid in scientific as well as natural discourse, which encompasses genders, sexes, and even gametes in a system of oppositions originating in the primal observation of the irreducible difference between the sexes.

I am placing myself at a very general level of analysis by considering the relationships between the sexes through these systems of representation without addressing the conceptual debate surrounding the categories of sex or gender. Nevertheless, the social construction of gender is a subject which interests me in two ways. Firstly as a general artefact based upon the division of tasks between the sexes, which along with the prohibition of incest (or the exogamic obligation) and the institution of a recognized form of union, constitute for Claude Lévi-Strauss[2] the three pillars of the family and society. Secondly, and in addition to the first, as a specific artefact resulting from a series of real and symbolic manipulations which affect individuals.

Certain New Guinean and Innuit societies serve as excellent examples of this point of view. Especially for the Innuit, identity and gender are not a function of biological sex but of the gender of the reincarnated soul-name. Nevertheless, the individual must subscribe to the activities and skills of their apparent sex (tasks and reproduction) at the appropriate time, even if identity and gender will always be a function of his or her soul-name.[3] As a result of his soul-name a boy can be brought up as and considered a girl until puberty, fulfil his male reproductive role when adult, and commit himself from that time on to masculine tasks within the family and social group, but he will keep throughout his life his soul-name, that is, his feminine identity.

I am bringing a general anthropological perspective from my own work and from the work of others to these questions of sex and gender. On several occasions I have looked explicitly to this work to try to make different audiences (doctors, lawyers, psychiatrists . . .) understand that the categories of gender, the representation of the sexed person, and the division of tasks in Western society, are not phenomena with a universal value generated by shared biological characteristics, but instead that they are cultural constructions. By means of a symbolic and universal 'alphabet' rooted in shared biological characteristics, every society develops its own cultural 'expressions' which are particular to it.

THE ALPHABET OF BIOLOGICAL FACTS

According to the naive perspective of naturalism, there exists a unique and universal way of transcribing, in a canonical form which legitimizes the relationship between the sexes, facts that are seen as natural because they are the same for everybody. But in reality the biological characteristics we observe in the natural world are broken down into conceptual units, and reassembled in syntagmatic associations which vary between societies. There is no unique paradigm. If it were possible to create a comprehensive list of these various associations, we would be able to map the whole landscape of cultural diversity. But this not the aim of my investigation.

It remains that, as much in the construction of systems of relationship (terminology, filiation, union) as in representations of gender, of the person, of reproduction, and of every part of the body, there are observable and recognizable conceptual units inscribed in the body, in the biological and the physiological, which are identifiable at all times and in all places throughout societies; these units are adjusted and reassembled in different cultures according to various logical formulae which are possible because they are thinkable. Inscription in biology is inevitable, but there does not necessarily have to be one unique and universal translation of the fundamental facts.

It is also easy to demonstrate that crude biological facts of an extremely simple nature are a consideration in determining filiation: namely, the existence of two anatomically different sexes which must join to produce offspring of each sex; an order of reproduction that cannot be reversed (whether it is a question of single cells or of individual beings, the begetter always precedes the begotten); and a succession in the order of brothers and sisters within the family, and thus the existence of collateral ancestry. Starting from these elementary facts, there are only six possible logical combinations that can result from the respective sexuated positions of parents and offspring: patrilineal, matrilineal, bilinear, cognatic, parallel, and crossed. The last two almost never occur, and there can be no others. But equally, there can be no fewer, for one single agency has not been able to dominate all human minds. All the logical, plausible, and realizable possibilities have been explored.

Examining the relationships of close kinship and collaterality (brother or sister, eldest or youngest, of a man or of a woman, of the father or of the mother of a man or a woman, etc.) by reducing them to their most basic units thus reveals a finite number of logical possibilities for mating (in spite of the variations which can be observed), which are derived from elementary biological facts, and which lead to terminological systems and types.

Because of this, I consider myself to be a materialist. In order to explain how social institutions and systems of representation and thought came to be established, I take biology as my starting point. However, I pose as a *petitio principii* that universal biological fact, reduced to its essential components, cannot have a single and unique translation, and that all the logically (in both senses of the word—mathematical and conceivable) possible combinations have been explored and realized by men in society.

THE DIFFERENTIAL VALENCY OF THE SEXES

However, it seems as though there has only been one translation of biological fact into the aspect of social reality that I have termed the 'differential valency of the sexes'.

In *L'Exercice de la parenté*, I wrote that to Lévi-Strauss's three 'pillars' mentioned above should be added the pillar 'differential valency of the sexes', which is no less an artefact than the others and which is not a fact of nature. This differential valency expresses a conceptual relationship oriented, if not always hierarchically, between the masculine and the feminine, translatable in terms of weight and temporality (anterior/posterior) of value. This conceptual relationship is easily identifiable in the terminological treatment of the central relationship of close kinship (the bother/sister, sister/brother pairings) and in the relationships which ensue, if one takes as an example those systems in which the logic of the rules of filiation—either patrilinear or matrilinear—is most strictly expressed, such as the Crow and Omaha systems.[4]

When I became particularly interested in the logic inscribed at the heart of the terminology of kinship, it became clear to me that in the matrilinear Crow system (which ought to represent the mirror image of the patrilinear Omaha system) in which the brother/sister relationship is understood as a 'father'/'daughter' relationship, the logic of inverse designation—whereby the sister/brother relationship ought to be translated as a 'mother'/'son' relationship—is never taken to its extreme. At a certain level in the generational system, the real relationships of seniority intervene and alter the inherent logic of naming. The older brother of a woman cannot be treated by her as a 'son', or as the equivalent of a son, even if her younger brother can be. Even if the Crow system essentially postulates a 'domination' of the feminine over the masculine at the heart of the close kinship between a brother and a sister, the full consequences of this domination are not realized—not even at the level of naming. Of course, this does not apply to the functioning of societies globally. In the Omaha system, the wholly conceptual 'dominance' of the masculine over the feminine in the brother/sister relationship is taken implacably and imperturbably to its extreme.

Thus, it seems that this conceptual relationship is inscribed within kinship, which is a profound social structure. The ways in which it is translated into social institutions and into the functions of different human groups are varied, but the social domination of the masculine principle is an observable fact. Let's take a brief example: for the Iroquois, with a matrilinear right, the matrons—mature, post-menopausal women—enjoyed considerable power, especially over women younger than they; however, this did not extend to the exercise of political power, or to equality with men in decision-making.[5]

Seeking the provenance of the 'differential valency of the sexes' and what would be the primary phenomena to explain its universal presence, I came to the hypothetical conclusion that it was less a question of feminine weakness (fragility, being shorter and lighter, the handicap of pregnancy and breastfeeding) than of a desire to control reproduction on the part of those who do not possess the power to give birth. This leads us to the question of procreation.

When discussing the categories of sex, one cannot ignore the many representations relating to procreation, the formation of the embryo, and the respective participation of the parents, and therefore the representations of bodily fluids: blood, sperm, milk, saliva, lymph, tears, sweat, and so on; furthermore, a close association can be observed between these representations and more abstract facts such as kinship and marriage.

Bodily fluids are always observable facts, subjected to intellectual manipulation, even if they are not always reducible to the same indivisible elemental core beyond the fact that they are fluid, and can be spilt and projected from the body.

It is well known that Aristotle attributed the weakness inherent in the feminine constitution to its characteristic moistness and cold-ness—the result of the loss of blood which women regularly endure without being able to do prevent it. Men only lose their blood willingly, so to speak, in situations where they have sought to do so: such as hunting, war, or competition. The loss of this substance does not therefore affect individuals of each sex in the same way. The loss of sperm can also be controlled, and many social and ideological systems recommend and regulate this control. In sum, it could be that in this inequality—controllable versus uncontrollable, willed versus submitted—lies the matrix of the differential valency of the sexes, which in this case would be inscribed in the body, in physiological functions, or more precisely, would be the result of observing physiological functions.

Although apparently tautological, this hypothesis can be further explored: the two sexes, which are anatomically and physiologically different are a natural given; in observing these differences, abstract notions of which the prototype is the opposition identical/different, ensue, and on these are moulded so many other conceptual oppositions which are used in discourse on all levels, and the hierarchical classifications implemented by thought and which have their own value.

Is this a constant, a universal category? Certain feminists and anthropologists working on the anthropology of the sexes contest this idea and seek to show that there could be or could have been societies in which the differential valency of the sexes did not exist, or in which it would work against what we know. But their attempts to demonstrate this remain unconvincing.

However, to say exactly why the differential valency of the sexes seems to be established universally, exactly like the prohibition of incest, seems to me to stem from the same needs. It is a question of constructing the social order and the rules which allow it to function. To the three pillars which Claude Lévi-Strauss defined as the prohibition of incest, the division of tasks between the sexes, and a recognized form of sexual union, I would add a fourth, so obvious that it has not been perceived, but absolutely essential to explain how the others function, since they are all based on the relationship of the masculine and the feminine. This fourth pillar, or if you prefer, the cord that links the other three pillars of the social tripod, is the differential valency of the sexes. Although this might seem to be a cause for despair, in reality it is not.

This discussion is situated at a very abstract and general level. Naturally, there are delicate and precise analyses to be made of the current evolution and role of beings in society. But it must not be forgotten that from primitive times up to today there have always been social beings, even if we have found it hard to decode their roles and the effects of these roles upon the fundamental representations of the categories rooted in the body. And the biased conceptual relationship is translated into inequality which is lived and experienced.

COGNITIVE CATEGORIES, INEQUALITY, AND DOMINATION

The striking thing, in spite of the various agents of social construction, is the constants. Although the difference in the experiences of each sex is currently dwindling, particularly in developed societies, and although we are seeing profound changes taking place, whether their origin lies in technology (biotechnologies) or in the evolution of our customs (the changes occurring in the heart of the family, in the practice of sexuality, etc.), it does not seem to me that we have yet reached the time when the relationship between the sexes is necessarily and universally conceived as an equal relationship, in intellectual and practical terms. And it seems to me that reaching such a point in time will be difficult, given the tight bond that exists between the four founding pillars of society.

Perhaps everything is beginning to come right and inequalities are lessening, but this is an effect of asymptotic regression rather than the disappearance of the problem. Even if women are more and more often taking on masculine tasks, there is always in the distance, in the future, a 'reserved masculine domain', in the highly select club of politics, religion, business, and so on. Obviously, this is not the result of particular competencies inscribed in the physical constitution of the two sexes. It is not here that the biological inscription of character-istics should be sought, but in those facts of a biological nature which are so fundamental to us that we lose sight of their biological nature. These facts are the origin of our cognitive categories: the functions of classification, opposition, qualification, and hierarchical arrangement forming the bars behind which the masculine and the feminine are imprisoned. These cognitive categories endure whatever their particu-lar content in each culture because they are transmissible, inculcated in us from an early age through our upbringing and our cultural environment, and reinforced through every message and explicit and implicit signal received in our daily lives.

One of the current functions of the so-called 'anthropology of the sexes' is to highlight the problems raised by masculine domination. There is no doubt that this task is legitimate and necessary. However, I doubt the potential of anthropological knowledge of these complex mechanisms to influence political decisions or other decisions, since objective situations cannot be changed through simple understanding or by decree.

Of course, there is the crucial role of 'social actors', of men and women. We can hope, therefore, to move towards an increasing equality of the sexes, since that is the current trend that can be observed. The role of men and women is far from negligible, and the positive evolution of Western societies is to their credit. But I doubt that we will ever reach an idyllic equality in every domain, to the extent that any society can only be built upon the tightly soldered framework of the four pillars: the prohibition of incest, the sexual division of tasks, a legal or recognized form of stable union, and, I would add, the differential valency of the sexes.

If we acknowledge this construction, even though it cannot be proved but only endowed with a powerful likelihood since this conceptual framework finds its source in the immutable facts which men have observed from the dawn of time—their bodies and their environment—then yes, the primary difficulty on the path to equality is to find the button which would blow apart these ancient associations.

THE BLOOD OF THE WARRIOR AND THE BLOOD OF WOMEN
THE CONTROL AND APPROPRIATION OF FERTILITY

There is no doubt, to any observer of Western society, that it is marked by a startling masculine domination.

Feminine subordination is evident in the domains of politics, economics, and the symbolic.

There are few female representatives of the nation in the organs of local and central government responsible for decision-making and administration.

On the economic front, women are most often confined to the domestic sphere, from which they can never escape absolutely: in fact, women with a salaried job must combine it with their domestic activities. When women have activities outside the domestic sphere, it is rare that they can reach the top, filling posts of responsibility, management, and prestige in their profession.

On the symbolic front, perpetuated by tradition and the way children are brought up, the valued and prized activities are those carried out by men.

Furthermore, a body of value judgements makes clear which characteristics observable in behaviour and performance are seen as the natural and therefore immutable 'qualities' or 'faults' considered to be the representative marks typifying the feminine sex.

A negative discourse exists, presenting women as irrational and illogical creatures, deprived of a critical mind, curious, indiscreet, gossiping, incapable of keeping a secret, addicted to routine, uninventive, uncreative especially regarding intellectual and aesthetic activities, fearful and cowardly, slaves to their bodies and their feelings, unable to master and control their passions, thoughtless, hysterical, changeable, untrustworthy and even treacherous, cunning, jealous, envious, incapable of being friends with other women, undisciplined, disobedient, indecent, perverse...Eve, Dalila, Galatea, Aphrodite ...

There exists another body of discourse, seemingly less negative. According to this, women are fragile, stay-at-home, lacking in intellectual and physical talent, gentle, emotional, seeking peace, stability, and the comfort of the home, fleeing responsibility, incapable of decision-making and of thinking in abstract terms, credulous, intuitive, sensitive, tender, and prudish. By their nature, women need to be suppressed, directed, and controlled by men.

In either case, and in spite of the contradictions between the two versions (the lustful woman, the frigid woman; the pure woman, the corrupting woman), this symbolic discourse refers to a morphological, biological, and psychological feminine nature.

These series of adjectives which qualify the feminine are marked as negative or devalued, while the corresponding series for the masculine are positive or valued.

The difference between the sexes is, always and in all societies, ideologically translated into a binary, hierarchical language. It is hierarchical even though we might logically expect that the two poles would be equidistant from a positive middle term. But the middle term is not positive, and it is often missing. Warm exists between cold and hot, and the combination of the two could be positive, but this is not the case regarding the sexes.

Only one of the poles is valued; and, what is disturbing is that the aspect considered as morally negative is often valued, while the positive aspect of the pair of oppositions is devalued *a contrario*. For example, all men in society say they prefer peace to war, but nevertheless, it is universally seen as better for a man to be a valiant fighter than a *'femmelette'* (this word is chosen on purpose).[6] The valorization of the negative pole indicates the forces at work in the relationship between the sexes. That which is morally superior can be socially decried or of low status.

John Ingham gives a remarkable example of this in a study on medicine and characterology in Mexican communities. As with the Samo, hot goes with dry, cold with damp, men are associated with heat, women with cold, and a certain number of other qualities are marked in this way. Thus, to be *macho* or to be avaricious is to be hot; to be good, generous, or naive is to be cold; the happy medium, the man who would enjoy a balanced relationship with others without being either too *macho* or too naive would be an ideal. However, such a man does not exist. There only exist the *macho* and the *tonto*, or the imbecile, who is in fact generous and naive. According to the popular imagery, it is good to be *macho* and bad to be *tonto*. In theory, generosity is preferable to severity, rain to drought, peace to war. But the reality of judgements and actions betrays these moral principles.

Therefore there is a major sex and a minor sex, a 'strong' sex and a 'weak' sex, a 'strong' mind and a 'weak' mind. Supposedly, it is this natural congenital 'weakness' of women which legitimizes their subjection to men even regarding their bodies.

The question is not posed here of knowing whether the unequal relationship between the sexes in Western society can and should change, and if so, how. Instead, we ask two totally different questions.

Can it be said that this masculine domination is *universal*? If so, where lies the *origin*, the explanation for this fundamental inequality between the sexes?

THE TOUCHSTONE OF FECUNDITY

In the majority of so-called primitive societies, sterility—that is, feminine sterility, since masculine sterility is generally not recognized—is the ultimate abomination. However, this is not always the case.

For example, for the Nuer of western Africa, a woman who is found to be sterile, that is after having been married and remained without children for a certain number of years (perhaps until menopause?), rejoins her family of origin where she is henceforth considered as a man. She is 'brother' to her brothers, and paternal 'uncle' to the children of her brothers.

Like a man, she is able to develop her own herd from the portion that comes to her with the title of uncle—the cattle given as dowry for her nieces. With this herd and the fruits or her own labour, she will, like a man, gather the dowry to obtain one or several wives for herself.

She enters into these institutional marriage relationships as a husband. Her wives serve her, work for her, honour her, and give her the marks of respect due to a husband.

She recruits a male servant from a different ethnic group, usually the Dinka, from whom she demands, among other services, sexual service for her wife or wives. The children born from these relations are hers, they call her 'father' and treat her as a male father would be treated. The biological father has no role except as a subaltern: perhaps linked emotionally to the offspring he has engendered, he remains nonetheless a servant, treated as such by the woman-husband, and also by the wives and children. He is paid for his services by the gift of a cow, the 'price for begetting', each time that one of the girls he has conceived gets married.

Sterility, whether it is absolute or relative (that is, caused by age/menopause), and the social body of institutions and behaviours that it leads to, can always be explained through the schemas of symbolic representation discussed earlier.

It seems, in any case, that the sterile woman is not, or is no longer, properly speaking a woman. Either in a negative or positive way, as a failed woman or a failed man, she is nearer to a man than a woman.

So, *it is not sex, but fecundity, that creates the real difference between the masculine and the feminine,* and masculine domination, which we will now attempt to understand, is fundamentally the control and the appropriation of women's fecundity, in the case that she is able to have a child.

The rest, that is to say the psychological elements, the particular characteristics which make up the portraits of masculinity and femininity in society's eyes and which supposedly justify the domination of one sex by the other, is a product of upbringing, and thus of ideology.

Simone de Beauvoir was right when she wrote: 'One is not born a woman, one becomes a woman' (just as one becomes a man or a father in certain societies in New Guinea). So, there is no maternal instinct in the sense in which it is usually understood, that is to say that maternity is a purely biological matter and that it therefore goes without saying that because of her nature, a woman has a vocation to look after children, and beyond that, to look after the home.

Maternity is a social fact as well as biological fact (and the same applies to paternity, Nicole Mathieu, 1974[7]), and there is nothing in the biological fact itself to explain the ineluctable chains which, through the idea of 'maternal instinct', bind women to domestic tasks and to the status of subordinate.

The appropriation of fecundity in the masculine body is bound to fail: there can only ever be an imitation of fecundity in the masculine body. Therefore appropriation becomes control: the appropriation of women themselves or of the products of their fertility, the sharing of women among men.

Women are fertile, inventive, they create life; on the other hand, it is seen as the lot of men to bring order and regulation, to impose limits, to determine the different spheres of society and to inscribe politics.

This control is made possible by the handicap which doubles the power of fecundity: a pregnant woman or a woman who is breastfeeding is less mobile than a man. It has been shown that for the Bushmen, hunter-gatherer nomads, without domestic animals to provide milk, a man covers between 5,000 and 6,000 kilometres a year, while a woman covers between 2,500 and 3,000.

THE TWO PIVOTS OF SEXUAL INEQUALITY

The obstacle to mobility caused by pregnancy and breastfeeding does not imply an inferiority of physical aptitude—neither, *a fortiori*, of intellectual aptitude—however, it has led to a certain type of division of tasks, at the heart of prehistoric societies of wild men, hunter-gatherers, who depended solely on nature for survival (it is known that agriculture and raising animals are relatively recent inventions in the history of humanity).

It was up to men to hunt big animals and to protect the unarmed against all kinds of predators. It was up to women to look after unweaned children and to collect more easily accessible foodstuffs than big game (it is not easy to hunt with a baby stuck to your side). This division of tasks was born of objective constraints and not of psychological predispositions of either sex towards tasks destined to them by fate, neither of a physical constraint imposed on one sex by another. This division does not include any principle of value.

The social control of women's fecundity and the division of work between the sexes are seemingly the two pivots of sexual inequality.

Still, it is necessary to understand the mechanisms which make of this inequality a valorized relationship of domination/subjection.

Kinship is the general matrix of social relationships. Man is a being who lives in society; society only exists divided into groups, based upon kinship and overcoming the original division through cooperation. The first institution which opens up the possibility of solidarity between groups is marriage. A group which relied solely upon its own internal strengths for biological reproduction, which practiced incest and only incest, would lead to its own disappearance, if only through the rarefaction of its members: a brother and a sister only produce one line of descent instead of two. The exchange of women between groups is the exchange of life because women give children and pass on their power of fecundity to others than their close relatives.

The fundamental linchpin of masculine domination, articulated in the economic constraints of the division of tasks, is without doubt to be found in the sacrifice of the benefit of the fecundity of their daughters and their sisters, of the women of their group, to the benefit of strangers. The law of exogamy which founds any society must be understood as the exchange of women and of their power of fecundity among men.

What is remarkable is the consistency with which there is always, through the rules of filiation and alliance, an initial appropriation by men of the specific power of reproduction of the women of their group, and of those women who are given to them in exchange for theirs. This is the only point at which violence and force can be identified as an ultimate explanation.

The appropriation of women's power of fecundity, a power which is vital for the constitution and the survival of any society and which is procured through the exchange of women between groups, is reinforced by the way in which women are restricted to the maternal role. There are two maternal roles: the Mother and the nursing mother.

All this is made even easier by the fact that the baby remains at the breast for many months. In societies which do not have artificial breastfeeding or modern techniques for feeding babies, babies are weaned at around two and half or even three years. The child knows its mother only as a wet nurse during these years and will continue to turn to her for food even after it is weaned. This occurs even more 'naturally' because the social confinement of women in the role of wet nurse, guardian, and maintainer, has taken place.

The status of the mother can be greatly elevated, very highly considered, and idealized—for example in the case of goddess-mothers—but this does not contradict the notion of masculine power.

The appropriation and the control of women's fecundity, the restriction of women to the role of wet nurse facilitated by the child's need for nourishment, the assumption of power over women, have been accompanied by the creation of highly technical specialisms, that is to say the exclusive practice by the masculine sex of certain technical professions which demand a period of either truly or falsely sophisticated apprenticeship, but for which nothing in the physical constitution of women explains women's lack of access to them.

In this way a reserved masculine domain is built, just as there is a reserved domain for women which is inaccessible to men: that of the ability to give birth.

To take one more example from the hunter-gatherer peoples[8] the Ona de Terre de Feu reserve archery solely for men. Men learn to make bows, arrows and even poison. They learn from a very young age to shoot and this apprenticeship is saved for them exclusively.

Chapman shows that, in this exclusive apprenticeship, adult women cannot, in the physical sense, use a bow, any more than a man who had not learnt how to use it in childhood could.

The reserved domain of highly specialized technical expertise, the corollary to the division of tasks between the sexes which is founded upon objective constraints, has the effect of further confining women to tasks which, although they require knowledge and know-how, will never be part of the reserved masculine domain since this knowledge is not particular to the feminine sex—men too can gather plant food in times of hardship.

Even if women manage to break into the exclusive domain, or if one part of this domain becomes progressively accessed by women, the important thing is that the exclusive domain continues to exist even though it is altered.

The above discussion sketches out the workings of thought, the ideological creation which we saw at work in the symbolism discussed earlier: an unequal value is attributed to the various tasks carried out by men and women which does not correspond to the quantity of work undertaken or to the expertise with which it is carried out.

Women's work of gathering represents sometimes more than 66 per cent of the food resources of the group in hunter-gatherer societies, but this fact is granted no importance: the real prestige is attached to the function of hunter.

Here we are confronted with the ultimate mystery. Since it seems to me that the primary material of the symbolic is the body because it is the first object to be subjected to the observation of the senses, and because for any problem there can only be solutions based on explanations relying on more and more simple facts until they hit against the most elementary evidence, I would suggest that the reason for the inequality between the sexes is a characteristic rooted in the feminine body (and it is not the 'inability to produce sperm').

What men value about men is without doubt the fact that they can spill their blood, risk their lives, and take the lives of others, through their own free will. Women 'see' their blood flow from their bodies[9] and they give life (sometimes dying in the process) without necessarily being able to prevent it.

Perhaps it is in this difference that lies the fundamental motive for all the symbolism grafted on to the origins of the relationship between the sexes.

Notes

1. F. Héritier-Augé, 'Les "sociétés traditionnelles" face aux épidemies', in Ordre des médecins, Troisième Congrès international d'Éthique médicale, Paris, 9–10 March 1991 (Les Actes: Paris, 1992), 293–9.
2. Claude Lévi-Strauss, 'La Famille', Annales de l'université d'Abidjan, series F, vol. 3 (1971).
3. Bernard Saladin d'Anglure, 'Iqallijuq ou les réminiscences d'une âme-nom inuit', Études inuit, 1/1 (1977), 33–63.
4. Names of North American Indian populations.
5. Judith K. Brown, 'Economic Organisation and the Position of Women among the Iroquois', Ethnohistory, 17/3–4 (1970), 151–67.
6. Translator's note: Literally meaning 'little woman', slang word for effeminate/homosexual man.
7. Nicole Mathieu, 'Propos critiques sur l'urbanisation des campagnes', In Espace et sociétés, 12 (1974), 71–89.
8. Anne Chapman, Drama and Power in a Hunting Society: the Selk'nam of Tierra del Fuego (Cambridge: Cambridge University Press, 1982).
9. The verb 'to see' used to be commonly used in French to mean 'having a period' ('avoir ses règles').

5 A Little Learning: Women and (Intellectual) Work

Michèle Le Dœuff*

Michèle Le Dœuff was born in 1948 in France. She completed her doctorate degree in philosophy in 1980 and has subsequently taught in the women's studies department at the University of Geneva and in the philosophy department at her alma mater, the *Ecóle Normale Supérieure* at Fontaney, where she also held the position of conference director. Le Dœuff is currently Research Director at the *Centre National de la Recherche Scientifique* (CNRS/National Center for Scientific Research). She published her first book, *L'imaginaire philosophique* (The Philosophical Imaginary), in 1980 and her second book, *L'Étude et le rouet* (Hipparchia's Choice), in 1989. Her work also includes the translation of Bacon's *New Atlantis* in 1983 and the translation and stage adaptation of Shakespeare's *Venus and Adonis* in 1986. In addition, she has also collaborated with the Théâtre de l'Aquarium on the play *Le Soeur de Shakespeare* (Shakespeare's Sister). Michèle Le Dœuff is one of the most recognized living French feminist philosophers, both in her own country and abroad.

Politically belonging to the generation of 1968 and the French feminist movement, Le Dœuff has remained throughout the years an outspoken social critic, especially with regards to the French government and national educational policies. Although much of her work has been on Francis Bacon, Le Dœuff's academic interests and commitments go beyond traditional disciplinary boundaries to accomplish a critical feminist standpoint that engages the intersections of philosophy, literature, and feminist theory in an innovative way. The diversity of the interests and forms of her work must not, however, be taken as a sign of a postmodern stance. On the contrary, her style is rather nourished by classical influences while her philosophical position is founded in a critical epistemology

* 'A Little Learning: Women and (Intellectual) Work' in Colin Blakemore and Susan Iversen (eds.), *Gender and Society* (Oxford: Oxford University Press, 2000), 97–115. Reprinted by permission of Oxford University Press.

    I should like to thank Simone Oettli and Richard Scholar, who kindly checked my English and turned this task into an occasion for shared merriment.

that she identifes in French enlightenment thought and the twentieth century writings of Koyré and Bachelard.

In her essay, 'A Little Learning: Women and (Intellectual) Work', Michèle Le Dœuff explores the cross-cultural and trans-historical implications of a sexuated determination of the meanings and practices of learning and knowledge within a sustained partriarchal, social tradition. Refusing the artificial gap between 'intellectual work' and the limited, or 'little', amount of practical knowledge deemed necessary for women to fulfil their gendered duties in an orderly and economical fashion, Le Dœuff argues that education for women has most often been figured as a means to an end rather than as an end in itself. Whereas the attainment of knowledge for men has been institutionalized as a first step towards professional training, either intellectual or otherwise, the relegation of women to the private, reproductive sphere of the home has produced a feminized knowledge with the sole purpose of ensuring that within the legal domain of the family, sexual morality and orderliness prevail.

In quite basic terms, Le Dœuff's discussion of the gendered (as opposed to sexed) nature of knowledge and learning returns us to the tired and perhaps seemingly collapsed distinction between productive and reproductive work. Returning to the works of theorists ranging from Fénélon to Engels, Le Dœuff proposes that despite the arguably substantial progress made by feminists over the past decades (or centuries!), women's work remains attached to the confines of the home. A controlled organization of space still serves to ensure monogamy and sexual morality on the part of women. 'Truth' and *real* work are relegated to the outer space occupied by men. Not until reproductive working hours become visible and literally 'outed' from the very physical space of the home might the 'little learning' of an artificially enforced regenerative sphere make way for the full knowledge necessary to the self-realization of a feminine subject.

When the Herbert Spencer committee honoured me with the invitation to give a lecture on women and work, I quickly realized that this is no longer a well-defined subject. It refers to a tangle of problems, and, what is more, the category of women's work itself may prove unstable, or ought to prove so. If, then, a brand new approach is necessary today, kindly consider this essay, which will broach the topic primarily from the perspective of intellectual work, as just a contribution to the necessary redefinition of the theme—a redefinition that will require many an indirect analysis. And let me tackle mine in a roundabout way.

The United Nations conference held in Cairo in 1994 made it plain that more and more agencies and governments feel concerned with the steep increase of population worldwide. Whatever the reasons for constructing the world's population as a major concern may be, this debate happens to have a side effect which will be my starting point: people in charge in the west are now realizing that 70 per cent of the children deprived of schooling are girls, and women the better part of the illiterate. How is it that a concern about population makes the issue of schooling for girls suddenly more visible? The answer is that a correlation between female illiteracy and larger families, or between female literacy and smaller families, is suggested. Furthermore, this correlation is being accepted as a causality, with the result that a miracle cure is said to be in view: let us educate girls *a little* and this will work wonders.

A sample of this creed appeared in an issue of *The Economist* published in September 1994, at the time of the Cairo conference. The editors first challenged a survey carried out by demographers who had argued that 'differences in contraceptive prevalence' explained about 90 per cent of the variation in fertility rates. *The Economist* declared they could not believe this, or to quote, that they found it 'preposterous to identify contraceptive supply as the main determinant of family size'. And they claimed that 'the single most effective and enduring way of moderating population growth, even more than by the diffusion of contraception, is to give women more and better education'. As if it was either one or the other, either making contraception available or giving education to girls. As if the latter appealed to the men in charge, but not the former. The article was illustrated by a diagram, entitled 'A little learning'. Based on statistics provided by the World Resources Institute (WRI), it was supposed to show that the fertility rate drops as female literacy increases.[1]

Sometimes, statistics happen *not* to be particularly relevant or indeed reliable from a mere mathematical point of view, as in the famous quip used in epistemology classes: 'Parisians who pay a monthly rent of 8,000 francs or more tend to go skiing more frequently than people who pay a lower rent; therefore, when all the rents go up, skiing will become accessible to all'. In a similar way, with the alleged correlation between a little learning and a drop in the fertility rate, it may be simply that a higher rate of female literacy derives from a factor which also involves some drop in the fertility rate. It may well be a package: when the situation is somehow better for women, we gain access to some civil rights, to some reproductive rights, and to some schooling, along with some free speech in the household and outside it, and to some access to skilled labour outside the household, women becoming thus financially, practically, and mentally more independent. But why not ask family planning counsellors their opinion? Their experience tends to show that, when a woman has some schooling, it is indeed easier for her to choose the type of contraception she will feel happy with—the Pill or a diaphragm, or whatever—and she will handle the technique she has chosen with fewer errors. But this must be qualified straightaway: the main knowledge required is that of her own body, and some of us can still remember a time when we learned a lot about the digestive or respiratory apparatus, while the syllabus left a blank on genitalia and the reproductive process.

As a tribute to Herbert Spencer's memory, I could offer a twofold comment on this debate. *Point one*: our century believes in science, and even newspapers think it essential to offer views based on scientific or supposedly scientific data, but then they can dismiss one set of results and choose another, according to their own preference. In the example given, editors decided not to accept a demographic survey and to endorse other statistics. A major debate concerning women's lives is then offered to public opinion formulated as a learned debate, as a problem that ought to be confined in a scientific construction and left to learned experts. But the construction is based on a non-scientific element, since one set of figures was dismissed just because the editors could not believe in them—as if belief ruled science. Moreover, a critique of statistics may cast a serious doubt on the set of data produced by the WRI, with the result that we are left with the feeling that we need extremely competent feminist scientists, women who would have reached the highest level in the subject and could therefore carry out a good critical survey; namely, who could bring mathematical control to bear on the construction. It is not a *little* learning we expect from women involved in intellectual professions, but the refined capacity that makes it possible to sort out what is serious and what is not in constructions offered in the name of scientific authority.

Point two: women's liberation is not just about subtle intellectual debates, nor the critical contributions feminist scientists could make to important controversies. Women's liberation is equally about, or even more about, everyday life for every woman, whatever her social class or level of education. Now, although a basic knowledge of one's own body has been heralded as *the* crucial issue that it indeed is in every woman's life by many a feminist since at least Mary Wollstonecraft, this crucial knowledge has not been integrated to the schooling system until very recently. Some women of my generation have acquired highly sophisticated learning—in, say, Latin grammar, algebra, or Leibniz's metaphysics—while growing up with no knowledge at all about the facts of life—our life. If no knowledge for ourselves was given by the education system, it did not make much difference whether we obtained a large portion of knowledge or just a small one.

Be that as it may, the philosophy behind the concept of 'a little learning for Third World women', used as a self-evident notion by (mostly male) decision-makers in the twentieth century, should give rise to some questions. Why just a little? Why not equal access to schooling? What do they call a little learning? How is the acceptable or apposite measure of learning determined? And who will determine the portion of learning which is good as opposed to the portion of learning which would be irrelevant, or possibly bad, and bad for what? When the matter discussed is what measure of learning a certain group is to be endowed with, then this limited portion of learning is always considered as a sheer means to an end, certainly not an end in itself. Moreover, it is a means not for the woman herself, but for politics, which may have little to do with her moral or practical claims. Learning, here, is seen as a mere tool in the hands of people who know its purpose and determine it.

This could be discussed in the light of Herbert Spencer's philosophy. In one of his *Essays on Education*, entitled 'What knowledge is of most worth?', he puts forth a concept which, although looking somewhat similar to 'the little learning', has in fact nothing to do with it, and obviously enough, the difference is based on gender. Spencer used the phrase 'to have some acquaintance with', stressing, for instance, that 'For the higher arts of construction, some acquaintance with the special division of Mathematics is indispensable',[2] and indeed he offers a generalization of this view, when stating that, 'to such as are occupied in the production, exchange, or distribution of commodities, acquaintance with Science in some of its departments, is of fundamental importance'.[3] This is true even for shareholders, he claims: since you buy shares in industry, and since industry is linked to technological hence scientific research, your profit or loss will depend on your understanding of the sort of sciences bearing on the business. Therefore, an acquaintance with science is vital in order to be among the survivors in an industrial society.

In Spencer's argument, this 'acquaintance with science' was clearly related to men. The vocabulary he used made that quite obvious. No wonder, then, that he added a special section for women, and discussed what they need in order to be more competent mothers. But what did he mean, by his concept of 'acquaintance with this or that'? Not full possession perhaps, not mathematics as a mathematician would practise it, or chemistry as a chemist would, but a knowledge of elementary principles, data, and findings that would enable every man to carry out his profession and also to be a successful shareholder, since according to him, every man above the labourer is somehow a capitalist. Therefore, this is knowledge with practical aims; again, not the complete learning that scholars would have, each in their own field, but a due proportion of preparation, with social and practical activities in view. And the result of this is that one cannot discuss work without discussing education, and one must discuss education in relation to work, work as it is in a modern society.

This concept has nothing to do with 'a little learning' as defined for girls and women by a time-honoured tradition. The concept of 'some acquaintance with' means 'enough, just enough, as long as it is enough'. A due proportion, because complete knowledge is not possible. It is better to have a moderate share of more than one subject than exhaustive information bearing on just one field, and total lack of acquaintance with knowledge in other respects, Spencer claimed. Therefore the restriction is simply pragmatic: since one cannot give a boy comprehensive knowledge in all subjects, one must define portions that can be acquired fairly easily. Moreover, there is no gap, no difference of nature, between an elementary knowledge of, say, chemistry, for those who will be involved in this occupation and a full knowledge of chemistry for the scientist. There is a good continuity between the knowledge necessary in work, whatever the occupation or job, *and* knowledge as laboured in intellectual professions, just as an elementary understanding is an understanding of elements of the whole.

In contrast, all we know about the western tradition concerning education for girls points to a difference in nature between what ought to be taught to them, and knowledge *as it is*, when it is described as full knowledge: teach her this, but, for goodness sake, do not teach her that. Teach her the tradition of moral thinking, both Christian and philosophical, but do not teach her history, literature, or latin. Or teach her literature, a smattering of moral philosophy and the fine arts, and of course housekeeping, but no sciences. Give her an ornamental education, but not professional training. The definition of the right syllabus for girls may vary, from one century to another, even between editions of the same book. But until recently, it was defined in such a way that it never was, nor could be, the first step leading us to intellectual work, by which I mean both the practice of an intellectual profession, as a scientist, academic, writer, researcher, *and* the practice of any profession as described by Spencer, granted that he claimed that most or virtually all jobs in a modern society involve some intellectual preparation, and this applies to a plumber, an electrician, just as much as to a lawyer, anyone running a farm, a shop, or an artisan business, a nurse just as much as a technical engineer, since everyone needs intellectual skills. A little learning for girls was never defined as a portion that would be sufficient for making a living, or for what Spencer calls self-preservation; nor was it a portion granted provisionally, with the promise of full knowledge in the future. A difference was always marked between 'a little learning' for girls and free access to the learning of the learned, but the difference also meant that women were earmarked for unskilled labour.

Let me bring an example of this pattern from a rightly forgotten book, which was influential thoughout Europe from the Renaissance to the nineteenth century. Written in Latin, it was soon translated into more than one European vernacular, and I choose it because the phrase 'a little learning', '*un petit sçavoir*', is to be found in one of the three early French translations. The author was Vivès, a Spanish humanist based at the English Court, as tutor to Princess Mary Tudor. His book, the *De Institutione Feminœ Christianœ*, launched an awkward tradition, namely the idea that a tailor-made portion of knowledge for females is to be defined, in order to make us more submissive to patriarchal law, more virginal before marriage, more strictly faithful during marriage, more compliant with any and every decision or wish of our husbands, and better mourners when widows. Vivès' plan was based on the idea that, with a carefully selected allocation of learning, women would be more decent, more docile, and more chaste, than with no learning at all, because, for instance, by giving them some kind of intellectual interest, it would be easier to keep them at home, and they would want to go out, dancing or socializing, less often. Also, because learning keeps the mind occupied, whereas an idle imagination may wander and come to mischief. But mainly because they would be given access only to books that would teach them in detail the conduct they were supposed to follow, books that would enforce duty in a deeper and more refined way. It is not necessary to give them literacy, by the way; they may listen to someone read books. And Vivès suggested a parallel between that occupation—reading or being read edifying works—and other techniques to enforce duty. Ancient Egyptians used to deprive women of shoes, so that they stayed at home; and many have thought it a good idea to deprive women of silk, pearls, and ornaments, in order to diminish their wish to go out and show off. Spinning keeps a woman at home, and when you teach a little girl her letters—if you do so, that is—she should start spinning at the same time, so that she will understand that it is one and the same thing. A little learning, therefore, is an equivalent of spinning, of being locked in, of being deprived of shoes, and I take it that Vivès recommended the use, not just of one, but of all these strategies at the same time. A little learning is viewed as a prop, among other things to enforce submission, perhaps the best of them, since it will make women internalize the demands of chastity and submission. A little learning and less freedom, in any case.

Is this idea utterly obsolete—that is, in our part of the world? Of course it is, and the younger generation would certainly laugh at the idea they could be kept at home, with no shoes, under lock and key, reading or being read edifying material, with a limited set of books and no right whatsoever to explore a library or the world of learning as they wished. Most young women would also offer some sarcastic comments on the demand for virginity. But could we, women of an already older generation, swear on oath that nothing at all of such a plan was present in our early education? I doubt we could. I suspect the demands made by schooling (learning lessons and writing essays at home in the evening, going to bed early in order to be fit the next morning) provided our parents with a formidable pretext not to allow us to go out as teenagers, and this was true even when they did not contemplate any professional outcome for our schooling or when they said we were not bright. Schooling made nice girls of us all, or was thought to help make us so, therefore it did not matter whether we found any intellectual development through it or not, and many parents thought it better we did not. Many girls of my generation were sent to school with such a double bind: learn your lessons, but learn nothing; your lessons are not devised to give you any learning, nor indeed to train you for a profession, but just to keep you in order. But this was a twofold order: we had to be nice girls, we had also to be attractive to men, and there is a long tradition of male complaints against learned women. In Spencer's words

'Men care little for erudition in women; but very much for physical beauty, good nature and sound sense. How many conquests does the bluestocking make through her extensive knowledge of history? What man ever fell in love with a woman because she understood Italian? Where is the Edwin who was brought to Angelina's feet by her German? But rosy cheeks and laughing eyes are great attractions'.[4]

MICHÈLE LE DŒUFF

Education sacrifices the body to the mind, he warned, and in a woman the body is what matters to men. We seem to be inheriting a culture which has always discussed a woman's intellectual development in relation to her sex. I say 'sex', for 'gender' would be far too polite or vague a term here. If what is at stake is rather her sex-appeal and her sexual morality, or perhaps the conflicting demands of sex-appeal and sexual morality, this must be said in so many words.

Therefore there was, or is, a huge and structural gap between intellectual work and the small ration of learning specially devised for women, a structural gap that may be noted either in theories upheld by old books or in recent practice. Some schools did their best to stick to the pattern of a specifically defined teaching for the female of the species. But, even in French State-run girls' schools, in which the syllabus was copied from the syllabus for boys, the underlying purpose, meaning and value of going to school could be quite different, and I believe children grasp the real reason why they go to school just as readily as they understand any portion of trigonometry, if not more readily. Similar syllabuses may well take on a completely different meaning, if the dominant view is that women should learn as little as possible or even that restrictions matter more than anything else.

According to Fénelon, a seventeenth-century writer who granted that a woman must have some education in order to govern her household, keep domestic accounts, and educate her children, there should be, in women, a sense of shame or modesty about knowledge, almost as keen as the sense of shame which inspires us with a horror of wantonness. Modesty about learning here means avoiding contact with pagan fables or other unwholesome stories and steering clear of any temptation to take a critical view on religious matters. It also means that women must not use knowledge as an adornment. And it must mean something much more than that or else Fénelon's vocabulary could not be accounted for. Furthermore, when he discusses literacy, a subtext tends to show through. A girl should be taught to read and write with correctness, she should never be at fault with her spelling; accustom her to using a neat script and making straight lines on the paper. She should be exact in her grammar, always use proper and accurate terms, neatly express her meaning, in an orderly way, etc.[5] As if acquiring literacy were nothing more than learning tidiness, a virtue most important in women according to the author.[6] What is acquired, then, is a virtue and not a skill, the virtues of cleanliness and propriety and certainly not the beginning of intellectual accomplishment. When you come to think how dreadful the handwriting of some male authors was, and how casual their spelling, and what a mess their manuscripts were, you may wonder whether something important is not at stake here. Descartes said about spelling that he could not care less about it, for it was the printer's job, not his, to know whether or not you should write *corps* with a *p* in it![7] All he was concerned about was to make the metaphysical distinction between this *corps*, the body, and the mind. Perhaps it was *infra dig* for a philosopher to know how to spell, perhaps he assumed that creative skills in the intellectual world implied a certain amount of untidiness, or at least the right not to bother too much with orderliness. Again, younger women today would simply laugh at the idea they should prove themselves tidy and law-abiding by having neat handwriting, correct spelling, and perfect grammar, but I believe this is so recent a change that many women schooled during the 1950s could bear witness that common practice was for a long time consistent with Fénelon's ideas. Even literacy, then, may function, not as a skill, but as a mere token of conformity. I believe this is the ideology at work in the World Resources Institute's views, taken up by *The Economist*: with a little learning and some literacy women create less disorder, and they internalize the order imposed upon them more readily. And since the increase of population is now being seen as a major disorder, let us conclude the syllogism and give all women a little education, which is safe anyway. It is as if a western myth were being prescribed to the rest of the world. And it is certainly a mythical medicine for overpopulation, if literacy is given instead of birth control, and not together with it. If under-population was found to be a disorder, perhaps they would recommend the same remedy, and claim that mothers with a little learning tend to reduce the infant mortality rate.

Another detail shows that western executives share past masters' ideology: when they refer to Third World women's access to work, they refer to cottage industries, such as sewing at home. Women must be kept at home, and if they must work, let this be at home or *close to home*, as Christine Delphy and Diana Leonard entitled their book about women's work.[8] For we should all be aware that women do indeed work. According to the United Nations, women are responsible for two-thirds of the working hours on this planet. Nonetheless, the current image does not fit with those figures, for the view remains that women do not work, or only rarely, or even that there is something unnatural about a working woman, that is about a woman working outside her rightful place. Discounting most of the work done by women is achieved by a simple trick: just deem that what is done at home, or close to home, is not real work, but just something you do naturally perhaps, and certainly invisibly.

The link between home and women may explain a lot, as far as this image is concerned. It seems to be created by the demands of patriarchal fidelity. Again, virgin brides and faithful wives, fulfilling the demands of monogamy, are better kept as close to home as possible. Traditional sexual morality implies an organization of space, namely, a distinction between the space in which control may be exercised, and the outer space or the world at large. This is even true when discussing access to intellectual accomplishments or skills. Consider the Platonic myth in the *Phaedrus*: eleven gods and goddesses fly to a space beyond the sky, where they feast on the contemplation of truth, justice, and wisdom; eleven deities out of twelve, because Hestia remains at home on her own. Hestia, the housewife goddess, cannot travel, and is thus deprived of access to the outer world and to truth. The way knowledge is constructed in our culture is made plain by this Platonic myth: it has something to do with going out and circulating in the widest space possible; not being confined within a domestic space or household. I wonder if this myth is not inspiring us academics, when we long for an international lifestyle, and reject the idea of belonging just to a limited parochial community. It can even inspire female academics, since after all, five goddesses are involved in the Platonic trip, although this may not be considered acceptable. For, in contrast, it is thought proper that women should be part of the household and should belong—in the literal meaning of the term—to a given restricted community. Therefore, the gendered distribution of space is the same, whether we discuss intellectual life or work acknowledged as such. Truth and what counts as work are to be found away from home in some outer space which is for men, or mostly for men. For decent women, what remains is a confined inner space, where no truth is, and where the only learning possible is not the real kind. And work done there is not considered real work.

The link between women and home, whether considered as natural or enforceable, could even explain how a separation between the arts and sciences took place. From the Renaissance onwards, some innovative fathers thought it possible to give their daughters not just a little learning, but a reasonably comprehensive education in the arts or humanities, since this could take place at home. On the other hand, the emergence of modern science and research was taking place outside the home, and contacts with scientific circles often implied some travelling abroad. Of course, humanities for girls gave them no future in the professions, at a time when men with such a training could become lay administrators. But for a few and brilliant exceptions, women's education in the humanities was, as Lisa Jardine has pointed out, mostly ornamental or again supposed to be a means for accomplishing virtue.[9] Modern science began as a more clearly masculine activity than the humanities, thus separating itself from the arts. This must be understood in relation to the distribution of space— science out of the home, humanities within.

If, then, the topic 'women and work, intellectual or not' must involve the consideration of 'the home', perhaps one should add that home must be understood as both a physical place (the appropriate site for a woman's work that is not work) and also a legal space, by which I mean that the fruit of her work has long been understood as belonging to the household. This was so much the case that, even when the work took place somewhere else, the wages were paid to the husband or father. In Europe, until the beginning of this century, women workers were not handed their own wages, and they often needed a husband's or a father's permission to work as servants or factory workers. The result was that even work outside the household did not help them to become more independent. It was a major breakthrough for women to be seen as the owners of their own working capacity—outside the home, that is.

Another step has taken place more recently, in some countries at least. It does not concern housekeeping, as yet, but productive work carried out by women very close to home. A baker's wife may sell bread in the shop twelve hours a day. Nonetheless, she used to be counted as a 'married woman with no profession', which implied, *inter alia*, that none of the social protection granted to an employee, in terms of pension, health insurance, risks of redundancy, and so forth, was granted to her. Artisans' wives, women involved in agriculture, lawyers' or doctors' wives acting as secretaries, have been seen as their husbands' helpers, not as the active workers they are or as participants in a family business. It is thanks to feminist sociologists that this major issue has been raised and addressed, through changes in legislation, at least in some countries. And with the increase in women magistrates and barristers, it is now possible to have such work taken into account in the divorce courts, so that a woman may get, instead of alimony, something like a retroactive salary. The court makes an estimate of what the work for her husband amounted to, and then she gets her due, instead of becoming somehow a 'kept' woman after the fact. This recognition of women's work as their husbands' employees is a good example of how intellectual work, carried out by women researchers, and some women's access to learned professions such as the law, may change the very concept of work, when used to describe women's work, thus improving the social status of thousands of women. From a narrow definition which counted out many working hours, we have moved to a broader one, which now includes what is done close to home.

To these practical and moral issues concerning social and legal recognition of women's work close to home, a theoretical debate is to be added. I suggested earlier that the association of women with home is a way of enforcing traditional sexual morality, with the production of a legitimate offspring at stake. That is consistent with Engels' *Origin of the Family, Private Property and the State.* But some Marxist feminists have claimed it is the other way round. According to them, exploitation of women's working potential by their husbands, or extortion of free labour, in housekeeping as well as in home-based productive work, is the core of the structure, whereas the construction of the family code and ideology is basically a technique to trap women into a position where they will work for nothing.[10] Male-centred society uses the 'bliss of motherhood' to attract women into family life, the same society deprives women of reproductive rights in order to press them into matrimony, so that they work as their husbands' employees for free.

Whichever theory is right, and perhaps we should knit the two together, certainly one theoretical finding is currently accepted by all: you cannot discuss women's work without discussing in detail the sexual contract that determines the family, or without discussing reproductive rights, at least today, when birth control can be obtained by many women. Such a theoretical principle, implying that both work and sexual contracts must be discussed together, has also been taken up by some feminist historians—let me simply quote the title of a book by Bridget Hill, *Women, Work and Sexual Politics in Eighteenth-Century England.*[11] The title itself indicates a full recognition that one cannot have 'women and work' as an independent entity or consider 'sexual politics' separately—both must be examined in relation to each other. And we would all agree that the location of women's work, namely, at home or nearby, or in the legal domain of the family, is connected with sexual reproduction and sexual relations as defined by formal or common law marriage, and sexual morality. Again, this is not gender, but sex; in this case, of course, heterosexual sex, as a relationship likely to produce children. For, when we reason in terms of gender, we tend to look for differences and to adopt only a comparative perspective. But here we must reason in terms of relationships, with the idea that the relationship between the two terms, namely, women and men, creates the social standard for both; unequal social standards of course, since one is made a dependant of the other.

And just as this situation implies an organization of space, it also involves an organization of time that must be questioned. In our culture, we believe that the daily twenty-four hours are to be divided into three parts: one for work, one for sleep, and one for leisure and all sorts of miscellaneous activities, such as trips from home to work and brushing your teeth. Such a division of time, into three parts and three parts only, has been challenged as gender-biased by Italian feminists, but let me explain the problem in my own words. This timetable could describe only a traditional man's day, the day of a man served by a wife or a mother. The only work it takes into account is productive work (as done in the office or factory) and not what we call reproductive or regenerative work as done in the home. It is clear that from day to day the energy required to work and to live needs to be restored, obviously enough by eating. Since the clothes that a worker wears form part of his or her working potential, office workers need a clean shirt or blouse each morning, and even a mechanic's overall must be taken care of. The nation and the labour force need to keep going from one generation to the next, therefore the birth and upbringing of children is contained in the programme of what ought to be called reproductive work. Currently, most of this cooking, washing, ironing, and bringing up children falls on the shoulders of women, but this does not need to be the case forever. Therefore, a daily organization of time, from the point of view of women, or men with no female helper, and ultimately of couples who live according to the principle of sex equality, ought to be a partition not into three but into four parts—one for sleep, the length of which is not negotiable, one for leisure, one for productive work, and one for reproductive work.

Otherwise, time and energy for this yet unacknowledged work are stolen from women's leisure, sleep, and capacity to be involved in independent productive work. Making reproductive working hours visible and acknowledged means no longer calling housework by that name, insisting that some tasks could be carried out outside home (think of crèches and nursery schools within this framework), and discussing how we are to reduce the standard length of productive work, so that everyone can do their due share of reproductive work and have an independent productive work position. It would also alter the structure of further education. Further education is a way of renewing or increasing a person's working potential; it is an opportunity to have this potential restored. It is often denied to women, especially women with young children. On the other hand, when granted to a man, it often takes place at the expense of his wife, since he would cease to carry out the small fraction of reproductive work he used to do. It is not just the employer or the state that pays for it, then; it is also the female partner who is, again, working in order to help a man maintain his work potential.

This concept of reproductive work may prove revolutionary in the future. It could put an end to the endless debate for and against payment for housework. It could also settle a question concerning values. Because, after all, do we human beings love work so much, and do we believe it is the only road to salvation, as Max Weber would put it? Are women identifying with men's values when we assume that access to the labour market is an important aspect of our liberation process? Problems like this should not be discussed in these terms, but rather described on the basis of a full recognition of how things stand. Productive and reproductive work do exist, and there is a limit to the quantity of working hours a human being can stand, day after day and year after year.

To conclude, I should like to leave the floor to Immanuel Kant and to some women in developing countries. Kant claimed that professional people with a university education, clergymen, lawyers, and doctors, were instruments of government, their function being to enforce regulations concerning spiritual, social, or bodily well-being, as defined by the State. From such a perspective, it was clearly unsafe to allow women into higher education, since some of us have, after all, questioned the conceptual framework of the rules, instead of duly putting them into operation, and since we still work to redefine them for the benefit of all women. Also, please note that I have not mentioned the research carried out in social and legal studies about sexual harassment in the workplace. There is a lot to be said about the broadest learning of women who know what solidarity with others means, a lot about their real commitment to intellectual work. But there is also a lot to be said about the smallest portion of learning, as long as it is not provided to make us 'nicer'.

Some years ago, at Queen Elizabeth House Oxford, UK, I heard a lecture on teaching literacy to African adult women. The speaker mentioned that, at the end of a course, she asked her trainees what benefits they thought literacy was giving them, and the answers included the ability to read the printed instructions on medicine boxes and sorting out administrative paperwork. What is at stake here is no less than taking care of the body and dealing with the State or civil society. I remembered fondly my two grandmothers, who belonged to the first generation of girls sent to primary school in Brittany, and who were delighted at acquiring literacy. It boosted their self-esteem, was useful for many practical matters, and for reading newspapers, and, above all, it was fun, just as doing philosophy is pleasurable for me. We do not need to see a gap between a little learning and intellectual professions for women, if—but only if—the portion secured, whatever it is, opens a door to a larger and more vivid world.

Notes

1. *The Economist*, 3 Sept. 1994.
2. 'What knowledge is of most worth?', first published 1859, reprinted in *Essays on Education* (London: Everyman's Library, 1911), 15.
3. Ibid. 19.
4. Ibid.
5. Fénelon, *Oeuvres complètes* (Paris, 1851–52), reprinted (Geneva: Slatkine, 1971), v. 593.
6. Ibid. 592.
7. Descartes, 'Lettre à M . . . mars 1638', in *Oeuvres de Descartes*, ed. Adam and Tannery, *Correspondance*, v. II (Paris, 1898), 46.
8. C. Delphy, *Close to Home: a materialist analysts of women's oppression*, trans. and ed. Diana Leonard (London: Hutchinson, 1984).
9. See Anthony Grafton and Lisa Jardine, *From the Humanism to the Humanities* (Cambridge, Mass.: Harvard University Press, 1986), ch. 2, 'Women Humanists: Education for what?', 29 ff.
10. This view was held by Simone de Beauvoir in the 1970s, at a time when Feminists were fighting for the right for birth control. See her Preface to *Avortement: une loi en proces; l'affaire de Bobigny* (Paris: Gallimard, 1973), reprinted in *Les Écrits de Simone de Beauvoir*, ed. Claude Francis and Fernande Gautier (Paris: Gallimard, 1979), 508–9. The views the text expressed may very well have been as much suggested to Beauvoir as actually held by her. For although she was never the feminist movement's spokesperson, she occasionally acted as our mouthpiece in public and we were only too glad to be her think tank.
11. B. Hill. *Women, Work and Sexual Politics in Eighteenth-Century England* (Oxford: Blackwell 1980).

The Meaning of Equality

6

Julia Kristeva*

Julia Kristeva was born in 1941 in Bulgaria. She was educated by French nuns, studied literature, and worked as a journalist before going to Paris in 1966 to do graduate work with Lucien Goldmann and Roland Barthes. While in Paris she finished her doctorate in French literature, was appointed to the faculty of the Department of Texts and Documents at the University of Paris VI (Denis Diderot) and began psychoanalytic training. Currently, Kristeva is Director of the Department of Science of Texts and Documents at the University of Paris VII, where she teaches in the department of Literature and Humanities. She also shares the Chair of Literary Semiology with Umberto Eco and Tzvetan Todorov at Columbia University. In April 1997, she received one of France's highest honours 'Chevalière de la légion d'honneur' for her thirty years of intellectual work which has been translated into ten languages. In addition to her work as a practising psychoanalyst and her theoretical writings, Kristeva has written three novels.

Kristeva continues to have a critical relationship to feminism and feminist movements. She objects to what she calls 'herd' feminism.[1] And, she rejects some feminists' stigmatization of maternity as the ultimate exploitation of women.[2] She counters that 'it is difficult to speak of motherhood without being accused of normativism. Yet it is precisely in this experience that woman's specific relation to meaning and to the other is achieved, refined, and differentiated: to an other who is the child, neither the object of erotic desire nor the object of psychological need, but another subject'.[3] This is the love of difference that makes 'love thy neighbour as thyself' imaginable. Not only are all women different and all mothers different but also women as mothers make it possible to imagine loving difference.

Kristeva insists that women's movements should demand attention to individual differences, especially sexual differences.[4] She suggests that there are as many sexualities as there are individuals.[5] In 'Women's Time' she describes the

---

* 'Female Genius: General Introduction', in *Hannah Arendt*, trans. Ross Guberman (New York: Columbia University Press, 2001), pp. ix–xv; and 'The Meaning of Equality', in *Crisis of the European Subject*, trans. Susan Fairfield (New York: Other Press, 2000), 95–109. Reprinted by permission of Columbia University Press and Other Press.

Women's movement and feminism in terms of a Hegelian dialectic: Universal-Particular-Individual.[6] The first wave of feminism argues that abstract universal rights, the rights of man, be extended to women. The second wave of feminism argues for women's particularity and difference from men. The third wave of feminism, a kind of post-feminism, argues for the singularity of each individual against both the universal and the particular. Kristeva's individualism takes us beyond equality to singularity. She describes her project in the trilogy *Female Genius* as 'a call to the singularity of every woman'. She argues that the genius of extraordinary women like Hannah Arendt, Melanie Klein, and Colette help all women to see what is extraordinary in their own ordinary lives. Conversely, she maintains that the genius of everyday life is women's genius, particularly a mother's genius. In creating new human beings, mothers are each singular innovators, reinventing the child anew all the time. Kristeva suggests that mothers might represent the 'only safeguard against the wholesale automation of human beings'. Each mother, and each mother–child relation, is singular and unique.

In 'The Meaning of Equality', she describes this individualism as 'a *singularity* that remains, today more than ever, beyond equality and, with it, the goal of the advanced democracies, that is, those based on consent in the negotiated handling of conflicts'. She rejects any notion of equality that would equalize differences; rather she endorses a notion of singularity with an emphasis on radical individuality. At the same time, she says that sexual difference 'is the foremost and irreducible to the others because it is the foundation of the inevitability political live of our species'. Indeed the species depends upon sexual difference. Yet, Kristeva insists that although the sexual difference is natural, it cannot be reduced to biology; rather, she says that 'social factors and the particular relations of the two sexes to Meaning' or to the Universal have as much to do with sexual difference as biology. Once we acknowledge the social aspect of sexual difference only then do we see the necessity of equality.

....

FEMALE GENIUS: GENERAL INTRODUCTION
....

> One of the most fervent passions is the genius's love of truth.
>
> (LaPlace)

"What a genius!" Our recent claims of discovering "genius" within ourselves—whether in the form of a talent, a natural gift, or a prolonged search for truth—have put an end to the ancient deification of personality. At first, the divine spirit charged with watching over the birth of the future hero was transformed into a viable means of innovation.[7] As Voltaire put it, "this invention in particular appeared to be a

91

gift from the gods; this *ingenium quasi ingenitum* was a sort of divine inspiration." Whether by simple metonymy or by analogy, "a genius" later became someone who "displayed genius," if not someone who simply happened to influence someone else.[8]

Hannah Arendt, one of the protagonists of this three-part work, made light of "the genius," whom she considered to be a product of the Renaissance. Tired of being reduced to the fruits of their labors, the men of the Renaissance became increasingly munificent, and as they lost touch with God, they grafted His transcendence onto the very best among their ranks. Since that time, the *divine*, disguised as a genius, has made up for this loss by producing a mystery play that has transformed the creator into something unique. Does this mean that the absolute has descended upon us? Or that we should consider this loss to be a challenge to humanity? Is it a demand from a superman? Or is it a refusal to lower ourselves to the level of "products" or "appearances" in a society plagued by "consumption" and the "spectacle"? Suffice it to say that "genius" is a therapeutic invention that keeps us from dying from equality in a world without a hereafter.

Even so, do we dare speak about "genius" without ignoring the "evil genius" who devoted all his resources to deluding Descartes himself? In our day, it would appear, the word "genius" stands for paradoxical occurrences, unique experiences, and remarkable excesses that manage to pierce through an increasingly automated world. The troubling, even formidable, emergence of such phenomena helps us understand the meaning of human existence. Does this mean that genius helps substantiate the meaning of life? The protagonists of this work believe that it does not: as we shall see, my geniuses consider life to be substantiated through more modest means indeed. They do suggest, however, that our existence can be perpetually revived by that which is extraordinary. Significantly, however, this brand of extraordinariness is not achieved by gaining entry into the hallowed halls that record the rigorous ordeals of history. Like the ancient Greek heroes, my geniuses displayed qualities that, while no doubt exceptional, can be found in most of us. And they (the geniuses, which in this case are three *female* geniuses) did not hesitate to make mistakes and to let us know their limitations. What distinguishes these geniuses from us is simply that they have left us to judge a body of work rooted in the biography of their experience. The work of a genius culminates in the birth of a subject.

Each of us leads some sort of existence, and many of us have lived through adventures, often interesting ones, that can provide fodder for family legend and sometimes for the local newspaper or even the nightly news. Yet such experiences are not the stuff of a noteworthy biography. Let us agree here to use the term "genius" to describe those who force us to discuss their story because it is so closely bound up with their creations, in the innovations that support the development of thought and beings, and in the onslaught of questions, discoveries, and pleasures that their creations have inspired. In fact, these contributions touch us so intimately that we have no choice but to moor them in the lives of their authors.

Some works of art have an impact that is greater than the sum of their parts. The way these works affect us depends ultimately on the historical disturbances they bring about and on the way they influence other people and their followers—in sum, their effect depends on the way *we* respond to them. When someone finds himself at this juncture and capitalizes upon it, he becomes a genius—even if all he ever did was be born into the world, work, and then die. We endow him with a biography that fails to explain the excess, the indulgences, or the invasiveness of his life. Still, the reason we afford such a biography to geniuses, and not to just anyone, is to sound an alarm: regardless of whatever creation, work of art, or deed has come about, someone has lived. Are we someone? Are you someone? Try to be someone!

A Mozart concerto, a funny Charlie Chaplin scene, and Madame Curie's discovery of radium were all events as unusual as they were inevitable, and as unforeseen as they were indispensable. Since "it" took place, we cannot imagine a world without "it," as if "it" has always been with us. The temporary shock caused by such acts and works makes us want to explain "it" away by conjuring up the superhuman and by contemplating the destiny or the genetics that preside over the birth of individuals. That is, when we do not make "it" into an everyday occurrence by proclaiming, as did Buffon, that "genius is endless patience" or, for the more romantic among us, by repeating Valery's words: "Genius! O endless impatience!" At the same time, when geniuses demand that we endow them with a life that amounts to less than their "genius" itself, they play another trick on us: they make us look at ourselves in a way that is just as ingenious as the way they locate their extraordinary character between their own pleas and the unpredictable opinion of the human beings who respond to them and who ordain them. At heart, they are geniuses for us—and for eternity, so much so that we become geniuses ourselves, the sort of geniuses that accompany "our own" geniuses.

And what role do women play in all this? Is it true, as La Bruyère and others have written, that women have "talent and genius . . . only for handiwork"? Of course, it has long been asserted that women's only genius is the genius of their patience, whereas style is the exclusive province of men.

The twentieth century has put an end to the notion that women are the birthing half of a species of mammals. The growth of industry, which demanded a female workforce, and then the growth of science, which has slowly increased our knowledge of procreation, have effectively freed women from the constraints of the life cycle. Although these trends have been underway for thousands of years, only privileged minorities and a few exceptional personalities have been able to take advantage of them thus far. The twentieth century has made this emancipation accessible to the majority of women, particularly in the industrialized world, and we have every reason to believe that women in Asia, Africa, and Latin America are prepared to follow a similar path. For better or for worse, the next century will be a female one—and female genius, as described in this work, gives us hope that it might be for the better.

The feminist movement is the third stage in the progress of women (the first being the suffragist movement in the late nineteenth century and the second being the militant struggle for equal rights in all aspects of life, as described in Simone de Beauvoir's manifesto *The Second Sex*). The feminist movement, beginning with the unrest in the late 1960s, focused with a heartfelt violence on this newfound freedom and on the unforeseen differences that such freedom laid bare: the existence of another sexuality, another language, and another politics. But this rejection of tradition did not avoid falling prey to excess, the most troubling example of which was to see motherhood as the ultimate proof that women have been exploited by every imaginable form of patriarchy since time immemorial. In the manner of libertarian "movements," the feminists have assembled "all women" into an emancipating force, or even a revolutionary force, as is the case with the majority of proletariat groups and developing countries. These downward drifts, far from being a thing of the past, have become tainted with a reactionary conformity that manages to discredit any notion of feminine specificity or freedom that is not based on seduction—which means not based on reproduction and consumption. Putting that aside, and putting aside the balancing act that characterizes all manner of social mores, much evidence points to a revival of women's emancipation.

One example may be found in the prominent (and growing) role that women play in the political life of democracies. We can safely assume that this display of political and economic competence will only become broader and more widely accepted, not only in the Western world but also in developing countries.

Motherhood, which has benefitted from scientific progress and which was demeaned at one time in certain quarters, has since emerged as the most essential of the female vocations. In the future, motherhood will be desired, accepted, and carried out with the greatest blessings for the mother, the father, and the child. Will mothers become our only safeguard against the wholesale automation of human beings?

In the end, the particular accomplishments of each woman and her personality, which cannot be reduced to the common denominator of a group or a sexual entity, have become not only possible but also proclaimed with great pride. It is because I am myself, and specifically myself, that I am able to introduce the contributions of women to a large segment of the world.

This particularity is where we shall find the sparkle of female genius. Recognizing the substantial contribution made by a few extraordinary women whose life and work have left their mark on the history of this century is one way to call attention to the singularity of every woman. Is it not true that going beyond your own limits presents a more appealing antidote to the various forms of "groupthink," whether they be generously libertarian or sensibly conformist?

We still must acknowledge that, no matter how far science may progress, women will continue to be the mothers of humanity. Through their love of men, too, women will continue to give birth to children. That fate, though tempered by various techniques and by a sense of solidarity, will remain an all-consuming and irreplaceable vocation. Everyone knows that women, through an osmosis with the species that makes them radically different from men, inherit substantial obstacles to realizing their genius and to contributing another specific, if not ingenious, talent to the culture of humanity that they shelter in their wombs. Many people have thumbed their noses at these insurmountable natural conditions that appear to banish female geniuses for good—and such caricaturists have not always been wretched misogynists. Think of the marvelous Mlle de Merteuil, who thought that certain women, such as the Présidente de Tourvel, would never amount to "more than a type of species." Joyce, that unsurpassed wordsmith who knew his Molly from personal experience, believed he was in the right when he accorded time to men while reserving space and the species for women: "Father's time, mother's species." And Baudelaire, the most disdainful of them all, scoffed at "the childish side of motherhood."

These views are not wrong, but they fail to tell the whole story. Mothers can be geniuses, not only of love, tact, self-denial, suffering, and even evil spells and witchcraft but also of a certain approach to living the life of the mind. That approach to being a mother and a woman, at times warmly accepted and at times outright refused or wrought with conflict, bestows upon mothers a genius all their own. Women, greater in number and in confidence than ever before, have proved this beyond cavil: though curled up like children in space and in the species, women are also able to work toward unique, innovative creations and to remake the human condition.

The three women who are the subject of this work are by no means the only women to have left their mark on the increasingly diverse pursuits of our time. My personal affinities are what led me to read, enjoy, and choose Hannah Arendt (1906–1975), Melanie Klein (1882–1960), and Colette (1873–1954). I hope that by the end of this work, the reader will be persuaded that my personal choices are worthy of a more objective selection.

The twentieth century was one in which the accelerated progress of technology revealed, more forcefully than before, both the excellence of humankind and the risks of self-destruction that lurk within it. The Holocaust alone proves this to be the case, and it is hardly necessary to add the atomic bomb and the dangers of globalization to the list.

With value systems fallen by the wayside, we now deem life to be the ultimate good. It is both a threatened life and a desirable life—but in the end, what sort of life is it? Hannah Arendt was consumed with such thoughts when she responded to the death camps of two totalitarian regimes by setting her hopes on a respectable political activity that would lay bare the "miracle of natality."

But Arendt did not wish to believe that language could turn mad and that the "good sense" of humanity could conceal the threat of lunacy. It would be up to Melanie Klein to investigate these chasms of the human psyche and to devote herself to studying the death drive that gives life to the speaking being from the onset, although melancholia and paranoid schizophrenia question the primacy of that operation.

The sensualists and seductresses who become intoxicated with the flesh of an apricot, with the arum of their lover's member, or with a schoolteacher's lilac-scented breasts have not, for all that, abandoned the atomic age. If the twentieth century turns out to be more than just a terrible memory, it will be in part because of the pleasure and immodesty of the liberated women that Colette described with the impertinent grace of the insurgent that she was. A zest for words, when grafted onto the robots that we have become, may be the most wonderful gift that female writing can offer the mother tongue.

I include here two German-speaking Jewish women who explored, in the English language and in London and New York, the weightiness of politics and the limits of human nature. I also include a French countrywoman who rekindled the fire of the materialists and a sophisticated debauchery. The genius of these three women has restored, with a complexity that complements the truths they tell, the many faces of modern Time.

These three women lived, thought, loved, and worked with men—with their men, sometimes by tolerating the authority of a master or by depending on his love, and sometimes by running the risks inherent in rebellious acts that are tinged with an unimpeachable innocence. In each case, however, these women were able to maintain more or less respectable independence.

It may come as a surprise that this book discusses, among Arendt's other writings, the political works on anti-Semitism and totalitarianism that made her famous. Tracing the development of her work seemed to be the most fruitful avenue, tracing the portrait of the woman-thinker whose substantial contributions to political thought have been either praised or criticized by others before me. I also consider how Arendt gave voice to Heidegger's concept of *Dasein* [Being] and yet replaced the solitude of the "being-thrown-in-the-world" with the virtuosity of the "appearance." Heidegger's concept of errancy, when cast against the anonymity of the "they," becomes suddenly unrecognizable once Arendt focuses on the miraculous "birth of each person" into the "frailty of human affairs," that is, into political life. Though she always remained attentive to the great philosopher's work, Arendt, that lover of pure thought, was able to move beyond it and to become a political theorist in a class by herself—one who has been discussed at length and yet who remains just as topical today. Not only was Arendt the first person to link the two totalitarian regimes because they both destroyed human life but also she made it known that the "appearance" is a condition intrinsic to humanity: she reveals the irreducible singularity of each person, provided that he finds the courage to partake in the common sense of those around him. After all, the media frenzy that has shaken up the world since Arendt's death amounts perhaps to more than just a curse, particularly if we examine it through the lens of the genius of this woman who revalued political meaning as a "taste" for showing, observing, remembering, and recounting.

Freud had just discovered the unconscious as well as the relationship between mental illness and sexuality. He was surveying the pitfalls of pleasure while settling scores with the social conformists who did not want—and who still do not want—to admit that the human body is a being of desire. To this concern for Eros and Thanatos, the founder of psychoanalysis added far more strident battles with his disciples that were primarily Œdipal in nature. It was at that time that Melanie Klein devoted herself to studying decompensation. Caring for children had taught her that in the beginning is the urge to destroy, an urge that eventually is transformed into madness but that always remains a conduit of desire. Freud had already said as much, but it was Klein who fully developed the notion. A more radical pioneer of child psychoanalysis than was Anna Freud, Klein created the real possibility of a psychoanalysis of psychosis, one that could circumvent the spiritualism of Jung that had wandered, against Freud's teachings, into that very domain.

Despite the dogmatism of the ferocious explorer that she is accused of being, Klein's work lends itself to a popular readership. Her work has been carried forward by original and fruitful developments that proved her right all along: W. R. Bion and David W. Winnicott were not her disciples but her followers. Without them, and without the modern psychoanalysis of psychosis and autism that dominate her work, we still would not understand the distinguishing mark of modern culture that is the ever-present risk of madness and the wide range of treatments we can use to stave it off.

The idea that pleasure is not only organic but also emerges in words, as long as those words become sensory, has never been articulated more effectively than by the French geniuses after Rabelais, particularly by the eighteenth-century sensualists and libertines. And yet it is Colette who can claim the privilege of saturating the French language with the pagan tastes that make up the charm of our civilization, all the while telling us how this sort of sensuality is rooted in the sexual antics of the well-bred or in the poignant pleasures of the common folk. To realize her genius, Colette, unlike Arendt and Klein, did not first have to overcome a master: she saw her husbands, Willy, and then Jouvenel, as primarily a source of assistance and protection, and in the end, an annoyance. Rather, Colette had to face the authority of the

mother tongue, which forced her to confront both reason and femininity, to love both of them equally, and to transmute one into the
other. Colette's only real rival would prove to be Proust, whose narrative search has a social and metaphysical complexity that goes well
beyond the adventures of Claudine and her counterparts. And yet
Colette far surpasses Proust in the art of capturing pleasures that have
never been lost.

These three experiences, these three truth-telling works were produced at both the heart of this century and at its margins. Though
Arendt, Klein, and Colette were not truly excluded or marginalized,
they nevertheless lay outside the norm. These women manifested their
freedom to explore without heeding the dominant trends, institutions,
parties, or schools of thought. Arendt's work is interdisciplinary (is it
philosophy? political science? sociology?), and it delves into religions
and into ethnic and political groupings; her work avoids the main-
stream views of the "Right" as well as the "Left." Klein, for her part,
challenged the conformity of the Freudians, and without fearing the
consequences of being disloyal to the prevailing psychoanalytic orthodoxy of the day, she broke entirely new ground in the study of the
Œdipus complex, fantasy, language, and prelanguage. At first provin-
cial and outrageous, and then worldly while remaining a woman of the
people, Colette was never fully part of the literary establishment until
she developed her insight into social mores and her sensual rebellion.

Though innovative in its refusal to conform, the genius of these
women came at a price: rebels glean their stimulation from their
genius, and they pay for it by being ostracized, misunderstood, and
disdained. That fate is common to all geniuses. Is it also common to
women in general?

Life, madness, and *words:* the three women relied on them to become
lucid and passionate investigators while drawing on their existence as
much as on their thinking and while sharing their unique perspective
on the most important issues of our time. I attempt to study these
women without limiting myself to the well-known themes always
linked to their names. Hannah Arendt is more than just "the banality
of evil" and the Eichmann trial, and more than just the linking of
Nazism and Stalinism. Melanie Klein went further than the "preco-
cious paranoid projection," the "want and gratitude" commanded by
the "part object" that is the mother's breast and the "multiple splitting" that culminates in endogenous psychosis. And the provocation of
the little urchin who acted outrageously in order to prevail at the
Académie Goncourt does not fully account for the magic of Colette.

These themes are no more than a few trees obscuring forests that are far more appealing but that are also dangerously more complex.

Of course, the zeal of the experts has already put to rest these commonplace associations: our three protagonists, often misunderstood or even persecuted during their lives, have since acquired their own set of commentators and fanatic adherents. I do not devote a great deal of time here to the work of the many specialists who have already spent much energy, with scrupulous attention to detail, on reconstructing various controversies and on clearing up the inevitable misunderstandings that shaped the paths of these three women.

Instead, I limit myself to studying these three women carefully and faithfully so as to reconstruct their individuality while putting each in her proper perspective—not to liken what cannot be likened, but to portray, amid the resonance that will sound among these three compositions, the complexity of twentieth-century culture as well as the major role played by women in its most vulnerable arenas: life, madness, and words.

Do we owe these uncommon forms of genius and these unforgettable innovations to these women's femininity, so unusual in itself? It is a question worth asking, and the title of this work implies that we do. At this early stage, however, I would rather not respond to the question. I began this study with the hypothesis that I knew nothing, that "woman" is an unknown, or at least that I preferred not to "define" what a woman is so that an answer might emerge out of a careful accumulation of examples. So perhaps, after accompanying each woman into her own genius, we will strike a chord that appears to bring them all together. We may hear some music composed of singularities, dissonant keys, and counterpoints that go beyond the fundamental tonalities. Perhaps that is what female genius is—that is, if female genius even exists. For now, I suggest that we reserve judgment until the end of our journey.

THE MEANING OF EQUALITY

The French Senate's adoption, at long last, of the governmental proposal on male—female equality, and its acceptance on second reading by the National Assembly, run counter to the fears expressed by the champions of universalism. This seems to be a good time to take another look at the presuppositions behind those fears, and to offer as a contrast another vision of the symbolic pact that will henceforth serve as a basis for our society, since equality now appears virtually in Article 3 of the Constitution, pending the definitive vote of the Congress at Versailles.

POWER AND POLITICS

Nowadays we equate "power" and "politics," so much so that when men or women of *power* speak out, many people decode this as the expression of a *political* thought. Let us consider, on the contrary, that politics is the experience of a debate in which free individuals come forth and measure themselves against one another in their plurality, so as better to think about the public interest. And in fact this is the inherited ideal of the Greek city, dear to Hannah Arendt, taken up once again in France today with discussions on equality (and on Europe): let us understand politics, then, as living interrogation and polemic, life of the mind remote from all archaism, investigation that can shed light on other peoples as well.

Women and men of power—to be distinguished from those who would like to make politics their life—have set themselves in opposition to equality. Whatever their personal talent may have been, their road to power was surely made smoother by the support of a family, a husband, a lover, or a clan, so that (unless they have been too quick to forget) they were not cruelly exposed to the ostracism of a political battle whose harshness is applied with special virulence precisely to the female sex. These women or men hoped that the "good will" of political parties, prompted by some encouraging measures, would be enough to change such negative discrimination. But don't we see, behind their optimistic vision, ambitions and privileges that are harder to admit?

METAPHYSICS OF THE UNIVERSAL

This divergence is coupled with a discord of a more metaphysical kind. No time was lost in mocking the typically French, if not Parisian, style of the debate: it hardly matters whether or not the universal is gendered, it was said; no one cares about that apart from the Sixth

101

Arrondissement and a few purists of republican Jacobinism. The question is more serious, since it touches on what is fundamental about the Republic, in the sense in which republican universalism is, in fact, the *foundation* of public jurisdiction as well as public morality. Removed, ever since the Revolution, from religious authority, freed from divine right, and having managed to inscribe in its laws the separation of church and state, the Republic has no foundation other than that of the universality of the citizen. That is to say that Universality is our God; it is what guarantees each citizen—regardless of sex, origin, faith, and so forth—equal access to the law, to all laws. Tampering with this universality amounts to tampering with what is sacred about the Republic: this is a fundamental question, the same as the question of the relation of women to the foundational, that is, to the sacred.

Now, we must not forget that the universalist principle—a sacred principle whose generosity has proven itself, though not without revealing its limits—descends in a straight line from the One, the unity of Intellect and Being that, beginning with Plato's metaphysics and passing through the autarchy of late Hellenism, constituted the foundation of Roman citizenship. Two thousand years of politics have been inspired by it, though it is not possible to enumerate here its multiple declensions, more or less felicitous, that form the basis of religious or partisan institutions. The founders of the Republic, among other descendants of the Universal, achieved the boldest translation, the one best adapted to history in progress, by modifying it in the form of a universal citizenship. The sacred, thus established in political legislation, consecrated democracy and made the French Republic one of the most egalitarian regimes in the world, along with the one that resulted from the American Revolution.

It quickly became clear that this sacredness excluded strangers: the prosperity of nation-states over the course of two centuries, with a dynamism still vital today, allows us at the present time to ask only cautiously and sparingly about the citizenship of migrants and other "undocumented" people. The metaphysical universal, like its republican variant, also excluded women; is it necessary to recall the numerous studies on the discrimination against women in post-Revolutionary society, especially in left-wing parties and syndicates? The regression with regard to the spirit of the Enlightenment is due not only to a mistrust of women as, allegedly, willing dupes of the Church, but also to deeper philosophical and sexist prejudices. There has also been criticism of the Western, European, limitations of this universalism on the grounds that it ignores other cultures.

But it is metaphysics itself, underlying universalism, that is made this way: the body, and with it sex, gives way, or rather is assimilated, to the One: Unity of Intellect and Being caught up in the quest for the True and the Beautiful. The cult of the One celebrates unity of thought as invisible activity, able to master the "universe" as well as the human beings "unified," globalized, by it; and it is expressed, in monotheism, as the cult of a single God. Whether it is explicitly One paternal God or One abstract principle, the universal is a sacrificer, in the sense that every mental representation (sign, idea, thought) abandons, loses, or sacrifices matter, the thing, or the object to which the representation refers. This is why the philosophers of antiquity could think of this universalizing One as turned toward death, "death-colored": in the Indo-European languages the sacred is a unifying "sacrifice" (from the Latin *sacer*) that separates, interdicts, and pacifies the social contract. A second type of sacredness, however, is suggested in the same societies by a term that means "overflowing life" and "growth" (from the Avestan *spenta*) and refers to fertility and the power of the spirit. Rites of phallic veiling and unveiling in the Mediterranean mysteries, and finally the celebration of paternal power in the monotheistic religions, complete for our civilization the panoply of universalist metaphysics. And even when a Chinese tradition like Taoism recognizes two universals, the *yin* and the *yang*, the feminine and the masculine, the rational administration of subjects and affairs under the aegis of authority necessitates, with Confucius, recourse to a certain dominating and hierarchical universalism.

Development and technical changes in social bonds were required in order for this founding universal to be inflected toward plurality. And also so that, in the wake of the problematic and risky dismantling of metaphysics, the inscription of sexual difference in the universal could finally make its appearance as a most decisive gesture: not as a rejection but as a recasting.

It is precisely here that there arose the feminine aspiration to equality within republican universalism. As speaking and thinking beings, women take part in this sacrificial universality, this "being for death" on the metaphysical level, and they take part in the citizenship that is equally constraining and protective for all on the level of human affairs. Nevertheless, and in so far as political life is neither contemplation nor domination, women as potential, and increasingly real, agents of this plural life demand to be recognized in their difference.

And indeed, a political life is not established solely on the basis of submission to equality, however salvific it may be. A political *life* that is

JULIA KRISTEVA

not political *power* can be established, without repudiating the universal principle, by including recognition of different agents. "God created them male and female," says the Bible. Jesus, the figure par excellence of the man of action, insists on the conjunction "and," the sign of difference: this innovator, according to the Christians, needs different beings in order for the action he is inaugurating, religious and political, to be oriented through debate toward freedom. Saint Paul, in contrast a man of salvation, privileges the alternative meaning "or" to designate the faithful saved in the universality of the faith. It is only from this initial difference between the two sexes, and despite the later dogmatisms that were so often repressive, that the singularity of each individual, as well as his or her respect, was proclaimed by Christianity and by human rights in the secular mutation of Christendom. A *singularity* that remains, today more than ever, beyond *equality* and, with it, the goal of the advanced democracies, that is, those based on consent in the negotiated handling of conflicts.

As soon as the One is incarnated, and metaphysics timidly attempts to show concern for humanity that is alive because it is plural, metaphysics moves toward the recognition of differences, of which sexual difference is the foremost and irreducible to the others because it is the foundation of the inevitably political life of our species. That this difference is *also* natural in no way reduces it to biology: social factors and the particular relations of the two sexes to Meaning (which are their relations to the Universal) structure the female "gender" on the basis of the female "genital" and the male "gender" on the basis of the male "genital."[9] A review of the elementary structures of kinship from so-called savage societies to our own is all that is needed to see that it is the recognition of sexual difference that constructs and specifies human culture, which gives it its meaning.

Is the female difference pure biology, or at best a subtle sensitivity, but without significant impact on the thinking and the behavior of women? The opponents of equality seem to have presupposed this, calling upon ... Freud. And yet, in contrast, the founder of psychoanalysis constantly affirmed the symbolic distinctions accompanying biological destiny, perhaps sometimes yielding to a misogyny that discredits women, but without ever underestimating their difference! Does psychic difference, then, have no influence on thought and citizenship? To be continued. Wasn't it urgent to grant to half of humanity the means to fulfill themselves, primarily in politics, so that the other domains might thereby be transformed even more effectively than they are within their own logic? In the hypothesis of a symbolic, professional, or political identity of women with men, the universalist principle will be considerably enlarged by taking into account this half of humankind that has hitherto been set aside.

This is so even if it is feared that the dominance of technology will confirm the metaphysical tendency to uniform standardization result-ing from universality, and that women, good daughters and good pupils, will enter the political space only to administer the power of the city and of business as well as, and sometimes even better than, but not differently from, men. This is not the only hypothesis in this case, and nothing prevents women politicians, in the future, from being something other than their fathers' brilliant daughters whom we have seen, in the last decades, governing states as though they were men, "real" ones.

As for the *difference* of women—difference of sexuality, of bisexual-ity, of thought, of relation to meaning and to political power—it is unjust to assert that it is a new claim. After Simone de Beauvoir, the French feminist movement since 1968 has clearly expressed these positions and, whatever its errors or excesses, it has left its stamp on the battles of women on the planet through its psychoanalytic and political affirmation of this difference.

NEW MOTHERHOOD

Motherhood itself, through the voice of some women if not through that of the movement as a whole, has also been claimed, since that time, as a free fulfillment of each woman and an essential contribution to civilization. Religions and the various fundamentalisms have so brutally assigned women to reproduction alone, and, in counterpoint, libertarian movements have been so fiercely opposed to this "repres-sion," that today—against all evidence—it seems difficult to speak of motherhood without being accused of normativism. Yet it is precisely in this experience that woman's specific relation to meaning and to the other is achieved, refined, and differentiated: to an other who is the child, neither the object of erotic desire nor the object of physiological need, but another subject. The beginning of that otherness, that enig-matic love of the different, to which we are invited by the formula: "Love thy neighbor as thyself." If the precept seems unfulfillable at this point, could that be because it translates (in addition to exceptional

105

mystical love) the optimal—but so difficult—bond of the mother to her child and vice versa? It is not impossible that in strengthening this bond, in becoming aware of its risks and its depth, women will transfer it from private intimacy or esthetics, to which tradition has confined it, and adapt their speech in the civic sphere to its measure. This would not be their least contribution to a politics that remains to be constructed, as a regime not of authority and domination but of harmonization of differences—which is precisely the goal of modern democracies.

For obvious economic reasons, those women who, up to now, have devoted themselves to women's liberation, and especially to the discussion of equality, are often childless, or else they share masculine identifications in such a way that motherhood seems oppressive, inappropriate, or at least of secondary importance to them. In contrast, when the supporters of equality put the valorization of the maternal calling front and center, they promise, in the long run, a political destiny for the large majority of women and mothers who would wish for one, thereby threatening in imagination the masculinized militants who control "their" private domain of women's liberation. But let it not be said that the changing of the Constitution will be of no help to the basic housewife in becoming a political woman. On the contrary, the law, and in particular the highest law of the Republic, has a symbolic and educational value the effects of which are major because they entail a cascade of concrete measures; as the source of public debate more than any other legal disposition, it works deep changes in people's minds.

Finally, since equality applies to so-called ordinary women, to mothers of families, it inaugurates new thinking about the human race. Are we destined to "artificial" or "assisted" reproduction, or to "cloning" in "families" that are more and more "modern" and "reconstituted"? Perhaps, but then this is another humanity that emerges, quite different from the current *Homo sapiens* with its sexual differences, its prohibitions, and its codes of meaning and morality, unless women continue to give birth to children with men, but while being recognized "as equals" by the latter and hence capable of participating fully in the construction of the meaning of the political space to which they destine their offspring.

The mastery of procreation has not rendered women superfluous, nor has it made them identical to men as has apparently been believed or feared. Paradoxically, in freeing themselves from natural accidents, women have become decision-makers both about reproduction and about human fate on all the levels of their professional competence. On this account their importance in social and political life now and in the future goes far beyond the value they may have had in matrilineal societies, and, without any relation to a new type of matriarchy, this importance entails a necessary symbolic and political recognition. What is at issue is no more and no less than the future of the human race.

We see that sexual difference in this sense cannot be confused with the identitarian demands of various groups constituted by biology, history, or behavior. If by chance such a threat were to exist, the law-maker could easily prevent it by means of a restrictive clause reserving positive discrimination to women, excepting every other social, religious, or political category—which they are not. The truth is that we have no "values," on the eve of the third millennium, other than that of life; that we expect politics to go beyond the administration to which it has condemned itself so that it may open up the meanings of human lives; and that, this being the goal of the recasting of the republican pact, its universality be realized for two.

What equality ultimately reflects, then, is a humanity given back to its constitutive and increasingly sovereign duality. A humanity that has not lost the sense of the sacred—neither the sense of sacrifice nor that of procreation—but one that explicitly joins women in equal measure to the sacred and as a result modifies the bases of the social contract by inviting men, in exchange, to regain for themselves a new equilibrium in a universality that has been twofold for a long time but without admitting it.

The shifting meaning of "female" and "male," along with their concrete realizations, can only be extended and promoted in this way: psychoanalysis, ahead of other approaches to the human in its knowledge of psychic sexuality, will also find here the occasion to counter the relative disrepute in which it is currently held.

As for France, which for two centuries has taken the initiative in dealing with metaphysics in the political arena, it has the privilege—by inscribing equality in its Constitution—of formulating for the entire world this awareness that is tantamount to a change in civilization.

Notes

1. Editor's note: 'Interview with Julia Kristeva', in *Women Analyze Women*, ed. Elaine Baruch and Lucienne Serrano (New York: New York University Press, 1980), 135.
2. Editor's note: *New Maladies of the Soul*, trans. Ross Guberman from *Les*

Nouvelles Maladies de l'âme (Paris: Librairie Arthème Fayard, 1993) (New York: Columbia University Press, 1995), 201–24.

3. Editor's note: *The Crisis of the European Subject*, trans. Susan Fairfield (New York: The Other Press, 2000), 105–6.
4. Editor's note: 'Interview', 133.
5. Editor's note: 'Julia Kristeva in Conversation with Rosalind Coward', *Desire, ICA Documents* (1984), 24.
6. Editor's note: *Les Nouvelles Maladies*, 201–24.
7. The Greek *daimōn*, and then the Latin *genius*, watched over the birth of men and their works. Women, for their part, were granted a *juno*, a profoundly protective double of the self.
8. The *Robert* dictionary traces the latter evolution to 1689.
9. Translator's note: *le sexe* means both 'genital organ' and 'sex', so that the ambiguity of the relationship between 'gender' and 'sex' is in play here.

The Difference between the Sexes, a Historical Difference

Geneviève Fraisse*

Geneviève Fraisse is a research associate at the National Centre for Scientific Research (CNRS), where she produces a distinctive blend of philosophical, historical, and feminist analyses. In 1974, Fraisse helped to found the Centre for Research on the Ideologies of Revolt at the University of Paris VIII—Vincennes, from which *Révoltes logiques* (Logical Revolts) was launched in 1975. Following in the wake of the revolutionary and socialist fervour of the Parisian student revolt of May 1968, this journal devoted itself to writing history not from the perspective of the victorious few, but from the lived experiences of the oppressed classes, including women. Fraisse was also a founding member (in 1974) of one of the first (and even now, few) enclaves of feminist theory within the French academy, the Groupe d'études féministes (Feminist Studies Group) housed at the University of Paris VII—Denis Diderot. From 1979 to 1985, Fraisse helped to found and served on the editorial board of *Pénélope*, a journal of women's history published through the Centre for Historical Research of the École des Hautes Études in the Social Sciences.

Fraisse's best known work is *Reason's Muse, Sexual Difference and the Birth of Democracy*, in which she argues that the democratic ideal of equal human rights supports the inclusion of women in the public sphere and politics. More provocatively, she also argues that the concept of liberal feminism (for which she provides a historicized analysis that is exemplary of her unique, interdisciplinary approach) will need to give way in the advent of a truly inclusive politics; in short, if it accomplishes its goals, feminism will become unnecessary. Fraisse is also known for co-editing volume IV, *Emerging Feminism from Revolution to World War*, of the five-volume series *A History of Women in the West* that was commissioned by the Italian Publisher Laterza. A collection of thematically organized essays, this fourth volume is dedicated to the nineteenth century—the rise of industrialism, Darwinism, socialism, and the first wave of feminism.

'The Difference between the Sexes, a Historical Difference', begins from the

* La Différence des sexes, une différence historique', in *L'Exercice du savoir et la différence des sexes*. (Paris: L'Harmattan, 1995), 13–36. Reprinted by permission of L'Harmattan.

assumption that the difference between the sexes is a natural fact that has been largely misinterpreted as ahistorical and unchangeable. Reading the texts of philosophy from the outpost of history, Fraisse sets out to think the relation between the two sexes conceptually; but approaching the question is difficult since the relation between the sexes is not a proper philosophical phenomenon (*philosophéme*). Nonetheless, psychoanalysis offers a concept of gender from which Fraisse hypothesizes. By inscribing the psychoanalytical concept of gender within philosophical texts, it becomes possible to see the appearance and disappearance of various representations of sexual difference in philosophy.

The logic of its appearance and disappearance exhibits disorder and fragmentation, which, according to Fraisse, is the very effect of the suppression and domination of sexual difference within philosophy. Philosophy presents us with a false choice between the erasure of difference in the name of universality, or its exaltation in the name of difference. Fraisse reasserts the obvious in return: the sexes are *both* similar *and* different. History serves as the pretext for the interpretation of the natural fact of sexual difference *not* as an oscillation between two extremes, but as a relation of mutual dependence—at once a political and metaphysical, abstract and concrete, necessity.

Sexual difference is a natural fact, the possible history of which it is hard to imagine. Still less do we think of this fact as having happened—that is, as being caught up in events, or being marked by a historical event. The same is said of women as a social group—that they were previously deprived of a history. However, more recently a history of women has been constructed based upon the idea that the sexual relationship and the lives of women are subjected to the historicity of the world. No doubt certain people will highlight the voluntarism of such a statement. However, they should refer to the evidence of facts and representations.[1]

Today the history of women is still mentioned less to ratify its particularism, its 'regionalism' on the map of human history, than to leave open the question that it poses: that of a perhaps specific chronology, that of the weight of image and representation, that of the political, scientific, and religious events which are the original influences in the lives of women ... As she is a human being, the historicity of a woman is a matter of evidence; the history of women adds a further possibility to that of evidence—the possibility of questioning the historicity of the relationship between the sexes. I would like to broaden this perspective here through the reading of philosophical texts, in order to discover which reading of sexual difference is permitted by history within the sphere of philosophy.

To come back to the first difficulty: the difference between the sexes is not a philosophical phenomenon. Properly speaking, no philosophical object provides evidence for it in any of the philosophers' texts. However, it would be a mistake to conclude from this that the notion of the feminine or the masculine, or the reality of gendered beings or of the sexual relation, are missing from philosophy. Rather, it appears simply that these issues have no status in philosophical investigation.

The textual space most suited to a discourse on the sexes and the difference between them, on the war and peace endlessly played out between them, is literature.[2] Up until modern times, literary writing was the only writing to approach the issue frankly. Further, the relationship between the sexes occupies a central place in poetry and in the novel. Here, the relationship between the sexes *is* represented, but the very word 'representation' leaves open the question of the modes of thought which all representation creates. Without doubt, one of the essential tasks of literature today is to question the theoretical approach to these representations. The prerogative to be the privileged place in which the eternal double image of the love and war between the sexes is expressed is not lost in the process, and this expression can be read in the many different forms of writing that exist.

Attempts are sometimes made to pass from the act of representation to its conscience, or in other words to the representation of representation. This is especially the case in the domain of psychoanalysis, a disruptive force in the history of thought. The idea of the unconscious disrupted the history of theories of knowledge, and the meaning of sex life disrupted the history of sexuality. From then on, sexual difference became a crucial stake in human discourse. If psychoanalysis is inscribed in the history of philosophy, in the chronology of philosophical 'systems', then it is reasonable to decipher from this the emergence of the 'difference between the sexes' as a philosophical phenomenon. At the same time, a century of psychoanalytical texts and discourses show that this fundamental disruption in thought does not necessarily lead to a transformation of the meaning of discourse relative to the feminine position in the relationship between the sexes. The epistemological revolution combines easily with the political reassurance of the patriarchal tradition and of the most trivial representations of the relationship between the sexes. The fact that psychoanalysis takes up again, especially from Freud to Lacan, the former treatment of sexual difference is worth thinking about, although it is beyond the scope of this paper. One would need to examine the history of psychoanalysis, its link with older medical theories, and the diversity of theoretical positions on femininity from Freud onwards. In order to do this one would have to distinguish between the content of a question (*quid* of the relationship between the sexes), and its status as an object of philosophy. This would only be possible after having described the different elements of the problem. Therefore I will confine myself to a rather summary but important observation: psychoanalysis has in common with literature the presupposition of the immutability of the relationship between the sexes, the certainty of the eternity of the elements of this relationship; in short, the belief in the ahistorical nature of their difference; even if in each case the stakes are different, which is an advantage for literature but a disadvantage for certain psychoanalytical dogma. To envisage or imagine that sexual difference is a philosophical phenomenon necessarily undermines this representation of the relationship between the sexes as immutable; this at least is my hypothesis.

ON THE OBJECT

Describing the disruption created by psychoanalytic discourse invites us to return to the history of philosophy. It quickly becomes clear that philosophical texts are not silent upon the question of the sexes; sometimes they even have much to say on the subject. Although it lacks the status of philosophical object, sexual difference appears or disappears according to the precise logic of the particular discourse. Therefore, I refuse to say, as feminism formerly stated, that sexual difference remains unthought, that it is subjected to a process of foreclosure inside philosophical work. As Michel Foucault put it simply: if sex is censored, this occurs outside discourse, not inside discourse.

Therefore, I will avoid any declaration in favour of the return, after a long absence, of the problem of the sexes to philosophy. The task at hand is totally different—instead, we must begin with the nature of the presence of the sexes in philosophical texts, with the *modes* in which the sexes appear. We must treat the presence of the sexes in philosophy as a phenomenon subject to logical conditions of emergence and disappearance. Working on these modes of apparition would allow us to mark out a vaster field of thought than has previously been imagined. Three directions are briefly indicated below, which, from the smallest to the greatest, seem to span the whole sphere of philosophy.

First, there is a movement from scholarly commentary, that untimely intervention of the real within philosophy, to the treatment of the two in metaphysics. Spinoza's remark about the difficult freedom in language is illustrated by the image of several types of people seen as less capable than others: for example, 'the delirious person, the gossip, the child' (*Ethics*, III. 2). At the outer limit, sexual difference can serve metaphysics because the duality of the finite and the infinite is eventually represented by the finitude of the sexuated individual caught in the infinite process of the reproduction of the species.

The second direction is from ideological digression to ontological metaphor. In his first book on ownership Proudhon affirms the absence of 'society' between men and women and the eventual necessity of putting woman in reclusion (this a judgement made in passing, not in the main body of the text, but in a footnote). At the outer limit, this is the idea of truth as a woman which is so strong in Nietzsche, for whom woman and truth meet as two similarly inaccessible objects.

With regard to the implication of the subjectivity of the philosopher as a masculine being assured by an asexual discourse, Kirkegaard inscribes his sexuated being in his philosophical writing, recognizing that woman's position is different to his own. At the limit, the usual discourse of philosophers, for example the Kantian discourse (in *Anthropology*), which identifies sex in general with the feminine sex, makes its own sex absent from philosophical thought.

Sexual difference is not a philosophical phenomenon because it does not constitute a philosophical object. Instead, there exist places within thought where sexual difference appears and disappears, textual instances in which sexual difference may be read and its way of functioning deciphered. It is certainly possible to make statements about sexual difference within the field of philosophy. It goes without saying, however, that reconstructing the modes in which the question of the sexes is expressed is not an end in itself—investigating the ways in which sexual difference is elaborated is a sufficient objective. The interest lies in the consequences of the readings that are thus made possible. First, the immediate effect of locating the appearances and disappearances of sexual difference within philosophy is that one reads something other than the eternal repetition of the war and peace between the sexes. The ahistoric representation of the relationship between the sexes is undermined by the contexts in which the relationship between the sexes appears.

The second consequence is that the sexes (or women—we will

come back to this double meaning) are often related to something else, clearly linked to a philosophical problem, either political or metaphysical.

The third consequence, then, is that it is not important to list the ways in which sexual difference appears and disappears in philosophy, to put philosophical objects in order (from the ideological clause to the metaphysical debate), or to organize that which is disordered. The important thing is not to bring order to the disorder, but first of all to assess the disorder in which the physical becomes entangled with the metaphysical, and where the social reality of women intersects with the use of the female metaphor to express the idea of Beauty or Truth. Assessing the disorder would help to eradicate *a priori* readings and reductionist interpretations; for example, it would be profitable not to read the violent misogyny of Schopenhauer, which is both a hatred of women and a refusal of sexual equality, solely for itself, but also to read it in the light of its metaphysics and its treatment of sexual difference. This metaphysics endows men with will and women with intelligence, thus inscribing itself *a contrario* to philosophical tradition, which is unwilling to accord the power of intellect to the female sex, and still more unwilling to suppose that this intellect is superior to male intellect. Perhaps a link exists between these two registers, these two discourses; and if in fact this link does not exist, the reader is nonetheless able to ask questions. We should not put words into the mouths of philosophers, but we can ask them questions. Above all, the easy argument which consists of dismissing the misogyny of a philosopher as one of the various prejudices of his day is rendered invalid by the approach. Misogynist texts are also philosophical texts.

Various statements about sexual difference can be linked up without necessarily putting things in order. Building logical links within such a subject is provocative because we know why the disorder exists: the repression of the sexes and masculine domination are at stake. Repression and domination: these are two reasons which explain why sexual discourse always tends to appear in fragments, in pieces of meaning; quite obviously, the meaning of masculine power and human sexuality are hidden in this way.[3] My choice to investigate how rather than why the disorder exists stems from this, and this work is carried out in the hope of finding material to act as a catalyst for change. The aim is to read the disorder, to uncover its mechanisms, and perhaps to perceive a way to speak philosophically about sexual difference.

ON KNOWLEDGE

Without an object, can there be a knowledge? Are there elements of knowing able to appear as a knowledge, marking out a domain of thought? In fact, certain fragmentary analyses suggest that a knowledge might be constructed, or might be in the process of constructing itself, in spite of the absence of a clearly defined object. Thus study and work are necessary in order to raise the issue of the object and to question the possibility of the concept as I do below. But the field in which these pieces of knowledge are inscribed lacks representation. On the other hand, these pieces of knowledge sometimes come from discourses which stand firm on the nature of sexual difference, on the essence of this difference. If the philosophical object is missing, how can a truth be produced, how can a philosophy of sexual difference be elaborated? I will leave this question unresolved, pointing only to the classical alternative in which these staunch philosophies are expressed. The alternative is simple: either sameness or difference will prevail between the sexes, between men and women.

Where sameness prevails in certain ideological standpoints, it is in the hope of putting an end to masculine domination. Sexual difference is not denied, but neutralized to the benefit of the representation of non-sexuated beings (outside the field of sexual relationships). This desexualization of individuals is represented as the culminating achievement of universalism. Masculine domination had a beginning, and it will have an end. Any thought of a feminine nature (or essence) different to a masculine nature was, in the past, ideology, a mechanism of this domination; nowadays no pertinent questioning could result from the belief in a feminine essence.

On the other hand, where difference between the sexes prevails, it enriches the criticism of masculine domination by debating its content and the poverty of its ideals. Instead of effacing the difference between the sexes, one can exaggerate them and show the utopian nature of feminine values in a world subservient to the rationality of the Enlightenment. The thought of the end of domination is presented as the thought of a redemption by women, and for women themselves as the only opportunity for true liberation.

I believe that there is nothing to choose between the two extremes of neutralizing and exaggerating sexual difference, for in this domain ideology prevails over philosophical questioning, since political strategy as much as personal conviction is present in theoretical

115

statements. Thus even if one accepts that one certainty prevails over another, it would be shameful to be satisfied with this. For these choices are strategies, convictions, beliefs—in a word, values. Value is certainly an important thing, but only if it becomes an integral part of the analysis, an element of its content, and not a presupposition of the analysis.[4] Clearly, if political choices are necessary,[5] it is out of the question that they should exclude the theoretical risks of the difficult statement on the basis of which I propose to work: that is, that the sexes are similar AND different. I believe that very little is known in this regard.

The philosophy of sexual difference appears problematic to me as long as the alternative between sameness and difference, which really seems paradoxical, is not analysed as such. Rather than a pair of philosophical solutions, this opposition is a component part of the philosophical question itself, especially since the modern era. The sameness of the sexes and their difference have been thought of as a function of each other. This mutual dependence could serve as the point of departure for a philosophical enterprise.

While the philosophical object is lacking, knowledge is probably also missing; that is, naturally, knowledge constituted by a tradition. We are concerned here to describe the conditions and means by which this knowledge is produced. In this undertaking, we should not expect to find certainty, and history will play an essential role. We will begin by studying the appearances of sexual difference in philosophical texts, and how these appearances are brought into play within thought. I mean to distinguish between the registers in which the sexes intervene: the philosophical text can deal with the question of the sexes or not; in other words, sexual difference appears for its own sake or for something else; it is the end or the means of a discourse. For example, sexual difference may relate to the place of women within the human community, or at the limit, of the role of love in knowledge, or to the familial or urban social space in which the sexual hierarchy is thought, or to the metaphysics which uses the two of human reproduction to question the very nature of Being. The philosophical text can deal with men and women, or with the masculine and the feminine; or again, with beings and their characteristics. Sometimes beings are stripped of all characteristics and become human beings in general. Sometimes the opposite is true, and beings are qualified primarily by different 'essences' of masculinity or femininity. And again, sometimes the masculine and the feminine are thought without any relation to individual support, perhaps as values independent from human beings.

While the philosophical text continues to support the aporia between sameness and difference, the possibility of ideological bias should be seriously considered. The political choice of the philosopher regarding sexual equality is often the reason for his or her philosophical choice between sameness and difference (but also, inversely, the philosophical influences the political). The phrase 'victim of the prejudices of his day' is often penned by commentators alarmed by the misogynist ranting of their favourite philosopher. It is no doubt because of this that feminists suggest an analysis of the sexism of the philosopher as a philosophical reading. A process of denouncing the masculine domination at work in a theoretical text, this undertaking often has a cleansing effect, even stimulating and encouraging in the reader the authority to think, to legitimate a theoretical method. But to denounce is always a limited enterprise, which should never be practised outside true philosophical research; otherwise there is a risk of never questioning the meaning of appearances of sexual difference in philosophy.

ON THE CONCEPT

Highlighting the absence of the philosophical object 'sexual difference' might mean that it is truly inconceivable that sexual difference could ever be a philosophical object. Contemporary psychoanalysis perfectly exemplifies this idea and it would be worthwhile to reinscribe psychoanalysis in the philosophical tradition in order to see the almost paradigmatic way in which this unthinkable philosophical object is narrated in psychoanalysis. It is as though psychoanalysis has produced the object of 'sexual difference' the better to show that it is theoretically impossible.

The concept of gender created by the Americans could compensate for the absence of philosophical object: perhaps the philosophical object might be recognized as such through this concept. Beyond the linguistic ease of using one short word instead of a periphrase such as 'sexual difference', 'relationships between the sexes', or instead of an exact term, such as women (or history, philosophy, etc.), gender is also undoubtedly a concept. But the difficulties begin when we realize that gender is used in two different contexts: biological and grammatical.

In the English language, the concept of gender is intended to be distinct from the purely biological sense of 'sexual difference'. In French, the phrase 'difference between the sexes' does not necessarily relate to biology, and, furthermore, the concept of gender (*genre*) is understood in the context of the term *genre humain* ('humankind'), a term which takes the two sexes together and expresses their unity in the human species—in sum, the contrary of what 'genre' is supposed to produce—a distinct perception of the categories masculine sex and feminine sex.

The difficulties increase when one considers the question of grammar, for in this case gender signifies one sex or the other, and never both sexes taking into account their difference. The fact that English only applies gender to human beings while French also applies gender to things changes nothing. The important thing is the division of the grammatical world into two genders, the masculine gender and the feminine gender. This is illustrated by French where gender sometimes denotes the universal, or human kind, and sometimes denotes the particular—the masculine or feminine sex; it is either one asexual gender or two sexuated genders. This ambiguity might appear to be very promising, endowing the concept of gender with a multiplicity of perspectives. However, the duplicity of gender shows precisely the difficulty encountered in the tradition of the representation of the female sex: whether excluded from universal ideas (for example, in the nineteenth century universal suffrage meant suffrage for men); or whether reduced to the particular as when in literature woman is the only sex of humankind: *the* Sex, the Beautiful sex. In fact, the constant slippage from the general to the particular is a mechanism essential to the discourse of sexual difference. The opposite movement, from the particular to the general, is rarer. It occurs, however, in Foucault when he uses the 'speaking sex' of Diderot's *Bijoux indiscrets*—clearly the female sex—as a metaphor for gender in general. This is astonishing given that this image is at the heart of the first volume of the *History of Sexuality*.

Beyond this problematic relationship between the general and the particular, the concept of gender, which is essential to a new questioning, can appear to be a voluntarist strategy when the concept as such is forced; to have the concept would be to have the object. This is a nominalist proposition which requires further comment.

First, concerning the use of the concept of gender. The concept of gender is an answer to a question that has not yet been asked—it has not yet even been explained why and how this concept has up to now been missing. The concept of gender therefore reinforces the belief in the autonomy of feminist thought—it supports the certainty that this thought occurs independently within the intellectual world. This seems to me an illusion. In the euphoria that accompanied the left's succession to power, much was made of the 'epistemological disruptions' caused by feminist research.[6] Since even one disruption would have been remarkable in the history of the thought surrounding sexual difference, these disruptions seemed to invoke their opposite: relations between things. Would it not be more striking to demonstrate the dependencies and theoretical borrowings of a thought system in search of itself? The point is not to be nervously assimilated with the authority of some philosopher or other; rather, it is to understand the transformations of the dominant philosophy from which a new way of seeing might spring, to understand by what use of various theories the work on sexual difference might flourish.

The second comment is analogous to the first. Rather than isolating the question of gender, I think it is important to study the issues close to it—to be precise, the question of women. Woman is never really thought of in isolation, but is associated in discourse with others, her friends in emancipation or brothers in servitude: children, mad people, slaves, workers, Jews, the colonized, the stupid... Aristotle, for example, deals simultaneously with gender and skin colour, and Kant brings together women, children, and servants, or gender, race, and people.[7] These multiple inscriptions of sexual identity require work on their context, on their inscription in the whole of philosophy.

The third comment relates to the issues of means and ends. Sexual difference sometimes actually forms the object of discourse, and sometimes it serves as a pretext for another topic, becoming the subject of an argument which does not concern the sexes. For example, the question at the end of the Middle Ages of whether women had souls was seemingly part of a theological dispute.[8] To take another example, Feuerbach criticized the three of the Hegelian dialectic in the light of the two of sexual difference—the ideal medium for a metaphysical confrontation.[9] Quarrel, dispute, confrontation: perhaps we should see the war between the sexes as the archetypal image of other wars, especially the war of words?

Perhaps the processes through which sexual difference forms part of philosophy are infinite, either in the discussion of sexual difference or the discussion of other matters. It is a bit like the game of 'pass the slipper', in which the object appears and disappears as it is passed from hand to hand. Is sexual difference a means of exchange or an object of exchange? Or is it both, like money, which exists both in itself and for something else? The question of sex might be a currency of discursive exchange, and hence, *a priori* unthinkable, or, at least, impossible to grasp.

My two points of departure in confronting the difficulty of grasping sexual difference as an object are (*a*) to establish the modes in which the question of sex appears and (*b*) to scrutinize the discursive game between the ends and the means of philosophical discourse in the sexes.

HISTORICITY AS HYPOTHESIS

These two points of departure (modes of appearance and discursive game) can form the object of a reading, a philosophical reading of the mechanisms through which sexual difference functions in a text. It is above all a reading because it is important to me to engage with tradition, to bear in mind, in keeping with the past, that the object is lacking, that there is no philosophical phenomenon, no concept. Therefore, I intend to elaborate a new knowledge based upon this awareness that the object is ungraspable, and in the light of a reading of multiple instances of the question of sex in philosophy.

I began by recalling the idea that the absence of a philosophical phenomenon is fundamentally linked to the idea that the relationship between the sexes is immutable, that the love and war between them are eternal. Literature and psychoanalysis are particularly well placed and disposed to express this; and philosophy to remain silent on the subject, natural activity prevailing over symbolic activity. To elaborate a new understanding complicates this divide and its consequence is to alter modes of representation, to put them into context, in short to historicize them. This is my hypothesis inferred through the production of a new knowledge.

Everyone knows that by going back over the history of a problem, a resolution to the problem can be found, and its history left behind. Historicity would, in effect, be a welcome opportunity for the possibility of change; the only solution to the domination of one sex by the other, the subordination of one sex to another. This is certainly true. But a militant expectation of this kind would not allow the full potential of a historical knowledge to be exhausted. For a historical knowledge offers sufficient diversity to thwart such aggressive commands.

These are commands which it is convenient for philosophers to obey in order to close any debate on sexual difference. They jump feet together on the problem of sexual inequality and invoke the necessity of action (bringing an end to sexual inequality) rather than the need to think. They say it is a matter of politics and not of philosophy. So between the two extremes of unthinkable difference and practical politics, building a new knowledge based on historicity is to requestion the usual treatment of sexual difference. It is a sort of gamble, balanced between a plan of action and a theoretical assertion, the development of a knowledge and a principle of a way of thinking.

For me, history was a way of proceeding, a necessary detour in the face of clear philosophical difficulties. In particular, the history of feminism as a place of disruption and political invention, and as a space for discourse and for criticism of sexual inequality, is ideal for identifying the points at which theory enters the problem: identity/equality, private/public, nature/mind, reproduction/production, etc. The history of feminism is part of political history and the history of thought, and as such is a field of speculative investigation. Allowing as it does a body of texts to be developed, this history is a prerequisite for the constitution of a philosophical understanding. The texts of a history of feminism are various in nature—literary, political, scientific, etc., and their homogeneity stems from their historical date. This history was a prerequisite for me because it is based upon the historicity of the man/woman relationship and on the possibility of transforming it. This history rallies freedom through its multiple possibilities.

The initial response to the philosophical difficulty was, then, to remain outside the field of philosophy. Support for this was found in the work of Michel Foucault when he played truant from philosophy in examining the history of representations, where he was more interested in problematics than in systems, in knowledge in relation to how it is practised than in philosophical ideas. I was in some sense 'condemned to the Foucaldian method' because of the absence of a philosophical object, and by the inevitable link between history and the political practice of feminism and feminism's theoretical endeavours. I introduced elements of one method into another problematic, one in which conflict is key. Further, the historicity of his history of sexuality is a problematic in which Foucault met with unusual difficulty—conscious of the modern break from tradition, he nevertheless felt it necessary to turn away from the contemporary era and to engage with the ancient world in following his line of enquiry,[10] as though history were escaping him. In sketching the conflict between men and women,

121

because he was unaware of the mechanisms of this conflict, or because he sometimes denied the reality of sexual difference (for example, his misunderstanding of the 'speaking sex'), he was mistaken.

My study of history as a point of view outside philosophy was a necessary detour and today seems in two ways like a preparation for more profound studies: first, as a means of access to philosophical questions, and now, as a philosophical proposition.

Certainly, going back to the history of the sexes is not such a new idea. In fact, any thought of liberating women presupposes a historicity, that domination has a beginning and an end. In the nineteenth century, the theory of evolution was used to question the origins of the relationship between the sexes and the primitive seizure of power by one sex over the other, either in the form of patriarchy or matriarchy. The idea was to locate the origin of servitude in order to be able to eradicate it. Also in the nineteenth century the end of domination was described in utopian discourses, and whether the utopia was a world of equality or a world saved by women is of small importance. The discourse of utopia shares with the idea of locating the origin of domination the desire to have a history, and shares the same difficulty that origin and utopia are non-places in history; and worse, their claim to history results in the elimination of their history. The same feeling of ahistoricity comes from reading the discourses of political history which analyse the domination of women and outline their emancipation. Effectively, the arguments about domination and emancipation echo each other to a great degree: a discourse questioning the mind of women and one reaffirming the importance of their bodies are very similar; and similar too are two feminist texts written a century apart both demanding the right to have full control of oneself, to be a social and political subject in one's own right. However, unlike the discourse of domination, the discourse dealing with the emancipation of women presents itself as a historical inscription. And in fact, the history of feminism actually happened, beginning in the nineteenth century and continuing through subsequent scansions and ruptures. But if the history of feminism has difficulties being recognized, if it is regularly effaced, it is naturally necessary to incriminate those who dominate... and to examine feminist practice itself. Women often present themselves as the beginning and argue that there is a 'year zero' of feminism, convinced of the absence of the past which they themselves help to erase.[11]

These comments are intended to express the difficulties of conceiving of the historicity of sexual difference, and to underline the importance of doing so. The return to history proves to be as necessary as it is problematic. Foucault had to turn to a different era to explore the history of sexuality; the nineteenth century thought in terms of the beginning and the end rather than the evolution of the relationship between the sexes; and feminism draws its energy from forgetting rather than remembering its history. The historicity of the question of gender is not obvious and any effort to uncover its genealogy meets with resistance on various levels. History, which was a method of proceeding, must return to its object, and beyond genealogy must put into perspective the historicity of sexual difference.

HISTORIES

The development of a textual corpus is a prerequisite of the elaboration of a knowledge, and these texts, philosophical or otherwise, are the place where history, or the historicity of representations, can act as philosophical investigation. I will give four example of this, four possible paths to follow. These are only limited examples, and are not intended to be exhaustive—they are simply an evocation of four experiences in which, from history to the history of philosophy, sexual difference takes the form of a philosophical issue. They are examples, and not categories, in which history is an event, and thus an opportunity to redefine sexual difference, and in which history is a moment, a semantic crystallization of thought; in which history is a pre-text, producing from philosophers an adapted discourse. The nineteenth century, the advent of history, is a particularly rich source of these examples.

One event, the French Revolution, coupled with the advent of democracy, necessitates a redefinition of the sexual contract (following the redefinition of the social contract). I have studied the reformulation of the relationship between the sexes that occurs with political regime change in *Muse of Reason*. Here, history is an opportunity, a place of new discourses which create and then justify change. Because these discourses emerge at the time of important historical disruption (revolution, war, etc.), their logic is often visible, the tension between the desire for emancipation and the renewal of domination is very apparent. This hypothesis about the relationship between historical disruption and the redefinition of the sexual contract should be considered in isolation from the contemporary era.

History is a moment, a sequence of time in which semantic associ-ations are made and unmade; an opportunity, or not, for certain thoughts, certain theses about the sexes to be formed. An example of this is the link between women and slaves, which is both real and metaphorical. In the ancient world, this was a historical reality: women and slaves shared certain characteristics, or non-characteristics, especially the exclusion from citizenship. The overlap of these cat-egories of exclusion undergoes radical historical change, as indicated earlier. These overlaps can become blurred without disappearing from thought—thus, the metaphor of slavery has often been used in the feminist struggle. At the same time, the real debate about ending slavery and the progressive abolition of slavery at the end of the nineteenth century upset the use of slavery as a metaphor. This can be seen in the quarrel over whether 'slave' was a suitable term for women. John Stuart Mill and August Comte disagree on this subject, and Darwin and Freud also dispute the use of the term. The definition of sexual difference would profit from thought being devoted to the game of qualification of categories of exclusion between real and imaginary groupings and analogies of situation and representation.

History is also temporal, but what kind of temporality is this in the face of official history? The history of women sometimes results in the need for an official history, which is a paradoxical anachronism in the temporality of the era in question. For example, the Marxist cri-tique of the rights of man (ownership) did not apply to women, who were still at that time caught up in a network of material and legal dependencies (as wife and mother, woman was a being relative to others). The subsequent critique of the subject was a foreign language as far as women were concerned, since they were still dreaming of becoming subjects themselves. Discussion of women can seem ana-chronistic, and above all highlights the impossible linearity of history: discourse about feminine nature (particularly reproductive nature) served at the beginning of the nineteenth century to reinforce mascu-line domination, but also to reconstitute the transcendence lost in the revolution. Man needs the Other, especially woman, to establish his humanity, and he needs an elsewhere: if God and the king are missing, then nature, including feminine nature can fill the lack.

These two examples of the subject and nature introduce movements in opposite directions compared to the traditional readings of modernity.

The three preceding examples use history as a place which is full of promise for the philosophical question. In does not matter whether history is useful as an event, as an evolutionary discourse, or as the analysis of a particular period. What is essential is that history offers many possibilities for thought, including the history of philosophy itself.

In this case, history is a pretext, or pre-text. Philosophy is able to discuss women or the sexes according to the evolution of its own importance and according to the history of the time. Between the 'destination' of the female sex anticipated by Kant, Fichte, or Hegel in their respective philosophies of law, which fix the role of women, and the 'destiny' of each woman, of the singular feminine individual in whom the biological meets the psychological as defined by Freud, philosophy is certainly enriched by history—by the history of women's emancipation and the birth of political feminism as well as by the history of philosophy: because the certainty of the self and the other is blurred, Nietzsche abandoned the discourse about 'all women' and turned to 'certain women', preferring, for better or for worse, 'destiny' to 'destination'.[12] The philosophical treatment of sexual difference follows social history as much as the history of philosophy, and the mingling of the two histories within philosophy seems to be inevitable.

These four directions, discussed all too briefly here, remain up to now little more than pathways. The different levels of reading already show the extent to which the hypothesis of historicity could not be satisfied by the desire to write the history of sexual difference, or even to establish the genealogy of the discourse about the relationship between men and women. The stakes are higher, they concern the very representation of sexual difference; to consider the historicity of this representation changes the very image of that difference. At the outset I united literature and psychoanalysis in their shared presupposition of the atemporality of the sexual relationship, a conflict whose terms are always given. More subtle nuances are necessary, psychoanalysis already having a sufficiently long history to be located in the transformation of the stakes concerning the definition of the feminine, and the importance of the gender of theorists in their conceptual development of sexual difference. But today where does the construction of the thought of sexuality and sexual difference occur? Foucault's attempts to find the thread of his thought show how difficult the task is; the remarks made in this paper about Foucault have sought to show this. From where should one start? From which place should the issue be addressed? I suggest here a rereading of the philosophical texts, but this does not mean that other methods are impossible. If sexual difference is to be read in philosophy, it is through the 'mode of appearance'; that equivocal status which recalls the impossible philosophical phenomenon of 'sexual difference' as much as it recalls the fragile reality of philosophy. The introduction of the hypothesis of historicity is significant at this point—to study the modes of appearance of the question of sex in philosophical texts is to rediscover a logic which has remained more or less hidden, to make the link between the most trivial and the most abstract philosophical writing, to bring together that which is usually separated in discourse. In this way, an effect of history is produced.

Notes

1. Cf. *L'Histoire des femmes*, in 5 vol., eds. Georges Duby and Michelle Perrot (Paris: Plon, 1991).
2. Cf. Georges Steiner and his analysis of literature as a place of expression of human conflict, *Les Antigones* (Paris: Gallimard, 1986).
3. It should be noted that even in the texts in favour of the emancipation of women and sexual equality, the appearance of sexual difference sometimes obeys the logic of disorder. For example, Condorcet's article dealing with 'the admission of women to the right of citizenship' treats the issue in digressions within the text.
4. This is why a woman researcher can be a feminist individual without using feminist theory—it is even desirable that she should be. There is no more a feminist philosophy than there used to be a proletarian science. Cf. the discussion of this issue in Françoise Collin's article 'Ces études qui ne sont pas tout', 'Fécondité et limites des etudes féministes', *Les Cahiers du Grif*, 'Savoir et différence des sexes', 45 (1990).
5. To take one example, it was necessary in France in 1989 to decide for or against the right for Muslim girls to wear a veil to school. This issue could be approached according to the matter of the lay State and religion, or according to the problem of sexual equality. Choosing the path towards sameness between the sexes or accepting the signs of difference between boys and girls is important, and the question continues at another level: how has the rise of jeans, worn by both sexes since the 1960s, become displaced towards a demand for cultural equality which challenges any other egalitarian achievement? Political choice leaves the theoretical issue unresolved.
6. Cf. Geneviève Fraisse, 'Sur l'utilisation du concept de "rupture épistémologique" dans le champ des recherches féministes', *Femmes, féminisme et recherches*, Actes du colloque national de Toulouse, 1982 (Lyon, 1984).
7. Cf. Geneviève Fraisse, 'Les amis de nos amis', *Lignes*, 12, 'Penser le racisme' (1990).
8. Cf. Geneviève Fraisse, *Muse de la raison, la démocratie exclusive et la différence des sexes* (Paris: Alinea, 1989).
9. Cf. Jacques Rancière, 'Sur la différence chez Feuerbach', unpublished, 1968.

10. Cf. Jacques-Alain Miller, 'Michel Foucault et la psychanalyse', *Michel Foucault philosophe* (Paris: Le Seuil, 1989).
11. Cf. Geneviève Fraisse, 'La Constitution du subject dans l'histoire de la pensée féministe', *Penser le subject aujourd'hui*, Colloque de Cerisy-la-Salle, (Paris: Méridiens-Klincksieck, 1988).
12. Cf. Geneviève Fraisse, 'De la destination au destin, histoire philosophique de la différence des sexes', *L'Histoire des femmes*, vol. iv (Paris: Plon, 1991).

8 Genealogy of Masculinity

Monique Schneider*

Monique Schneider was born in 1935 in Mirecourt, a village in Lorraine, France. After graduate work at l'École Normale Supérieure, she taught in Grenoble until 1970 when she was appointed director of research at the Centre Nationale de la Recherche Scientifique (National Centre for Scientific Research), in Paris. Schneider's thesis for the Doctorat d'État de Philosophie (1980) explores the connections between affect and the process of learning. Long interested in relations between philosophy and psychoanalysis, Schneider has been a practising psychoanalyst since the 1980s, and is affiliated with l'École de la Cause Freudienne (School of the Freudian Cause). Now director of research emerita at the CNRS, Schneider practises psychoanalysis in Paris.

Schneider works at the intersections of psychoanalysis, cultural critique, and philosophy. From her earliest writings, she has been concerned with the performativity of language and cultural domination, and with the status of constructions of sexual difference in social discourse. Schneider's critique of sexual division in patriarchy has concentrated on several key figures: Freud, Fliess, Ferenczi, and Lacan in psychoanalysis; Lévi-Strauss, Héritier, and Loraux in anthropology; Plato in philosophy; and Molière, Shakespeare, and Sophocles in literature. Thoroughly psychoanalytic in her symptomatic readings, Schneider has developed much of her genealogy of hierarchical sexual division through what she has called 'the detour of the master's consciousness, the viewpoint of men and men's fear'.[1]

Schneider has written extensively on psychoanalytic theory and the clinical process. Since her first book, *De l'excorcisme à la psychanalyse: le féminin expurgé* (From exorcism to psychoanalysis: the feminine expurgated) Schneider has called attention to practices of exclusion and expulsion by psychoanalysis as a Western cultural practice under male domination. 'I wanted to be an analyst after reading Lacan's *Écrits*,' she relates. In her research, however, she found that 'affect was situated at the outset in too marginal a way [in Lacan's reading of Freud], so that

---

* 'Vers d'autres "décisions" ', in *Généalogie du masculin* (Paris: Aubier, 2000), 339–76. Reprinted by permission of Aubier.

to work on the problem of the role of affect in the process of achieving consciousness couldn't be done in the Lacanian perspective'.[2] Schneider has proposed that
instead of expelling objects and affects represented as alien and toxic, psychoanalysis might act therapeutically by readopting that which has been rejected: a
'maternal adoption of the other and through the intermediary of the other the
adoption of a part of the self'.[3]

Généalogie du masculin (Genealogy of the masculine) analyses the cultural
repercussions and internal limits of symbols of masculinity, which Schneider shows
historically to be driven, in patriarchal theory, by a passion for cutting, dividing,
sectioning, or 'sexioning' the body. She argues that in reducing masculinity to
symbols of verticality, the erect penis, the intellect, and culture, patriarchal discourse sets up, under the slogan 'anatomy is destiny', a cleavage between the
masculine and a devalued feminine, which it associates with vulnerability, lack,
flesh, the sensorial, and nature. What men depreciate in their own constructions
of 'the feminine'—vulnerability (exemplified by the figure of the skin as maternal
envelopment), fertility, openness, fluidity, and uncontrollability—are those
aspects of their own embodied experience which they deny.

'Vers d'autres "décisions"?' ('Towards other "decisions"?'), the last chapter of
Généalogie du masculin, takes off from a reference to Freud's hypothesis in
Moses and Monotheism that a 'decision' marked the historical shift from matriarchy to patriarchy: the 'decision' that paternity is more important than maternity,
and that because paternity cannot be determined by the 'evidence of the senses',
intellection is more important than sense perception. Schneider's main criticism of
Freud and Lacan is that both attribute an absolute value to phallic sexuality and
ascribe a transcendent legislative function to 'the Father', moves which she diag-
noses as attempts to construct a 'pure' masculinity by expelling the feminine. In
Schneider's interpretations, Western constructions of the masculine and the feminine (exemplified here in her readings of Plato, Lévi-Strauss, and another, more
radical Freud) emerge as arbitrary, frequently reversible, and remarkably hetero-
geneous, evoking complex oppositional conceptions of femininity and alternative
conceptions of masculinity based not on transcendence, interdiction, and the
drive to divide and control, but inspired by processes of fertility, reciprocity, and
alliance. At the time of this writing, Schneider is working on a book entitled
Le Paradigme féminin (The feminine paradigm).

....

TOWARDS OTHER 'DECISIONS'?
....

Of the two logics proposed by Freud to tackle the question of sexual
division—the essentialist logic under the high authority of anatomical

'destiny', and the voluntarist, historicist logic based on the advent of a 'decision' (*Entscheidung*)—is not the second the more pertinent, taking into account the importance of systems of representation?

Further, the very term *Entscheidung*, situated by Wladimire Granoff on the threshold of his work on *La Pensée et le Féminin*, offers a singular contrast between the global meaning of 'to decide' or 'to resolve' and the concatenation of meaning at work in its etymology. Just as the feminine is kept at a distance in the decision to engage civilization in the direction of progress, it is present at the heart of this signifier, since *Scheide* refers, among other meanings, to the vagina. Taken literally, then, the *Entscheidung* would be the equivalent of a devagination or an evagination. If one is attentive to the unconscious, disdainful logic of negation, the presence of the feminine at the very heart of the operation claiming to distance the feminine becomes clear.

ÊTRE AU PRINCIPE

Because the masculine and the feminine are represented by separate entities or by characteristics present in one or other of the sexes, the image of two halves imposes itself. This representation is present in Plato, and the discourse of Aristophanes, and is found again in the design of the front cover of Françoise Héritier's book *Masculine/Feminine*:[4] the area of the cover is bisected by a median vertical line. The interpretation suggested by this schema is that each sex represents half of what is human.

But where is the being who determines this configuration situated? Can it be identified in the places suggested to it by the schema? In speculating on this game of places, the being can only overhang the field of observation, be outside itself. The configuration which reveals a structure animated by a principle of hierarchical superposition reappears. Does the highest level of this hierarchy consider itself to be part of the landscape that it takes upon itself to bisect and to organize? The assimilation of the masculine with a principle of exile and flight towards the top of the hierarchy might result in the organizing principle being situated beyond what it organizes. An architect would be unable to insert a diagram of his own body space into the plan of his architectural project. Because of the process of division which presents itself, everything which falls under the blow of determination is as a result suspected of femininity.

The attribution to the masculine sex of a function of control, forcing the masculine sex to transcend any given schema, is associated by Françoise Héritier with the exclusion experienced by the masculine sex in relation to the process of birth. Unable to represent itself as the sentient origin of a living creature, the masculine sex claims an originating function on another level:

The appropriation of fecundity in the masculine body is bound to fail: there can only ever be an imitation of fecundity in the masculine body. Therefore appropriation becomes control: the appropriation of women themselves or of the products of their fecundity, the sharing of women among men.

Women are fertile, inventive, they create life; on the other hand, it is seen as the lot of men to bring order and regulation, to impose limits, to determine the different spheres of society and to inscribe politics.[5]

In this way a demiurgical power is created which certainly accords a decisive authority to the masculine sex, but which at the same time chases the masculine sex from the field of the humanity in whose name it legislates. From this stems the role played by denial in defining the masculine sex on the basis of what it must not be. If the possibility is envisaged for this type of organizing principle to achieve incarnation by slipping inside the very configuration that it put in place, then a compromise can develop allowing at the same time for the quasi-immateriality of the principle and for the possibility for the principle to be inscribed at the heart of the organized space. In this case the organizing principle will be situated, not in one half of the territory of the body, but rather as the axis from which the body attains the vertical position. The image of an axial masculine sex has already been seen in the schemes presented by Françoise Héritier, where the masculine sex is envisaged as the lengthening of the spinal column.

Far from being the reserve of distant civilizations, this mythical configuration is potent in the constitution of Western social space. The story of Solomon's wisdom corresponds exactly with this structure. There is a Manichaeist division of the two mothers in the story, and Solomon acting as judge transcends in a radical way the field affected by desire and violence. Don Juan provides another, less edifying, model. Again, only the women are prisoners of the specular face-to-face confrontation, while the masculine figure is characterized by his remarkable power of evasion. In a sense, these two scenes are a reflection of each other, and far from the second adding to the first, it sketches out the way in which the first destroys the traditional rules of the system, to the extent that it acts as an implicit denunciation of

131

the illusion. In these configurations, the tension and the conflict are abandoned solely to the women, as though the scheme of dividing in two, which is sometimes used to represent sexual difference, were situated in the feminine territory. Is not the symmetrical axis of a diagram supposed to be deprived of 'thickness'—the same thickness assigned by Alain Roger in *Le Voyeur ivre*[6] to the female body?

Whilst remaining inside the scheme, various permutations of it are still possible. The masculine pole can relieve itself of all internal conflict or instinctual fight, by creating outside itself a confrontation within which two female characters will stage an agonising internal struggle. This dynamic relates to a process of denial which takes over, not the field of representations or internal impulses, but a socialized, feminized field. Watching this confrontation, the masculine pole can serenely occupy the position of arbiter or impartial judge, of well-meaning neutrality.

Are we dealing here with a stratagem, pure and simple, or with a trap set on a whim? The manoeuvre to relieve the masculine pole is not dissimilar to a motor scheme specific to masculinity—the projection of the self towards the exterior. Recalling the etymological root of the term 'sex' in the operation of sectioning, Sylvain Mimoun and Lucien Chaby underline, in relation to the masculine destiny, the way in which this sectioning bounces back on itself: 'But this "sexion" is also that which separates the sex from the rest of the body. . . . The exteriority of the masculine sex and its visibility confers upon it a status of "extraterritoriality"; they constitute its power and its weakness.'[7] In this sense the masculine sex is presented as both sexed and separated, that part which is devolved to the outside also representing a territory belonging to an element which supports various projections constructed on a double process of delegation and denegation. It is certainly not by chance that René Kaes, in analysing the 'pact of denial' which generally founds the cohesion of the group, suggests as a primary example the complicity between two men, Freud and Fleiss, to deny Fleiss's responsibility for Irma's haemorrhage. 'The institution of psychoanalysis', writes Kaes, 'places at the heart of its debate the *proton pseudos* and the question of the truth of the subject in his or her relationship with what represents him or her: for Freud and Fleiss as much as for Emma.'[8] It is not insignificant that this *proton pseudos*, which constitutes the unity of the group, sets up a female character as target. Further, this femininity is represented by a liquid element, blood, which is for many cultures the paradigm of femininity. As for the masculine, it is associated with a solid element, capable of verticality: bone.

Exploring the work of Saint-Denis Garneau, Anne Elaine Cliche foregrounds the correlation between various centres of gravity of a masculine experience sought in the attempt to be extracted from oneself so that in the end only the backbone would remain. In this way, the frustration of the passionate desire to see is made clear—a desire typical of the operation of becoming exterior to oneself and leading to, according to Cliche, 'the madness to see *the seeing*'.[9] Various fragments of the work of Saint-Denis Garneau are then quoted:

Under this hump there is a room where one can withdraw from everything, even from oneself, and sit down and watch. There, one has no longer anything to do with anything, one is a stranger. One merely looks.

The idea about bones consisted in getting rid of the flesh which can never be trusted. . . . Now, the idea about the backbone with its associated impression of an axe which (painlessly) removes the ribs, *the impression of being pruned* . . . Now it will be reduced simply to the vertical trunk, totally naked.[10]

Here the characteristic dimensions of the masculine path of flight are tightly knotted: the desire to see aggravating the claim to exteriority, withdrawal, the extraction of the flesh, the process of detaching, so many operations and negations leading to the permanent release of the 'backbone' and the resulting 'vertical trunk'.

This brand of axial purity finds its apogee in the representation of paternity which invites the man to become adequate to what is only his symbol, indeed what remains only as the trace of his symbol, his name. In *Les Formations de l'Inconscient* (*The Formations of the Unconscious*) Lacan reveals the transmission whereby the man enters a dialectic which, as he enters it, both mutilates and defines him: 'Nothing will be realized in what I have called this fundamental mutilation thanks to which the phallus will become the signifier of power, the signifier, the sceptre, but also something thanks to which this virility will be assumed.'[11]

WESTERN CULTURE AS THE PAROXYSM OF THE MASCULINE

How does the masculine being manage to distribute the totality of his powers after this ruthless act of 'fundamental mutilation'? Is not a divorce created between that which remains on the side of motivity, improvisation, of the realization of what is happening? If we measure the price to be paid—mutilation of the skin, the cavity, the flesh, the

133

liquid and all that within the body which is affected by redundant symmetry—we are able to configure the masculine being, as distinct from 'the masculine' which refers to an abstract specificity, as though it too is 'not all' caught in the phallic function, without the non-phallic and the feminine being assimilated. In effect the phallic function seems to be representative of the passage to the limit—to which is added a passage to eternity—of masculine power. When, among the various metaphors of the masculine emblem, including the branch and the shoot, the figure of the sceptre comes to eclipse the other modes of interpretation, the masculine risks becoming radically emblematized by this fixed verticality which in fact only represents one of the stages of its cycle. Further, this fixity may or may not become, according to cultural interpretation, the object of an exclusive celebration.

Is there not, in addition, a correspondence between the emphasis placed by Hegel and subsequently Lacan on the operation of ejection towards the distance, specific to the strong, and the strategy which Lévi-Strauss makes the prerogative of the Western world? In *Tristes Tropiques*, the return journey leads the ethnographer to propose a dichotomy not dissimilar to the one at work in sexual division, although it is not immediately presented as being so. In effect, Lévi-Strauss attempts to illuminate the strategy of rejection which affects, in the so-called civilized world, the practice of anthropology. In a strategy of reversal, he proceeds with a magnificent return to sender, in order to stigmatize the strangeness of the driving response valued by the West—that of throwing away, cutting, excluding:

> If we studied societies from the outside, it would be tempting to distinguish two contrasting types: those which practice cannibalism—that is, which regard the absorption of certain individuals possessing dangerous powers as the only means of neutralising those powers and even of turning them to advantage—and those which, like our own society, adopt what might be called the practice of anthropemy (from the Greek *emein*, to vomit); faced with the same problem, the latter type of society has chosen the opposite solution, which consists in ejecting dangerous individuals from the social body ... Most of the societies which we call primitive would regard this custom with profound horror.[12]

Thus we are led back to the dichotomy which, in Lacan's thought, gives birth to the parental characters. To the mother 'whom we suppose', according to Lacan, 'to have reached the pinnacle of her capacity of feminine voracity',[13] is opposed the father in whose hands the separating instrument is placed. In the light of Lévi-Strauss's comments, perhaps we might see Lacan's parental characters as the cannibalistic mother and the anthropemic father?

Lévi-Strauss's preface to the second edition of *The Elementary Structures of Kinship*, written in 1966, again questions the salvific value attributed to strategies of separation. The target is now the nature–culture separation so important to Western society. This separation is thrown into doubt by the presence, in the animal world, of communication processes 'sometimes bringing into play real symbols'. Lévi-Strauss denounces the separation between nature and culture as follows:

The question then is just how far the contrast between nature and culture may be pushed. Its simplicity would be illusory if it had been largely the work of the genus homo (antiphrastically called sapiens), savagely devoted to eliminating doubtful forms believed to border on the animal; inspired as it presumably was some hundreds of thousands of years or more ago by the same obtuse and destructive spirit which today impels it to destroy other living forms, having annihilated so many human societies which had been wrongly relegated to the side of nature simply because they themselves did not repudiate it (*Naturvolkern*); as if from the first it alone had claimed to personify culture as opposed to nature, and to remain now, except for those cases where it can totally bend to its will, the sole embodiment of life as opposed to inanimate matter.[14]

One cannot avoid surprise at the analogy which emerges between the argumentation of Lévi-Strauss and that which supports, in the field of analysis, the separating function attributed to paternity. The ethnographer calls into doubt the claim to unity linked to the strategy of division. Is not such an analysis diametrically opposed to that developed in *Moses and Monotheism* and in a rereading of Lacan? Lévi-Strauss continues his protest by denouncing the artificial character of the nature–culture division: 'Rather it [the contrast of nature and culture] should be seen as an artificial creation of culture, a protective rampart thrown up around it because it only felt able to assert its existence and uniqueness by destroying all the links that lead back to its original association with the other manifestations of life.'[15]

If one recalls the etymological roots of the word sex in the act of sectioning, one can take Lévi-Strauss's protest as relevant to the 'sexion' which leads to sexual difference as well as to the anthropological separation between so-called civilized and primitive peoples. The exacerbation of the strategy of separation aims to deny all the possible modalities of 'original association', even if this association were only detectable during certain moments of transition. The denunciation stresses the hierarchical ideology which subtends the passion for separation: 'Ultimately we shall perhaps discover that the interrelationship of nature and culture does not favour culture to the extent of being hierarchically superimposed on nature and irreducible to it.'[16]

It is significant that the denunciation of the separating mode of thought takes as its target 'the genus homo (antiphrastically called sapiens), savagely devoted to eliminating doubtful forms believed to border on the animal'. Ferocity is thus situated at the level of the theoretical efforts devoted to a notional purification, as though the intellectual strategies of hierarchical separation were able to bestow some kind of ultimate hygiene. Questioning the separating mode of thought undermines the paradigms according to which sexual division is legislated. The division between father and begetter is also found in the separation between nature and culture discussed by Lévi-Strauss.

Nevertheless, one objection could be raised against Françoise Héritier's comment regarding the laws of Western society which legislate on paternity: 'The essential element of the problem we have set ourselves', she writes, 'stems from the introduction of the criteria of biological truth, and more profoundly, of the criterion of genetic truth in establishing filiation.' Compared to so-called primitive societies which anchor paternity even further in a socialized process, permitting relief and delegation, it seems that the Western judicial procedure sanctifies the verdict of the laboratory. In the decisive value attributed to biology, Héritier sees an illusion at work: 'On the basis of these observations, I will say that the recourse to genetic "truth" corresponds to an illusion, to a fantasy of the natural which totally contradicts the definition of the social fact.'[17].

However, this apparent overvaluing covers up a process going in the other direction. Since bodily participation is considered in many current interpretations as the prerogative of women, the father is essentially characterized by the symbolic operations of recognition centred on the inscription of the name—the analytical statements radicalizing this dichotomy. Ultimately, paternity becomes symbolic and retroactive. The opposite applies to bodily participation, attributed by Héritier in the societies she studies, to the father: 'when intercourse leads to conception, the desire of the male seed is supposed to be extremely strong. It empties the man of his true substance. Jokes are made about the man who suffers from aches and pains in his knees, sides and back first thing in the morning, that he has literally "made a child"[18] in the night.'

We are now far from the partition which delegates to the woman alone the gift of the body and only asks a symbolic contribution of the man. In the Western world is it not because the male body risks being excluded from the process of gestation that the recourse to the observable fragment, the evidence of the laboratory, which is therefore part of the symbolic circuit is endowed with even greater value? The fragment acquires the status of a remnant that is overprotected in the manner of a relic. The place accorded to this remnant of matter will therefore function as a limit, the reminder of the existence of a natural regulation that we strive to deny. In *Frankenstein ou les délires de la raison* [Frankenstein or the Madness of Reason],[19] Monette Vaquin's analysis shows the extent of the project aiming towards the totally voluntarist, technological, and scientific creation of a child. The taking into account of a natural participation in conception is given a status analogous to that of a geographical outlier. The boundary whose purpose is to limit the passion for creation is made sacred. Lévi-Strauss notes in passing the function which is today accorded to biology: 'it is in the field of biological concepts that we find the traces of deductive reasoning still prevalent in modern thought.'[20] In order to become relegated in this way, biology has been eclipsed by the latent fullness of meaning accorded to the symbolic register.

It would be artificial to oppose in a general way Western thought to 'savage thought', because there is diversity among the various Western cultures. With regard to this, Fethi Benslama points out the gap between the Jewish system of filiation which, based on the descent from Abraham, privileges symbolic paternity, and the Islamic heritage, passed down through Agar, which privileges the real father: the paternal function is inscribed in the body of a woman occupying the position of servant.[21]

DISJUNCTION

In one of Freud's earliest texts, the *General Scheme*, a crucial passage deals with the emergence of the entity to which Lacan later accords a very particular status—*das Ding* (the Thing). Is the Thing a founding principle or a nascent entity of disjunction affecting an experience which has always been mixed? Far from imposing itself as an original entity as the Lacanian Thing does, the Freudian Thing is the product of an operation of separation or fragmentation. The 'subject' whose 'ideal genesis' Freud reconstructs, is confronted in the *General Scheme* with a being which is initially presented as undivided, the *Nebenmensch* or 'fellow human-being'. We should not be too quick to assign a sex to this being, of which Freud only determines the spatial position: it is *neben*, 'next to', and it will have the responsibility of being 'attentive' (*aufmerksam*)—a term which anticipates the eventual attitude of the psychoanalyst—to the needs of the child, and of helping him, compensating in this way for the situation of initial distress. How will this prosthetic being, the 'first object of satisfaction', be perceived by the child? Having suggested the *Nebenmensch* as 'similar to the subject', Freud dissects the encounter between the two in its globality:

> Then the perceptual complexes proceeding from this fellow human-being will in part be new and non-comparable—his features, for instance, in the visual sphere; but other visual perceptions—e.g. those of the movement of his hands—will coincide in the subject with memories of quite similar visual impressions of his own, of his own body, [memories] which are associated with memories of movements experienced by himself. Other perceptions of the object too—if, for instance, he screams—will awaken the memory of his [the subject's] own screaming and at the same time of his own experiences of pain.[22]

Experience opens onto two dimensions: the specular dimension, and the dimension of otherness. The specular dimension, rather than being related to the visual encounter with a mirror image, is fundamentally attached to two other registers—movement and hearing—both of which are connected to lived experience. The reference to lived experience is repeated several times to indicate the experience of 'movements experienced (*erblet*) by oneself' as well as 'experiences of pain' (*Schmerzerlebnisse*) inspired by the cry.

As for the 'visual sphere', it seems to impose an experience of distance and relative rupture. While the perspectives of the mobility of the fellow human-being condition the encounter with a being 'similar to the subject', the visual apprehension of the 'features' causes 'new and non-comparable' elements. This encounter is therefore related to the dimension of otherness rather than to the specular dimension.

The caesura separating the 'similar' from the 'non-comparable' other is inscribed in the wake of an experience of sensorial dehiscence, of inchoate dehiscence opening on to a phenomenon of disjunction:

> Thus the complex of the fellow human-being falls apart into two components, of which one makes an impression by its constant structure and stays together as a *thing*, while the other can be *understood* by the activity of memory—that is, can be traced back to information from [the subject's] own body. This

dissection of a perceptual complex is described as *cognizing* it; it involves a *judgement* and when this last aim had been attained it comes to an end.[23]

Thus the division separates that which, in the fellow human-being, is related either to mobility or to permanence, the 'Thing' representing a principle of inalterability and internal coherence. At the heart of the kaleidoscope of perception, the Thing, seen as 'features', is inscribed as a landmark, as a pole to which various qualities of sense and movement can be attached, just as predicates are correlated to a substance which confers perceptive and logical support to them. A problem is indicated here that will resurface in the later text, *Negation*. It is important to Freud to anchor the logical operation in the more ancient operation which dictates the senses. The logical distinction between subject and predicate finds its origin in the bipolar nature of the experience of the senses, depending on whether the facts amount to a pole of otherness, situated essentially in the 'visual sphere', or to a pole represented by one's 'own body'. The body would encounter the movements of the body of the fellow human-being as an echo of its own movements, the secular dimension thus being attached, at least in this ancient experience, to a scheme of motor functions.

Two structures are coupled here: the duality formed by the 'non-comparable' other and the subject's 'own body' is superimposed upon that which imitates in the experience of sense, the equivalent of dehiscence. The encounter with otherness occurs only in the visual field, while the echo effect—the repercussion of the perception of the other on the experience of the subject's own body—involves several fields at once: hearing and movement, which may find themselves reactivated by the fact of visual perception. This splitting of sensory experience in some way anticipates the dehiscence which will take place in Merleau-Ponty's analysis of perception. As for Freud, the visual pole sets up a principle of distance, allowing vision to autonomize the thing seen, while other sensory perceptions, finding their paradigm in touch, will outline a sensory experience of proximity and contact. It is, however, possible to perceive a gap between these two approaches, since for Merleau-Ponty dehiscence only relates to an inchoate bipartition which causes a phenomenon of chiasmus, of sensory reflection. At this stage of his analysis, Freud emphasizes the split on the basis of which the function of judgement will be exercised, in its power of relating the subject and the predicate, an operation which Freud names 'comprehension':

At the start of the function of judgement, when the perceptions, on account of

139

their possible connection with the wished-for object, are arousing interest, and their complexes ... are dissected into an unassimilable component (the Thing) and one known to the ego from its own experience (attribute, activity)—what we call *understanding*.[24]

Freud's analysis distorts traditional locations. The being participating in the experience—the being which Freud first calls the 'subject'—is lead, through the manifestations of its own body and the revival of motivating feelings it has already lived, back to the status of 'predicate', or rather to a shattered group of predicates. With the intervention of judgement, the subject is delegated; it becomes attributed to the 'Thing', encountered as the only centre of permanence. At the end of the analysis, the various sensory impressions, resounding in the memory of the subject's own body, become the predicates of the Thing. That which is decided through perceptual experience leads to a transferral of subjectivity, the Thing coming to represent, in the structure of judgement, the 'complex subject'. According to this perspective, the thing is characterized by a certain ideality due to the constancy conferred upon it by its pre-eminence in relation to sensory mobility.

In Freud's subsequent development of these ideas, there is a division analogous to the moment in *Civilisation and its Discontents* where Freud forges the hypothesis of a sensory dehiscence which will lead to the repudiation or 'foreclosure' of olfaction, linked to female menstruation, in order to promote vision linked to the upright stature and to the visibility of the male genitals. As in the developments of the *General Scheme*, a separation occurs which leads to the relegation of the sensory dimension—olfaction becoming *verwerflich* ('repudiated' or 'foreclosed') because it is linked to the feminine—and the promotion of a nucleus of visual perception, based on the perception of the masculine appendage. In the note to *Civilisation and its Discontents*, the privileged sense of vision is characterized, as in the *General Scheme*, by the possibility of its constituting a pole of constancy or permanence around which the family can assemble.

This arrangement of the senses is subject to the same finality which takes shape in the *General Scheme*. The essential thing is the appearance of a centre of stability: 'constant assemblage' (*konstantes Gefuge*) of the *General Outline*, encountered in the visual sphere and imposing itself as the 'Thing', is continued in the 'visual excitation' of *Civilisation and its Discontents* which exercises a 'permanent action' (*permanente Wirkung*) intermittently opposed to the sense of smell linked to the feminine. Does it follow that, in a retroactive reading, the pole of 'permanence' situated by *Civilisation and its Discontents* in the masculine register, allows the vector on which is inscribed the 'Thing' encountered as 'complex subject' to be delivered afterwards? Following the links made in Freud's text, it seems that the continuity communicates the need to bring out, through sensory experience, a visual pole characterized by stability, 'permanence' or 'constancy', and the inscription of a function pointing towards paternity. The pre-eminence of vision within the sensory register anticipates the pre-eminence of the *Geitstigkeit* (sphere of the mind) which, in *Moses and Monotheism*, is opposed to the whole of sensory experience. The separation at work in idealist philosophy between the diversity of the phenomenal field and the more abstract entities regulating the sensory manifestations structures the dichotomy underlying the sexual division in the parental couple. Further, the etymology communicates the noumenon presiding over the *'chose en soi'* ['thing in itself'] and the Freudian *geistig*, both terms referring directly to the regulation exercised by thought or the mind.

The ideal of representing the permanence, constancy, and ideality at the heart of a moving and intermittent sensory universe linked to the 'cry' in the *General Outline* and to blood in *Civilisation and its Discontents*, becomes the principle of an acting out, a role play, whose structure, according to Jacques Derrida, underlies the writing of *Beyond the Pleasure Principle*. The death of Sophie brings about a fracture which it is subsequently necessary to erase in order to reinstate an ideal and retroactive permanence. One would have to quote in their entirety the pages in which Derrida gathers together Freud's statements in order to make felt the construction of the inalterable. The inalterable nevertheless needs the support of the structure of the couple.

'As if she had never been' can be understood according to several intonations, but it must also be taken into account that one intonation always traverses the other. And also that the 'daughter' is not mentioned in the phrase: 'snatched away from glowing health, from her busy life as a capable mother and loving wife, in four or five days, as if she had never been'. Therefore the work goes on, everything continues, *fort-geht*, one might say. *La séance continue*. This is literally, and in French in the text, what he writes to Ferenczi in order to inform him of his mourning: 'My wife is quite overwhelmed. I think: *la séance continue*. But it was a little much for one week' . . . The work of mourning no doubt comes later, but the work of *Beyond the Pleasure Principle* . . . was not interrupted for a single day.[25]

Could the inalterable permanence be so celebrated if another entity by its side was not responsible for incarnating and ratifying the dimension of collapse? The statement 'My wife is quite overcome' allows for the possibility of another statement: '*La séance continue*'. An analogous structure, resting on the relationship between a pole of collapse, generally entrusted to a dependent figure—woman, child, disciple—and a pole of invincible stability, surfaces in another declaration addressed to Ferenczi: 'I have succeeded where the paranoid fail.' In many of Freud's dreams, it seems to me that there is a similar phenomenon of delegation, Freud entrusting to a woman or child the task of embodying, in a game of ejection through delegation, a place of vulnerability encountered in his own childhood. In the theoretical texts in which there is a scission between the principle of permanence and the fragments of mobility, the experience which presides over the fragmentation regularly places us at the heart of the apprehension of a threat or a cry for help. In the *General Outline*, the cry mentioned before the intervention of the subject–predicate fracture emanates from the *Nebenmensch* itself. This distress can be averted by delimiting, thanks to the fracture presiding over judgement presented as *Urteil* (original participation, since *Teil* means part), a support, a *subjectum*, traversing unchanged the various experiences of destabilization like the substance stretched out at the time of the apparent metamorphoses of the piece of wax. Further, it is regarding the flowing of blood that Freud brings out the phallic 'standing up', posed as an emblem of civilizing progress and as a pole of orientation.

BEING 'ITS OWN METAPHOR'—THE AIM OF THE MASCULINE?

In the case of both the couple of Freud and his wife and that which features in the correspondence, a duality commanded by a hierarchical principle is often encountered. The couple is possible only as long as the head, seen as a principle of direction and initiative, is unique. This is the paradigm of the 'monarchic body' promoted as a model of jouissance as it is analysed by Pascal Bruckner and Alain Finkielkraut. It is significant that this monarchic model leads to the partner being reabsorbed, by being neutralized, in the couple, and that the fundamentally rebellious bodily element which, in the Augustinian conception, refuses to obey the orders of the head.

Is not the phallic logic which presides over this centralizing and monarchic conception at work in the 'decision' made in *Moses and Monotheism* that 'paternity . . . is more important than maternity'? While in *The Infantile Genital Organization* Freud reveals beyond the phallic organization which only recognizes one sex, a genital organization open to the possibility of two sexes escaping the principle of differentiation by subtraction, there seems to be in *Moses and Monotheism* an insidious return of the monarchic primate in the question of a necessary preference between paternity and maternity. This question is posed and then frozen and leads to the staging of a quarrel for precedence: of paternity and maternity, which will triumph in the final tournament?

Setting up the respective powers of maternity and paternity in competition with each other, even if this competition is merely theoretical, is like staging a farce within a sex scene. Monique David-Ménard,[26] Genevieve Fraisse,[27] and Michel Tort renew the problem of sexual difference by refusing to confine it to an exercise of objectification and by asking questions about sexual difference which can be addressed to any discourse. In the introductory text, 'The Exercise of Knowledge and Sexual Difference', they question the various discourses, emphasizing their relation to their eventual audience with the statement that 'each sex is in a relation of address with the other':[28] 'because difference is not essential, the experience and fantasy of sexuality develops from a presumed knowledge of the identity of the other, and presented to the other. This dimension of otherness and address affects all discourse on sex, including psychoanalytic theory.'[29]

To whom is addressed the discourse which privileges paternity over maternity? Next to the game of seduction, a more ambiguous performance can be perceived. In the essay *Medusa's Head*, the goal attributed to the exhibition of the genitals—'I am not afraid of you, I have a penis'—is the exact opposite of achieving penetration, since Freud assigns to this provocative gesture the power to 'chase away evil spirits' either in the form of the devil or of woman. The context is the struggle between enemies, the confrontation aiming to make the enemy power disappear rather than to eventually meet it.

This structure is not dissimilar to the structure analysed by Freud in the ritual of rude jokes. If the woman occupies the position of target, she acts as a screen to mask another target: the woman exposed by the rude joke will be offered to the third man with whom can be established a masculine complicity. As in the 'relationship between cronies' the staging of masculine power over women is the medium through which an alliance is sealed between men. In his preface to *The Death of Oedipus*, Conrad Stein enlarges the scope of this structure by suggesting that the pillorying of the feminine figure, in this case Jocasta, is the foundation of the 'cohesion of the community'.[30] While in the theme of the death of the father, the father must pay the price to seal the fraternal alliance, Stein's interpretation reveals, behind the spectacular orchestration of the theme of parricide, the more insidious efficiency of a founding matricide.

Is not the theoretical enterprise backed up by a strategy of cancellation matching that of the promotion which accompanies the very process of symbolization? Isn't it possible to relate the phrase addressed by M.K. to Dora: 'My wife is nothing to me' to the theoretical construction which permits Lacan to reconstruct the whole symbolic apparatus on the sole basis of the masculine symbol?

I should say that strictly speaking there is no symbolization of woman's sex as such. In any case, the symbolisation isn't the same, it doesn't have the same source or the same mode of access as the symbolization of man's sex. And this is because the imaginary only furnished an absence where elsewhere there is a highly prevalent symbol. . . . The female sex in characterised by an absence, a void, a hole, which means that it happens to be less desirable than is the male sex for what he has that is provocative, and that an essential dissymmetry appears.[31]

We remain, therefore, confined within the tight circle of competition. Further, is it even proper to speak of the confrontation of two powers when only one of them is the object of official recognition and the other only constitutes the negative of the principle announced at the outset? In the insularity which characterizes his symbolic status, the masculine being sees himself deprived of one of his possible determinations. If the target that he can aim for is labelled as 'less desirable', then one of the metaphors illustrating one of the possible directions of his movement is removed. He ceases to be an arrow and becomes a fragment confined to a ceremony of self-celebration. This kind of closure had already been articulated by Lacan in *Les Formations de l'inconscient*: 'Insofar as he is virile, a man is always more or less his own metaphor.' This remark has a tone of derision, since its meaning persists in the following observation: 'That which puts upon the term virility the shadow of ridicule, which must nevertheless be mentioned'.[32]

Is the masculine symbol necessarily condemned to function in a self-referential mode? This type of celebration effectively corresponds to one of the stages of the journey, that of adolescence, and the fine arts have been able to capture the form of the body as fully erect, which makes superfluous the addition of an emblem to lessen self-celebration. In her commentary on Brancusi's work *Torso of a Young Man*, Marie-Laure Bernadac highlights the reason behind the form of this figure: 'The wooden torso of a young man, as smooth and flat as that of a young girl, has no sex because it is already in the shape of a phallus.'[33]

At its extreme, self-celebration has the effect of immobilizing, or sidelining, the symbol itself. Lacan comes back to the German formulation of M.K.'s remark to Dora, '*Ich habe nichts an meiner Frau*': 'The German phrase is particularly expressive, and has a particularly vivid meaning if we give the word *nothing* its full weight. What he says to her in fact removes him from the circuit he has set up.'[34]

Passing from one language to another subverts the location of the 'nothing'. While the French translation '*Ma femme n'est rien pour moi*'[35] puts the destitution of the woman first, destitution having the value of castration, the German text, at least if one makes a significant cut to isolate 'Ich habe nichts' (I have nothing), puts the destitution upon the speaker. Beyond the relation concerning the message in which M.K. designates his wife, is not the question that of the status of the masculine 'to have'? The text tightly links the *haben* and the *haben an* (to have for or to have in respect of, the preposition *an* indicating a destination). In this sense, presenting the construction 'to have' in a truncated way deprives it of its dimension of destination and transforms the arrow into an emblem. If the direction of the arrow is not inscribed upon it, then various penetrative journeys and trajectories can be imagined, and the arrow loses one of its powers in becoming, quite simply, a metaphor of itself, and thus being confined to a monadic structure. That which is lost relates to what Michele Montrelay attributes to a power of 'casting off', a term which indicates both a power of mobility and a curiosity oriented towards another place.

Putting into perspective in this way the masculine 'to have' has a place in various theoretical instances. For example, the story of the Trojan horse, exploited by Conrad Stein, or the expression used by F. Perrier to designate what the masculine emblem represents for the hysteric: the 'homing device' which, beyond the characterization of the masculine offers the representation of possible exploration of a different territory. All these perspectives work to shatter the monadic fortress. When his approach receives criticism, Lacan indicates the limitations of the theoretical apparatus that he constructs. His remark

145

about the 'shadow of ridicule' attached to the virile being wanting to be 'his own metaphor' responds to the question concerning his presentation of œdipal structures: 'We never highlight the relationship of the father to the mother.'[36] On several occasions in Lacan's landscape an amputation of the vectorial dimension occurs, which confines the message relating to the phallus and self-celebration.

THE PREHISTORY OF THE PHALLUS

If, in taking account of the masculine, the feminine does not appear to be correlated to a destination, then without doubt her masked presence acquires a more determining power if that which underlies the emergence of the phallus is envisaged. When the phallus is understood in its status of signifier, it represents essentially a differentiating sign, linked to the register of the detachable, the register of what the seminar on *L'Angoisse* [Anguish] names the 'divisible object', offered for symbolic retranscription. This perspective refers necessarily to a binary logic built around the duality presence/absence. In the Freudian approach, the differentiating perspective needs the confrontation between man and woman since the threat of castration becomes conceivable only on the basis of the perception of the female genitals. The postures of the masculine 'to have'—standing up or falling down— then become secondary.

The opposite applies in the Lacanian perspective which situates the passage to the negative in the actual becoming of the masculine performance. The need to invoke the feminine as a metaphor of the negative then disappears, at least in the approach applied in *L'Angoisse*. Lacan brings into play concerning detumescence the same logic that Freud correlated to the vision of the woman's sex. This reorientation of masculine destiny invites Lacan to cast a particular light upon the epiphany which constitutes the upright figure:

Just as in nature there are already certain reservoirs, there are in the signified a certain number of elements which are given in experience as accidents of the body, but which are taken up in the signifier and which give the signifier, so to speak, its first weapons. These are ungraspable yet irreducible things such as the phallic term—the erection, pure and simple. The standing stone is an example of this, and the notion of the human body as erect is another. In this way, a certain number of elements, all linked to bodily stature and not simply to the lived experience of the body, constitute the first elements, borrowed from experience, but totally transformed by the fact that they are symbolized. By *symbolized* it is meant that they are introduced into the place of the signifier as such, which is characterized by the fact that it is articulated according to the laws of logic.[37]

Thus in order to be promoted to the status of symbol, the phallus must pass through an understanding of itself as *Gestalt*. Lacan comes back to the importance of imaginary mediation when talking about the 'prevalence of the phallic *Gestalt*', which dictates the identification of the father, and about the 'prevalence of the imaginary form of the phallus . . . insofar as this form is itself taken as the symbolic element central to the œdipus complex'.[38]

The Lacanian insistence on the dimension of manifestation in its function as a stage in a cycle leads to the deployment of the paternal function on several fronts. While the emphasis on the signifier privileges the dimension of division, the attention to the conditions of operativity nonetheless helps us to see a bodily process under the sign of becoming. While for Freud paternity was supported by the duality which constitutes the domain of life abandoned to the mother, and the mind in which the idea of paternity is carried out, Lacan blurs this dichotomy by extending the field of manifestation to paternity. The figure of Booz invokes the relation to the living, which Freud reserved for the mother, to underline 'the creative drive, the creative force, the force of begetting' attached to the metaphor of the sheaf: 'It is something which, as it is substituted precisely for the father, releases the whole dimension of biological fecundity which was underlying the spirit of the poem.'[39] Although various subsequent statements in the *The Ethic of Psychoanalysis* seem to reduce the paternal function to the imposition of the name, the approach of 1957 inscribes in the field of paternity the kind of biological references which for Freud were essentially the privilege of the maternal.

But can an allusion to the power of fecundity remain bereft of any reference to the maternal? The session of 23 April 1958 sees in the Greek *phallos* 'that which, of life, manifests itself in the purest way as turgescence, as shoot', that which relates to 'the order of intrusion, of the vital shot as intrusion'. Seeing the *phallos* in the vital shoot makes necessary its confrontation with various entities—the goddesses of fecundity—who are presupposed to guard the field of fecundity:

In all ancient cultures, it is as one approaches the cult—that is, the signifying manifestation of the fecund power of the great goddess—that everything related to the *phallos* becomes the object of imputations, of marks of castration,

147

or of more and more accentuated interdictions; the character of the eunuch of
the priests of the great goddess, the Syrian goddess, being one of the most
widely recognized, found in all the texts.[40]

How can the joining of these two participants in fecundity be
achieved? Is it a question of an operation of relief based upon annex-
ation? In that case, the equivalent of the Greek turning point that
Freud includes at the end of *Moses and Monotheism* would be played
out: 'Athena without mother' seems to incarnate the denial of the
maternal participation in fecundity. This proclamation rests upon a
denial, since Zeus's act of giving birth was only made possible by his
first having swallowed the mother, Metis. This act of swallowing is
swallowed by Freud, who does not mention the correlation between
the swallowing of the maternal by the father and the subsequent possibility of a birth 'without the help of a mother'. Is the repeated claim,
essentially in Lacan's early texts, of a 'dimension of biological fecundity' inherent to paternity and witnessed by the Greek *phallos*, reducible
to paternity's act of swallowing maternity?

Although this hypothesis cannot possibly be accepted, it nevertheless reappears in another version. While the seminar of 27 November
1957 dedicated to the figure of Booz reveals the 'sharp edge of the
celestial sickle which evokes the intention of castration', the seminar
on *La Relation d'objet* suggests the 'trial of a logic of rubber' in order
to examine the plot between the sheaf and the sickle. This plot requires
the creation of a malleable logic. The springing up of the sheaf is in
effect made possible by the intervention of an act of substitution. But
while this logic of substitution intervenes regularly to realize the per-
mutation through which the father finds himself substituted for the
mother in the same movement through which he is mediated by the
mother, taking account of the dimension of fecundity places the father
in the position of target. Talking about Booz, Lacan says: 'It is here that
the sheaf come to take his place, and for a moment literally cancels
him out. We see again the schema of the symbol as the death of the
thing. Here is it even better—the name of the person is abolished, and
his sheaf is substituted for him.'[41]

Is not the power of fecundity the origin of the 'abolished' position
of the father? Given the correlation between the moment of conception and the announcement of a birth, does not the mother necessarily
become an agent or accomplice of the process through which the
father is 'abolished', and abolished by his own sheaf? The 'golden
sickle in the field of stars', thrown away by 'which god, which harvester

of the eternal summer', is identified by Lacan with the phenomenon of maternity:

The sickle in the sky is the eternal sickle of maternity, which has already played its little part between Chronos and Uranus, between Zeus and Chronos . . . It is power that is represented there in the mystic waiting of woman. With the sickle always in her reach, the female gleaner will cut down the sheaf from which the lineage of the Messiah will spring.[42]

It is understood retroactively that this approach has been placed under the auspices of a 'logic of rubber' that will perhaps allow the 'sheaf' to improvise certain strategies of bending is order to escape the threat of castration at the hands of the mother. In effect Lacan imputes to the female gleaner an action that the poem, in interrogative form, attributed to some 'god' or 'harvester'.

When this approach comes close to the realm of vivid tumescence, it is not certain that the appropriate instrument of logic should take the form of the sword. A central point of theory diverts the injunction of separation. Does paternity emerge as the prolonging of the vital turgescence or as that which, by abandoning the vital shoot to the woman—apparently Freud's preferred solution—provokes the abolition of the father or at least his relegation in the domain of the *Geist*? From the moment at which the scope of the 'eternal sickle of maternity' is grasped, the urgency of a maternal language which 'founds the father' is understood.

THE MASCULINE AND THE DIVINE

Is it to escape the dilemma—presenting the self as the power of fecundity or recognizing the risk of abolition stemming from the maternal sickle—that Lacan's thought on paternity in one of his subsequent theoretical trajectories privileges a sex other than that in which is inscribed the dimension of fecundity? The verdict of *The Ethics of Psychoanalysis* relates the crux of the paternal function to a different theme than that which in *La Relation d'objet* leads to the issue of fecundity: 'If Œdipus doesn't have an Œdipus complex, it is because in his case there is no father at all. The person who served as father was his adoptive father. And, my good friends, that's the case with all of us, because as the Latin has it, *pater is est quem justae nuptiae demonstrant*, that is to say, the father is he who acknowledges us.'[43]

The theoretical decree is presented here in a damning form, as though there were no other possible mode of access to paternity. The opposite is true in *La Relation d'objet* which constantly inspires a sense of vertigo as each approach regularly leads us to the edge of the 'unthinkable'. Lacan highlights the gap between the quest for the father and the entry of each individual being into the status of paternity: 'Asking the question *what is a father?* is different from being a father oneself, from acceding to the paternal position. If for each man the accession to the paternal position is a quest, it is not impossible to say that, ultimately, no one has ever really completely been a father.'[44] What remains unattainable for each individual father is however available on a cultural scale, as long as we come back to the field of religion:

The only one who could respond to the position of the father as Symbolic father is he who could say, like the God of monotheism, 'I am he who I am'. But this phrase that we find in the sacred text cannot be pronounced by anyone.

You will say to me then, 'You have taught us that the message we receive is our own message in an inverse form, so all will be resolved through the phrase "You are he who you are". Do not believe it, for who am I to say that to anyone else? In other words, what I am trying to show you here is that the Symbolic father is, properly speaking, unthinkable.'[45]

Confronted with an impossible demand, Lacan highlights, in little Hans's quest, an essential turning point, centred on the 'real penis'. What is put in place is 'the notion that at the level of the great Other, there is someone who can respond in any eventuality, and who responds that in any case the phallus, the real one, the real penis, belongs to him. He has the master tool and he knows it. He is introduced into the symbolic order as a real element.'[46] While in *The Psychoses* the status of the symbolic order confronts the questioning individual with an atemporal field, which does not acknowledge the 'singular existence of the subject', a mediation is offered in *La Relation d'objet*:

There is the Symbolic father, and there is the Real father. Experience teaches us that in the assumption of the male sexual function the presence of the Real father plays a vital role. In order for the castration complex to be truly lived by the subject, the Real father must really play the game. He must assume his function of castrating father, the function of father in concrete, empirical form, I almost said degenerate, thinking of the character of the primordial father and the horrifying tyrannical form in which the Freudian myth presented him to us. It is in the extent to which the father, as he exists as such, fulfils his empirically intolerable imaginary function ... that the castration complex is lived.[47]

It is rare that a phrase such as 'experience teaches us' flows from Lacan's pen. Equally surprising is the emphasis on 'lived', usually a proscribed word for Lacan. In effect, there is a reversal of the process of theoretical legitimization, since the symbolic function is itself dependent upon a propping-up in which the Real must intervene as well as the 'imaginary function'. From this stems the advent of a mythical father, playing with the categories attendant upon the divine, in the case of the bestowing of immortality: 'The father we are talking about', writes Lacan, in regard to the father of the primitive horde,

is not conceived of by Freud or anyone else, as an immortal being. Why must it be the case that the sons have in some way brought forward his death? ... He was only killed to show that he cannot be killed.

The essence of the major drama introduced by Freud rests on a strictly mythical notion to the extent that it is a categorization of a form of the impossible, that is, the eternalizing of a single, original father, among whose characteristics is that he has been killed. And why should he have been killed, except to preserve him? I note in passing that in French, and in several other languages including German, the verb 'to kill' (*tuer*) comes from the Latin *tutare* which means to preserve.[48]

The edification of the theme of paternity is thus in solidarity with the construction of an illusion, and is also joined to the function of defence against death which Lacan assigns to paternity. The paternal institution would therefore take over from the illusions underlying the field of religion. Drawing on the trajectory of little Hans, Lacan exposes the founding function devolved to the Imaginary father:

What does it mean that it must be an Imaginary father who sets definitively the order of the world, since not everybody has a phallus? It is easy to recognize that the Imaginary father is the all-powerful father, the founder of the order of the world in the common conception of God, the guarantee of the universal order in its most massive and brutal elements, that it is he who made everything.[49]

In order to deal with the risk of irremediable collusion between the status of paternity and that of the divine, Lacan introduces into the circuit an intermediary character, Professor Freud, as he simultaneously participates in human nature and divine privilege. In so doing, Lacan is happy to take Hans's account seriously and to make him a guarantee, drawing on the denunciative modality of Freud's interpretation.

Here Freud does not follow any kind of rule, he really takes up what I might call the divine position—He speaks to the young Hans as though from Mount Sinai and Hans staggers under the blow.

Understand that the position of the Symbolic father . . . remains veiled. To position oneself, as Freud does, as absolute master, relates not only to the Symbolic father, but to the Imaginary father, and it is in this way that Freud tackles the situation.[50]

Thus far from being denounced as an illusion, the Imaginary allows the 'articulation of the truth'. In this way Hans grants to Freud the status of God:

Naturally he believes in him as we all believe in God—he believes without believing. He believes in him because the reference to a sort of supreme witness is an essential element of any articulation of truth. There is someone who knows everything, and he has found him—it's Professor Freud. What luck to have found God on earth. If only we were all so lucky.[51]

Can we be sure that the writing of the paternal function, as it occurs in Lacan, does not bring us the substitute of the 'god' which comes to help Hans? In *Figuras del Padre*,[52] Sylvia Tubert relates many psychoanalytic constructions to a 'mystique of paternity'. It is true that the turning point in the analysis of little Hans is interesting in its presentation of a bipartition affecting the paternal function. God is not incarnated by the father, but in a character who is part of the cultural context. This gap limits the risk that the social will be swallowed by the familial, as it is profiled in patriarchal ideology.

The risk of being swallowed up is much greater when, beyond the moment of cancellation, Lacan presents the return of Booz: 'And Booz, after having been eclipsed, hidden, and abolished, reappears in the fecund influence of his sheaf. He knows no avarice or hate, he is purely and simply natural fecundity.' The figure which emerges is extended beyond proportion. This extension is depicted in 'the dream that will follow': 'He will soon be a father, that is to say that from his belly will issue a great tree at the bottom of which a king sang and at the top of which a God died.'[53] This is a collusion of the human and the divine confused in one unique epiphany. Far from restoring the rights of division, Lacan welomes this poetic production: 'It is a question of a substitution which maintains at the same time that which it substitutes. In the tension between what is abolished and suppressed, and what is substituted, there is a new dimension which so visibly introduces poetic improvisation. This new dimension, manifestly incarnated by the Boozian myth, is the function of paternity.'[54] The terrors attached to the 'eternal sickle of maternity' then disappear and the sheaf regains at its core the powers which were exposed to the risk of separation. The belly of Booz represents the place of origin.

FREUD AND THE RETRACTILE MASCULINE

Was this dishonest compromise between the father and the divine at work in Freud's text? The risk of being totally swallowed up is certainly active in Freud, and it culminates in the figure of the father of the primitive horde whose savage and 'degenerate' character is underlined by Lacan. But this type of engulfing appropriation is precisely what the union, which is essentially horizontal because it is fraternal, is supposed to put an end to. It is incontestable that this kind of sacralization haunts *The Interpretation of Dreams*,[55] but the dream text, sharing incidentally the logic surrounding 'Doctor Herod', strains at the same time to denounce all that relates to the abuse of power or mass destruction. In the wake of the all-powerful, ravaging father the silhouette is traced of what Conrad Stein names the 'mortal father', whose vulnerability is exposed. A pattern of breathing is established, and sets up a rhythm centred on the alternate apparition of the two figures, the 'mortal father' and the 'immortal father',[56] the reference to paternity itself being carried into this scansion which integrates the moment of vertical emergence and that of falling back down.

Freud's emphasis on the position of collapse prevents his construction proceeding, as Lacan does in asymptotic mode, to the falling back of the paternal on the divine. The shadowy figure which is supposed to rule the infernal world then appears—'Lucifer-Amor'—in whom Freud sees a representation of the dead father during his analysis of a case of possession. While Hans believes he can see in Professor Freud a substitute for God, it seems that Freud, in his own fantasy, is attracted towards a more disturbing figure of the supernatural world, a figure with whom he sketches the movements of parodic identification, arguing that cultural interpretation has assimilated the Jew and the devil. In presenting himself as 'Jewish infidel' Freud combines two adherences, in taking up again his paternal heritage he inaugurates a more transgressive operation. If, in dressing himself up as master, Freud inherits from a paternal figure touched with omnipotence, and evidence for this can be found in the analysis of François Roustang in

Un destin si funeste,[57] the position adopted by Freudian psychoanalysis towards the cultural field will resemble that of the rebellious son.

In bringing about the possibility of delimiting a place for the son, Freud is thus led to split the figures of the masculine. This problem is particularly manifest in the latest developments of *'Analyse sans fin, Analyse sans fin'* ['Endless analysis, endless analysis'], where an end point is exposed, the 'rock' on which the masculine trajectory stumbles: 'The man does not want to submit himself to a paternal substitute . . . does not want therefore to accept [*annehmen*] the cure from the doctor.'[58] The operation from which the masculine being removes himself is significant. Far from relating simply to a passive position and to the castration complex, it leads to a thematic opening and swallowing, implicating either an oral dimension or a female-genital dimension. Although the reference to castration is also present in this text, Freud tries to make possible for the masculine subject the use of a metaphorical mouth, an opening that seems incompatible with the essence of masculinity and that the cultural landscape situates in the feminine territory.

Again we find an allusion to an oral performance when in *Negation* Freud proposes a diagrammatic representation of perceptive exploration, seen as a model of judgemental activity. A comparison emerges with the strategic operations resting on the alternance of a rapid advance (*Vorstoss*: 'sudden attack', 'raid') and retreat. Intellectual activity would thus follow the rhythm which corresponds to the masculine movement during intercourse. Freud organizes an oral pause in this penetrative gesture, since an extended moment would allow one to 'taste' (*kosten*) that with which one has contact, in order to appreciate its value as well as its risk of danger. The comparison of psychical movements with those of the amoeba—throwing out pseudopods into the surrounding environment in order to change its form—appears on several occasions. In this configuration of the psychical operations, the phallic dynamic is associated, not with the exhibition of an erect form—an image celebrated by Lacan and symbolized by 'standing stones'—but to a mobile game making of retreat not a capitulation or an aphanisis, but the return to a protected position, the equivalent of a winter hideaway.

By elaborating a retractile masculine strategy, Freud thus reserves the possibility for the masculine to refer itself to a bifocal model, leaving behind the sacralization of the erected, petrified position. This position forms part of a cycle of positions, the masculine thus being identified less with the complex operation of *Gestalt* which, in a study articulating the analytical field and the aesthetic field, Jean Florence places under the sign of *Gestaltung* as Prinzhorn analyses it:

In that way his notion of *Gestaltung*, borrowed from Ludwig Kalges, proves its fecundity regarding the theory of *Gestalt* long considered to be incontestable in the psychology of perception. The defining link of *Gestaltung* to rhythm, to the game and to a relation to instinct recognized in its irreducible multiplicity is sufficient to distinguish the stasis of the structures released by the Gestaltists and to assess its pertinence in realizing the formal invention that is art.[59]

On several occasions, the aesthetic field is encountered in this approach as the purveyor of models which escape the tyranny of the dominant cultural prescriptions. Besides, Freud is not concerned to contest in a radical manner the imperatives which determine the definition of the masculine, but, in an ambiguous strategy to save the possibility of a master position which is not absolutely condemned to insularity. Hence the need to leave open to the disciple or the son access to a position of apprenticeship. Does not Lacan condemn the eventual inscription of such a place when he immediately links the statement 'You are my master' to its echo 'You are my wife'? In Lacan's perspective, masculinity risks running into an all-or-nothing logic, which make the processes of transmission difficult to understand.

Freud's concern to arrange a phase of apprenticeship seems to lead us to the Greek realm which he endlessly borders. Further, examining the Greek models causes us to relate the examination of sexual difference to a perspective which includes the cultural and historical dimension. Is not the fact of granting the father a function situated in the vicinity of the divine the other side of the retreat of the divine which characterizes modernity? Are the radical stakes attached to the promotion of the father the consequence of a phenomenon of displacement and compensation? Talking of the Imaginary father as he appears in Hans's quest, Lacan brings into play the theme of belief and faith. This dimension was already visible in the relationship to the father deployed by Freud, but belief was in strange company, since it was immediately associated with deduction and doubt. Thus the Lacanian construction of paternity radicalizes a movement sketched out by Freud.

The Platonic context presents the ambition to muddle the system of equivalences which regularly leads to the word for word pairing of various dichotomies. Here we enter a structure which is no longer binary, but ternary, which will perhaps allow us to escape certain traps inherent to Manichaeist logic. The tripartite structure of the soul permits us to complicate the couple by associating the function of mastery with servile docility. The head is in effect attached not to the whole of the animate being, but to the link that it maintains with a transcendent world:

We should think of the most authoritative part of our soul as a guardian spirit given by god, living in the summit of the body, which can properly be said to lift us from the earth towards our home in heaven, for we are creatures not of earth but of heaven, where the soul was first born, and our divine part attaches us by the head to heaven, like a plant by its roots, and keeps our body upright.[60]

Leaving aside the question of being rooted in a transcendent land so that the relationship to verticality is turned on itself, this disorienting psychical landscape is interesting because it weakens some of the evidence we have examined so far. From the moment that the masculine is no longer confined to the function which forced it to constitute the unique vertical location, a field of multiple mobilities opens in front of it. Plato situates thus the relationship between the bodily functions and the animation which presides over the sexual game:

What we drink makes its way through the lung into the kidneys and thence to the bladder from which it is expelled by air pressure. From this channel they pierced a hole into the column of marrow which extends from the head down through the neck long the spine and which we have already referred to as 'seed'; this marrow, being instinct with life, completed the process and finding an outlet caused there a vital appetite for emission, the desire for sexual reproduction. So a man's genitals are naturally disobedient and self-willed, like a creature that will not listen to reason, and will do anything in their mad lust for possession.[61]

To the extent that the question of relationships guaranteed through transcendence is resolved at the level of the head, the intermediary soul, dedicated to *thymos* and *eros*, can hand over to the 'unruly being' which presides over the masculine performance and to whom it is not asked to rival in dignity and bearing the stature of the Commander. We are far from the contemporary equation which assigns to the masculine, as he is charged with assuming to paternal function, a task of arbitration.

Does this mean that the masculine can only find the right to occupy a living place in a frame which attributes to the divine the function of control entrusted to the male representative at the beginning of the lay era? Could not other theoretical constructs, some of them based upon the analysis of the social field, suggest various interpretations of transcendence? Lévi-Strauss is not far from doing this when he rests the whole system of exchange less on what it forbids than on 'alliance', a word charged with reminiscences which it is important to bring to the surface.

Notes

1. Editor's note: *Le Trauma et la filiation paradoxale* (Paris: Aubier, 1988), 175.
2. Editor's note: 'Interview with Monique Schneider', in Elaine Hoffman Baruch and Lucienne J. Serrano, *Women Analyze Women* (New York: New York University Press, 1988), 168.
3. Editor's note: ibid. 171–2.
4. Editor's note: See Chapter 4, 'Masculine/Feminine: The Thought of Difference', by Françoise Héritier.
5. Héritier, *Masculine/Feminine*. All translations are by the translator of the chapter unless otherwise specified.
6. Alain, Roger, *Le Voyeur ivre* (Paris: Denoël, 1981).
7. S. Mimoun and L. Chaby, *La Sexualité masculine* (Paris: Flammarion, 1996), 11.
8. R. Kaes, 'Le Pacte dénégatif dans les ensembles transsubjectifs', in *Le Négatif: figures et modalités* (Paris: Dunod, 1989), 110.
9. A.E. Cliche, (1995). *Comédies: L'autre scène de l'écriture* (Montreal: XYZ, 1995), 94.
10. Ibid. 95–6.
11. J. Lacan, *Les Formations de l'inconscient 1957–1958* (Paris: Seuil, 1998). Session of 12 Mar. 1958.
12. C. Lévi-Strauss, (1973). *Tristes Tropiques* (London: Jonathan Cape, 1973), trans. John and Doreen Weightman, p. 388.
13. J. Lacan, *Les Formations de l'inconscient 1957–1958*, Session of 29 Jan. 1958.
14. C. Lévi-Strauss, *The Elementary Structures of Kinship*, trans. James Harle Bell and John Richard von Sturmer (London: Eyre & Spottiswoode, 1969), p. xxix.
15. Ibid.
16. Ibid., p. xxx.
17. Editor's note: Cf. Chapter 4, 'Masculine/Feminine: The Thought of Difference'.
18. Translator's note: The French phrase 'faire l'enfant' is used which means 'to behave childishly', although literally means 'to make a child'.
19. M. Vaquin, *Frankenstein ou les délires de la raison* (Paris: François Bourin, 1989).
20. Lévi-Strauss, *The Elementary Sturctures of Kinship*, 14.
21. Comment made by Felthi Benslama in the conference 'Dieu et la clinique', 1997.
22. S. Freud, 'General Scheme', in *Project for a Scientific Psychology*, the Standard Edition of the Complete Works of Sigmund Freud, trans. James Strachey, vol. i (London: The Hogarth Press, 1966), 331.
23. Ibid.
24. Freud, 'Attempt to Represent Normal ψ Processes', in *Project for a Scientific Psychology*, 366.
25. J. Derrida, *The Post Card : From Socrates to Freud and Beyond*, trans. Alan Bass (Chicago and London: Chicago University Press, 1987), pp. 329–30.

26. Editor's note: cf. Chapter 12, 'Is it Necessary to look for the Universal in the Difference between the Sexes?'.

27. Editor's note: cf. Chapter 7, 'The Difference between the Sexes: A Historical Difference'.

28. *L'Exercise du savoir et la différence des sexes*, 7. This question is taken up again by M. David-Ménard in *Les Constructions de l'universel* (Paris: PUF, 1997). [Editor's note] Chapter 12 of this reader is taken from here.

29. *L'Exercise du savoir et la différence des sexes*, 9.

30. C. Stein, *La Mort d'Oedipe: La Psychanalyse et sa pratique* (Paris: Gonthier, 1977).

31. J. Lacan, *The Psychoses. The Seminar of Jacques Lacan*. Book III *1955–1956*, trans., Russell Grigg (London: Routledge, 1993), 176.

32. J. Lacan, (1998). *Les Formations de l'inconscient*, Session of 22 Jan. 1958.

33. 'Feminine-Masculine', 67.

34. J. Lacan, *La Relation d'object. Séminaire*, vol. iv (Paris: Seuil, 1998).

35. In English and French the phrase shares the same structure 'My wife is nothing to me', so that both languages illustrate Schneider's point.

36. Lacan, *Les Formations de l'inconscient*, Session of 29 Jan. 1958.

37. Lacan, *La Relation d'object. Séminaire*, vol. iv.

38. Lacan, *The Psychoses. The Seminar of Jacques Lacan*. Book III *1955–1956*, 176.

39. Lacan, *Les Formations de l'inconscient*, Session of 29 Jan. 1958. Session of 27 Nov. 1957.

40. Lacan, *Les Formations de l'inconscient*, Session of 23 Apr. 1958.

41. Lacan, *La Relation d'object. Séminaire*, vol. iv.

42. Ibid.

43. J. Lacan, *The Ethics of Psychoanalysis 1959–1960. The Seminar of Jacques Lacan* Book VII, trans. Dennis Porter (London: Routledge, 1992), 309.

44. Lacan, *La Relation d'object. Séminaire*, vol. iv.

45. Ibid.

46. Ibid.

47. Ibid.

48. Ibid.

49. Ibid.

50. Ibid.

51. Ibid.

52. S. Tubert, *Figuras del Padre* (Madrid: Catedra, 1997).

53. Lacan, *La Relation d'object. Séminaire*, vol. iv.

54. Ibid.

55. Cf. 'Father, can't you see . . .?', in J. Lacan, *The Four Fundamental Concepts of Psychoanalysis*, trans. Alan Sheridan (London: Penguin, 1994), 34.

56. C. Stein, 'Le père mortel et le père immortel', *L'Inconscient*, 5 (1968).

57. F. Roustang, *Un destin si funeste* (Paris: Minuit, 1976).

58. '*Analyse sans fin, analyse sans fin*', in *Résultats, idées, problèmes, ii* (Paris: PUF, 1992), 267.

59. J. Florence, *Art et thérapie, liaison dangereuse?* (Brussels: Facultés universitaires Saint-Louis, 1997), 60.

60. Plato, *Timaeus and Critius*, trans. Desmond Lee (London: Penguin, 1971), 119.

61. Ibid. 120.

9 The Excess Visibility of an Invisible Sex or the Privileges of the Formless

Claire Nahon*

Claire Nahon is a clinical psychologist currently completing her doctorate in Fundamental Psychopathology and Psychoanalysis. Her research focuses on the notion of trans-sexuality, as opposed to transexuality. Through her clinical work with transexual patients she seeks to re-evaluate the commonly accepted usage of the term 'sexuality' within the field of psychopathology. Beyond the traditional Freudian concept of 'bisexuality' constitutive of a certain normativity with regard to the duality of the sexes, a normativity grounded in static modalities of desire anchored in anatomy, Nahon's elaborations of trans-sexuality destabilize socially acquired representations of sex and sexual difference. Contrary to common critiques, transexualism, on Nahon's reading, does not necessarily undermine psychoanalysis as a discipline but rather, through its situational commonality with the logical structure of the dream, allows us to think through the continuity of the sexes as well as the identifications that dream work, the work of psychoanalysis, consistently reveal. Transexualism operates as an autonomous psychopathological model that problematizes previous psychoanalytic taxonomies and their underlying dualities and introduces a trans-sexual dimension to our thinking of sexuality as a passage from one sex, one gender, one symptom, to another.

The following text, 'The Excessive Visibility of an Invisible Sex or the Privileges of the Formless', is taken from a collection entitled *On the Difference of Sexes among Women (De la différence des sexes entre les femmes)*, a series of essays based on a recent conference dedicated to the elaboration of discourses that seek to move beyond the identification of a unique vision of femininity as constituted through an imaginary binary opposition to masculinity. In this chapter, Nahon examines the ways in which the contemporary phenomenon of transexuality allows us to rethink the relationships between sex and gender from a decidedly psychoanalytic perspective whereby the unconscious and its drives can be seen to

---

* 'Le trop visible d'un sexe invisible ou les privilèges de L'informe', in *De la différence des sexes entre les femmes* (Paris: Presses Universitaires de France, 2000), 52–79, abridged. Reprinted by permission of Presses Universitaires de France.

159

make an uncanny, and quite visible, appearance on a violently shifting social scene. Whereas the obsessive linkage of sex and image within phallocentric culture has consistently figured the *one* (penis) of the masculine sex and the feminine sex as *not one*, a theory of an auto-erotic sexuality grounded in the transgressive, singular structure of the dream—beyond form and identity—demonstrates the truly dialectical, individual nature of a sexuality freed from the repressive cultural dysfunctions of traditional gender roles.

Transexuals, on Nahon's reading, embody the sex/gender distinction through their denial of the so-called 'normal' relationship between anatomy and its psychic inscription and sexuation; they maintain a *certainty* as to what constitutes sexual difference that takes us to the very heart of the representation of woman and her sex. Transexuals vividly realize the notion that *jouissance* transcends the materiality of the sexes and demonstrate the sexual logic of the unconscious. The transexual's excessive attachment to the sexual organ in its capacity to instantiate visibility and form, his or her insistence that gender identity might be equated to sexual identity (as formalized through a surgical affirmation of a male or female sex organ) replays a confusion between the unthinkable formlessness of unconscious sexuality and the physical 'organ', which organ becomes quite literally suppressed and denuded of its sexual function. The transexual, then, presents him- or herself to the interlocutor as a sort of dense dream image thereby displacing the unconscious and incarnating, *showing* the deformity of the formless as a transgressive spectacle.

With regard to the question of the relations between gender and sexuality, certain strains of feminism, on Nahon's reading, tend towards a desire for a sense of harmony between sex and gender that ultimately leads to a reductive theorization of feminine sexuality that negates individual differences among and between women. A feminism with an anti-identity politics, however, might recognize the transgressive possibilities of sexuality, the polymorphous nature of desire. Once masculinity and femininity as iron-clad identities are recognized as social constructs, the repressive nature of sex roles ceases to wield its power and the formless, dream structures of the dialectic of the unconscious remain. The social scene, then, having denounced artificially enforced gender roles, opens the emancipatory space that permits the 'trans-sexual' nature of sexuality to develop.

Have the secrets of œdipal torment and the mystery of femininity become so clear to us that we must leave behind the Graeco-Roman Antiquity so dear to Freud and look no earlier than the Minoan-Mycenaean civilization to which Freud refers when confronting the issue of the pre-œdipal sexuality of the young girl? Should we forget castration, psychic bisexuality, and the bedrock of biology and anatomy as destiny?! Should we forget Tiresias, as though the threat of his fate held only an outdated charm for us?! Sexual difference—is it really necessary to specify *between* the *two* sexes?—would then speak for itself, the terms 'man' and 'woman' would cover realities of which we could be certain, whose content, stable and indubitable, had been largely explored and carefully defined. The phallocratic era would have lost its prestige and power and the hour of women would have come. Finally, women would take centre stage, finally an interest would be taken in them for and according to themselves and no longer according to the ancient yardstick of an invasive masculine other; finally their identity, their specificity and the sexual difference *between women* would be examined. But who would risk believing in such a fiction? In fact, far from being finished with those questions dear to Freud, the title of this forum[1] takes them up again and turns them around, perhaps subverts them, because it is presented in the form of a pastiche, because it insists on parcelling and fragmenting, because it emphasizes division, because it tends to split even further that which from the first was presented as dual. It does this in an optic which is certainly postmodern,[2] but it continues nevertheless to acknowledge the perplexity into which these questions still plunge us.

In fact, while the most recent psychoanalytic literature never ceases to question the development of sexuality in culture in general and in the narrow sphere of psychoanalytic treatment in particular, it is easy to see, whether or not one is an analyst, the force of social transformation. The patriarchal structure is in rapid decline, the outward signs of sexual difference are decreasing in a startling manner so that transsexualism, which only a short time ago was seen as one of the strangest pathologies, is now almost typical of the changes occurring on the social scene. Furthermore, while this curious condition, based upon the unshakeable conviction of the individual involved that he or she belongs to the opposite sex, seemed to concern predominantly the sudden desire of the masculine sex to attain a convincing idealization of female being, it is remarked—and this is a trick of the phallocratic order!—that more and more women are claiming to be men, as a result of which, obviously, they are demanding male physical attributes. Some will say this is penis envy, others will say perversity or even perversion, the denial of castration ... This does not lessen the fact that these patients, through the most intimate suffering, are radicalizing a malaise which unfortunately seems to be characteristic of our society. By this, I mean the 'new maladies of the soul'[3] characterized by the weakness of the image—the unconscious image, the product of auto-eroticism and of its perfect metaphor. In these maladies sexuality, far from contributing to the foundation of a stable sexual identity, but perhaps closer to the true nature of sexuality, adopts the most singular, transgressive forms, or indeed those social performances which, to the contrary, privilege appearance through deliberate masquerade (*drag queens, drag kings* and other phenomena of *cross-dressing* or *gender-bending*[4]). The image, in its link to the sex organ, becomes a constant obsession in a civilization which, according to certain feminist interpretations, is marked by the hegemony exercised by the 'phallomorphic one'[5] over the 'sex which is not one'.[6] Is it therefore necessary to choose between an essentialism which excludes any difference between women and which must perhaps lead to the 'lesbian continuum' dear to American cultural feminism (to which we shall return), and, on the other hand, a constructionism which plays with possibilities of an imaginary emancipation of sexuality, so that the nature of auto-erotic sexuality can be fully deployed, and so that in reality sexuality becomes a singular, transgressive work, much like a dream? The alternative which presents itself seems to me to investigate the possible *imagin-ation* of the female sex, linked to an excessive attachment to form, and in this way to articulate harmoniously the relationship of gender and sexuality (*sex/gender*[7]).

In an article entitled 'The Discourse of Others: Feminists and Post-modernism' which exemplifies the questions surrounding the conditions of the representation of women in postmodern culture, Craig Owen makes the following observation: '[Still, if one of the most salient aspects of our postmodern culture is the presence of an insistent female voice . . . theories of postmodernism have tended either to neglect or to repress that voice.] The absence of discussions of sexual difference in writings about postmodernism, as well as the fact that few women have engaged in the modernism/postmodernism debate, suggest that postmodernism may be another masculine invention engineered to exclude women. I would like to propose, however, that women's insistence on difference and incommensurability may not only be compatible with, but also an instance of postmodern thought.'[8] This is precisely where work such as that of the American artist Cindy Sherman is relevant. Hers is strange work: embraced by the supporters of both feminism and postmodernism, it never fails to arouse surprise, embarrassment, and fascination through its forceful stigmatization of the isolation and tension underlying a representation which from the first is presented fundamentally as a copy, and most importantly, a copy without an original.[9] It is a representation which displays the female body conforming to the stereotypes prevalent in the cinema of the 1950s[10] and photographed using techniques which conform to cultural norms.[11] This female body then evolves, still through the same photographic techniques, into more and more monstrous figures: figures of beaten, hunted and prostrate women,[12] which soon begin to dissolve, literally, into a shapeless magma composed of the most horrible discharges. It is as though one were witnessing the progressive and inevitable decomposition of the human body, in this case the feminine body. Sherman's work leads us through a strange museum, from the protean young woman of the *Untitled Film Stills* to that hybrid, 'interregnum', being with the pig snout, lying limp in the mud,[13] of *Fairy Tales* and *Disasters*, to those other ridiculous, monstrous, and even terrifying creatures, all of which display the strange characteristics of a body which divides itself up, of a nightmarish corporal topography, enormous heads with grimacing faces,[14] with snouts instead of belly buttons and perhaps instead of genitals, and immense breasts.[15] And then the body disappears completely, and an apocalyptic vision reveals the filthy magma which constitutes this photography of extraordinary luminosity.[16] We are at once attracted and repulsed by the formal treatment of the archetypal shapelessness: spit, excrement, vomit, bodily secretions of every type, bloody viscera and organs are all mixed with the vermin which remain the object of a gaze, at the heart of the image: the remnant of a face contemplating the sad chaos, glasses still reflecting a horrified gaze, a luminous television screen,[17] or the pupil of an eye staring with a rare intensity. Thus, always, the image hesitates between maintaining itself in an endless vacillation and breaking itself down, continuing however to *show*, by affirming the primacy of the gaze over form, the primacy of the archetypal shapelessness, of the very material of the image of the dream, as Lacan describes it in relation to the mouth-chest-sex of Irma which also appears in the dream as the defigured image of the unrepresentable: 'a horrible discovery, the flesh that one never sees, the heart of things, the face inside out, the archetypal secrets, the flesh from which everything issues, the very kernel of the mystery, the flesh as it suffers, as it is shapeless, as its shape itself provokes agony'.[18]

The nightmare then adopts a new form in Sherman's work. In *Sex Pictures*, the living disappear to make way for strangely jointed mannequins, automatons displaying their sex in the crudest way,[19] organs which exist in their own right, almost detached from the actual body, often reduced to gaping orifices, sometimes oozing blood, harnessed, caught in pornographic poses. The grotesque and the tragic combine in a purely mechanical way, an assemblage of parts revealing

163

the inanity of the sex decontextualized in this way as well as the absolute autonomy of the sex, its power of imagination (of putting into images), which is expressed very clearly by Sherman: 'The shock (or terror) should come from what the sexual elements actually represent—death, power, aggression, beauty, sadness, etc. It's too easy to make an amusing or shocking image based solely on the appearance or the revelation of sexual organs (particularly those organs). What is difficult is to create images which are simultaneously poignant and explicit.'[20] The journey ends with the *Horror Pictures*, one of Sherman's most recent series: a monstrous family composed of fractured and tortured automatons, endowed with unbelievably piercing eyes or with a morbid mask which is beginning to fall apart, revealing the wounds of another face which is just as impalpable but which is still staring,[21] from the eyes of which we are almost unaware, so strongly does their gaze grasp us.[22]

'Cindy Sherman's work is inversely related to critical discourse because she understands that photography used to be the Other of Art, the desire of Art in our time. Thus her photography does not constitute an object of art criticism, but rather an instance of criticism. Thanks to photography, she is able to build a metalanguage which makes it possible to operate on a mythogrammatic level of art, simultaneously exploring the myth of creativity and the artistic vision as well as the innocence, the primacy and the autonomy of the "support" of the aesthetic image.'[23] This conception reveals very clearly the paradox of such uncompromising work—that it becomes the support of commentaries based exclusively on its most elementary material—that is, the image, and in this case, the image of woman and of the female body, and also that it constantly creates a tension, a distortion, so that the photographic form can never be a representation of an 'original' fact, neither, *a fortiori*, an illustration of pre-existing, perhaps militant, theories. The fact that Sherman's art—*a demystifer of myth, a de-myth-ifier*, according to Rosalind Krauss—is repetitively and abusively consumed as a myth, especially by Laura Mulvey, a feminist theorist who has worked on the masculine gaze ('Theory of the Male Gaze'[24]), is evidence of this major misunderstanding, this contradiction against which Krauss argues so forcefully. Krauss's attack is that Mulvey, who in her article dedicated to Sherman[25] remains convinced of the thesis that she developed in her inaugural article 'Visual Pleasure and Narrative Cinema',[26] constantly forgets to liberate herself from the immediately obvious ('to look under the hood', writes Krauss), and as a result never reaches the signifier itself. According to Krauss, Mulvey is ultimately only interested in the supposed message conveyed by the artist, that which would free itself from the mythical representation of the female body established by the phallocratic order, from the representation of woman reduced to nothing but image and masquerade in order to satisfy the desiring male gaze, deconstructing in this way the mechanisms of voyeurism/fetishism on which Hollywood cinema of the post-war era functioned. Thus, Mulvey analyses the *Untitled Film Stills* according to the male gaze, which in order to protect itself from the traumatic vision of woman—the very incarnation of sexual difference through the visible lack of penis—must turn to the characteristic mechanisms of voyeurism and fetishism to relieve the anguish of castration which the female body necessarily evokes.[27] Thus, through the threat that she signifies, woman—archetypal image—becomes at the same time the eroticized fetish sought by the male spectator. We can see, then, how Mulvey, loyal to the theory she had developed fifteen years earlier, reads in Sherman's work the deliberate will to stigmatize a representation which is subject to the tricks of a system of power in which women, the objects of male gaze and desire, have been dispossessed of their being, in some way stripped of their subjectivity. And Rosalind Krauss's virulent criticism is that the totality of metaphors to which Mulvey refers is inscribed in the field of 'verticalization'[28]—the verticality of the fetish, of the veil and of the phallus. Mulvey never ceases to adhere to this system of metaphors, continuing to interpret the content of the work according to a recurring and intangible form, so that Sherman's series *Horizontals* risks remaining invisible. According to Krauss this series initiates the movement of de-sublimation, deformation, and progressive dissemination of all the boundaries of the image, which Mulvey, in her 'fetishization of the fetish', seems incapable of recognizing, and which Krauss highlights, referring to psychoanalysis and Lacan in order to privilege, far beyond the image as such, that which Sherman makes apparent with such subtlety: that which cannot be imaged, that which has no shape. Thus, to the fetish charged with sealing the horror of castration Krauss prefers the lack, or the Lacanian object, which, in the realm of the visible is in fact the gaze,[29] so that, referring to the idea of the schism between the eye and the gaze developed by Lacan, she defines Sherman's work as the privileged site of a desire 'modelled in terms of a transgression against form. It is the force invested in de-sublimation.'[30] Through the dispersion of light, the effects of shining and light, of sparkling and radiance, of half-light and opacity, we reach, then, the 'formless pulsation of desire',[31] shapelessness itself.

Thus, the polemic surrounding the work of Cindy Sherman reveals various exemplary aspects of the thought inspired by the difficult question of 'the difference between the sexes between women'. For example, the possibility of a representation of the body of woman and of her sex, far from illuminating the nature of the feminine by indicating the path to a potential imaging of the female body, seems instead to display once again the fantasies of the opposite sex. While the theory of the male gaze claims to evade the systems of power responsible for the oppression of women, Laura Mulvey actually seems to develop, in her explicit reference to Freud, a theory of sexual controversy founded upon men's terror of castration. At the same time, her attachment to the visible, to form, to the fetish, to the phallus strangely assimilated to the penis, seems above all to indicate that her theory remains first and foremost a *sexual* theory, the way in which *a* woman claims to unveil *the* fantasy that men have of women. In this sense, Mulvey establishes as a theory something that can only be a prejudice, and, moreover, a phallic prejudice, repeating the idea that woman only exists to the extent that she is a fundamental incarnation of the wound, the gaping of the so-called 'invisible' sex, as opposed to the 'phallomorphic one'. From this point, Mulvey is a victim of her attachment to the sex organ, which I certainly do not consider to be 'that *form* of deformations recognized by the dream',[32] and her interpretation never reaches the dimension of a sexuality which, far from being suppressed, is in some way visualized *a contrario*, through the shapeless.[33] On the other hand, the sexuality to which Krauss implicitly refers, emancipated from the servile reference to form as an alienating force, would actually succeed in *imag*ining form, *deform*ing and transgressing it, thus allowing the dream images to flow and at the same time attesting to the fundamental indecision of the unconscious regarding sexual difference as well as to the free deployment of the partial drives which the unconscious permits, and which are sometimes assimilated to the feminine.

'In the psyche, there is nothing by which the subject may situate himself as a male or female being',[34] declares Lacan. Such would be this shapelessness (or the feminine as Freud dares to imagine it, when he speaks so cautiously of the 'dark continent'): the place where drives reign, a place of chaos, of lack and of the continual movement established by the dynamic of desire. To affirm, then, that transsexuals, because they so ardently deny the established link between anatomy and psychic inscription on the one hand and sexuation on the other, are closer to the logic of the unconscious, to the primary processes, to the formless, could be surprising and even shocking. In fact, more than anyone else, these patients, whether they claim to be women despite having a male anatomy (masculine transsexuals) or to be men in spite of their female bodies (feminine transsexuals), are certain of the real nature of sexual difference, since they inscribe it in their flesh through surgery. Transsexualism, either masculine or feminine, plunges us into the very heart of the question of the representation of woman and her sex. Through the distinction established by the suffering between identity and sexuality, through the denial of auto-erotic sexuality which its manifest discourse leads us to suppose, the sex organ becomes the centre of attention, and seeing becomes being. One's gaze occasionally wavers in front of these 'perfectly' feminine women as one listens to them, as they give off a signal which short-circuits the listener in an almost traumatic way, violently reminding us that this body remains that of a man, that the woman in question has a penis and testicles, and even, rarely, that her children call her 'dad'. Similarly troubling are those men who are clearly only at the beginning of the hormonal and surgical process, those men whose appearance is so masculine that it is very difficult to imagine them one day transformed, their demeanour and their way of talking and moving being so dissimilar to those of a woman. At this point arrives the complaint, the breaking into the psyche of the other: the useless ovaries must be removed, the womb must magically become the penis and testicles necessary for the ensemble to be complete. It is troubling to confront the 'heterosexual' couple in which the woman confirms the masculinity of her partner. No doubt the virility of this man with whom she has been living for so long has been proved, this man whom she would like one day to be the father of her children, who 'likes DIY, repairs things around the house, sure, he's a bit macho, but isn't that what a woman wants in a man?', she explains, irritated by the idea that people might think she is homosexual; she has only ever been attracted to men, and wouldn't it be pure madness to claim that her 'man' is a woman? Wouldn't you have to be completely *blind*? Certainly his sex is feminine in appearance, but in reality could there be a more virile partner than he?... We can see that it is here a question of the 'difference between the sexes between women', of the fundamental hesitation between a representation of woman (and of man) that becomes too attached to the sex organ and another vision based, on the contrary, upon the *transgressive nature* of anatomy, the auto-erotic capacity of the organ as such. In fact, what transsexuals affirm and even claim—all the while aspiring to the contrary—is that femininity is in no way dependent upon the physiology of the woman, that virility is absolutely not subject to the possession of male genitalia, and finally that sexual pleasure transcends the materiality of the sexes. And it is in this sense that they illuminate so clearly the logic of the unconscious. Inversely, what should also arrest our attention here is the strange fate that awaits the sex organ, a fate based in some way upon the distinction between *sex* and *gender* suggested by the English language and which Stoller, creating his own theory of transsexualism, sacrilized. His 'theorization reflection',[35] which mimetically reproduces the distinction established *de facto* by the transsexual patient between biological sex and psychic gender, consecrates a division which, in reality, denies the very notion of sexuality, obviously understood in the sense of *psycho*sexuality. Therefore we consider the problems of identity experienced by transsexual patients to be born of the inadequacy of gender and sex and, as soon as we can be sure of the primary transsexualism of the patient, we set off on a path of suppressing/transforming biological sex, which is in this case a scapegoat. In sum, the defence consists of becoming 'attached' in a paradoxical way to the 'de-libidinalized' organ all the better to sacrifice it, so that sexuality is finally suppressed. In effect, that which, through the magic of translation, becomes named 'gender identity'[36] is really the disguised form of a sexual identity (based on the distinction of the sex organs) stripped of everything which linked it to the sex drive. This translation which encourages an 'ideological' overturn—the privilege accorded to what is from then on the pathology of a narcissism radically opposed to that sexuality which, never understood in its unconscious meaning, tends to become confused with the capacities of sexual reproduction—authorizes the recurring assertions of the difficulties in explaining the psyche of the transsexual, of his or her unshakeable belief of belonging to the opposite sex in the face of which any psychotherapeutic effort is bound to fail miserably. It has already been said, the excessive attachment to shape is such that it aggravates the flesh and harms the psychic 'revolt', rendering extremely banal one of the most extraordinary pathologies, consenting hypocritically to subject the organ itself to public condemnation so as not to risk *seeing* the shapeless, although we are constantly threatened with this by the disturbing strangeness of (counter-) transference.[37]

'In the scopic relation, the object on which depends the fantasy from which the subject is suspended in an essential vacillation is the gaze. . . . From the moment that this gaze appears, the subject tries to adapt himself to it, he becomes that punctiform object, that point of vanishing being with which the subject confuses his own failure.'[38] I have already mentioned the visual trouble sometimes experienced when one meets a transsexual patient, as though the strangeness of a body which is belied by its speech suddenly surfaces, as though the being who is talking to us, and whose words resonate in us independently from the materiality of what we see—the body of the other—suddenly becomes the awful, monstrous figure of the Gorgon, commanding our gaze and then blinding us. Thus, confronted with the patient who we know has recently undergone the surgery to remove breasts, womb, and ovaries, we 'naturally' perceive and listen to him as a man—until, that is, he claims in one sudden gesture to reveal himself, to reveal the sex which is no longer one, which is not one, the sex which is now hybrid, shapeless. This is the nature of the disturbing strangeness which sometimes occurs in the relationship with the transsexual patient, this excessive, frightening putting-into-pictures, the fear experienced at the sight of that which, suddenly, for the stunned listener, can no longer be either a man or a woman, the horror of blindness permitting us no longer to see, or to think, or to name, the radical uncertainty, in sum, regarding the order of the living, of sexual difference, of the capacity of the gaze to make sense of the reality with which it is confronted.[39] 'The world is all-seeing, but it is not exhibitionistic—it does not provoke our gaze. When it begins to provoke it, the feeling of strangeness begins too. What does this mean, if not that, in the so-called waking state, there is an elision of the gaze, and an elision of the fact that not only does it look, *it* also *shows*. In the field of the dream, on the other hand, what characterizes the images is that *it shows*.'[40] In fact, by giving him or herself to the other fundamentally as image—an extremely dense image, moreover—the transsexual would literally represent the image of the dream, somehow throwing the unconscious out of the closed space of the psyche the better to incarnate it, to *show* it. Thus, to offer the other the possibility of imaging the sex, of animating this hybrid incarnation of unbridled shape, would be to have the archetypal shapelessness, that flesh which comes closest to the deformation at work in the dream, Irma's suffering flesh, that the transsexual could let us see, provoking the specular anguish which initiates the feeling of strangeness so similar to that experienced in the nightmare, the 'spectral decomposition of the function of the ego'[41] which knows that sexuality is the 'sexuality of the fantasy', the power of imagination and emancipation, the fundamental transgression of shape, of difference, of the organ.

'Transsexualism . . . raises many of the most complex questions feminism is asking about the origins and manifestations of sexism and sex-role stereotyping ... Transsexually constructed lesbian-feminists show yet another face of patriarchy. As the male-to-constructed-female transsexual exhibits the attempt to possess women in a bodily sense while acting out the images into which men have moulded women, the male-to-constructed-female who claims to be a lesbian-feminist attempts to possess women at a deeper level, this time under the guise of challenging rather than conforming to the role and behaviour of stereotyped femininity.'[42] Janice Raymond introduces us here to the sex wars that raged in the United States in the 1980s.[43] Raymond is a feminist denouncing the duplicity of a patriarchal culture illustrated by 'lesbian' transsexuals—men who, according to her, far from having given up their masculine prerogatives, have taken over the appearance of women the better to 'penetrate' them, to 'rape'[44] them even, through cunning, by pretending to adhere very intimately to the most authentic expression of being a woman—lesbian feminism. Raymond thus emphasizes a certain representation of 'the difference between the sexes between women' conceived immediately as sexual controversy between the two sexes (already seen in Laura Mulvey's perspective on Cindy Sherman's work), since femininity must necessarily be the prerogative of women, because women share, in a society based upon phallocratic ideals, values belonging to a culture whose coherence is based upon the possession and the division of one sex, upon an essence at the extremes of the foundation of the masculine sphere from which they want to be saved at all costs. It is also, then, a question of the difficult relationship between gender and sexuality[45]—which, as we have seen, is both inherent to the very notion of transsexualism, and has been to a large extent shaped by it: for 'cultural feminism', as termed by Alice Echols,[46] in reaction to the tendency of a radical feminism no longer determined to overturn gender relationships in order to end the oppression of women, but rather ready to confirm them—gender shares an essence common to women, a nature endowed with all manner of qualities, to which the ignoble, violent, bestial qualities of men evident in the (hetero)sexual act are obviously opposed. In this perspective, the sex/gender division is reinforced: gender is in absolute contradiction to sexuality, the archetypal place of oppression, at the same time leaning on a sex which, for women, loses to a large extent its libidinal or erotic value, but on the other hand guarantees consensual identity. In effect, if lesbianism is the other face of feminism,[47] if it is a matter of thereby affirming a political choice revealed by the notion of 'lesbian continuum' described by Adrienne Rich, this notion permitting a whole series of experiences specific to the woman who identifies herself as such (woman identified woman[48]) to be qualified, independently of any homosexual practice.[49] Evidently, this insistence on community and sharing tends above all to reduce differences between women, differences which stem from the very existence of a 'tamed' sexuality, when it is redefined in the terms of a truly feminine eroticism—'the erotic in female terms', writes Rich[50]—diffuse, tender, centred on the whole body, in opposition to a masculine sexuality obsessed with the genitals.[51] Thus cultural feminism aspires to the elimination of difference between women, it wants sex and gender to be a harmonized pair, and sexuality to be condemned outright as long as it authorizes the deployment of the power relationships inherent to heterosexuality—the expression of masculine supremacy—and monstrously aped, according to cultural feminism, by certain sexual practices defended by the 'pro-sex' contingent of radical feminism. These radical feminists are against the levelling of differences between women. More attentive to the possibilities of emancipation presented by sexuality than to the oppressive dimension of sexuality, they refuse the withdrawal of identity in order to reaffirm their desire to explore all forms of sexuality, with their respective components of 'pleasure and danger'. As a result, they are led to plead in favour of practices necessarily held in contempt by cultural feminism and by other feminists, who, because of their attachment to the idea of the social construction of gender relationships, see themselves as equally radical, but fight against those sexual practices accused of reproducing sexually masculine domination.[52] Hence, according to them, the division of roles at the heart of the female couple (butch/fem relationships) and the sado-masochist lesbian share the same sexist and degrading ideology as pornography, against which they battle.[53]

In sum, whilst sexuality was proscribed by cultural feminism, under the cover of a frigid lesbianism emptied of eroticism, whose purpose was to provide an identity, it returns in force, in spite of being shouted down, through those sexual practices aimed at reintroducing difference; for, what the pro-sex feminists seek is the ability to explore their desire in all its forms, and especially those forms which are linked to regimes of power: in this optic, lesbian sado-masochism[54] as well as butch/fem relationships, because they effectively allow liberation from sexual stereotypes by simulating and parodying them, because they are based precisely upon the subversion of these sexual roles and identities, because, finally, they consist of the acting out of certain strategies of desire. They not only constitute the place of experimentation of the polymorphous nature of desire, but also illustrate the transgressive component of sexuality, its liberating potential—that which, if not queer theory, at least Judith Butler truly systematizes by questioning the very notion of identity, insofar as that identity, far from sharing a supposed 'naturalness', is riddled with the same mechanisms of power. If, following the example of what is revealed by the phenomenon of drag, identity is parodic imitation,[55] an ostentatious performance; if the process of becoming a subject is reduced to identifications which are to say the least fragile; if the categories of sex and gender are no longer valid; if, finally, the notions of masculine and feminine, of man and woman, need no longer be covered with tangible reality since their artificiality and their performative character have been demonstrated, it must be admitted that it is now a question of the shapeless as described above, of the logic of the unconscious and of dream images! It is as though the anti-identity politics had to come back—even if it was not their aim—to a definition according to which only the visual nature of the fantasy—since it eludes the mechanism of power—has any value, independent of the sex and its visibility.[56] In effect, once the mechanisms of subjection through which gender relationships as sexual conduits are constructed are exposed and denounced, it is the responsibility of individuals to produce individuality! Certainly there is emancipation from pre-existing social categories and a fundamental transgression of the roles assigned to men and women; the dialectic of the unconscious remains, however ...

Finally, by following the example of what transsexualism *shows* us, and according to a logic which undoubtedly borrows from the pleasure principle, the social scene, both denouncing and mocking the coercive character of sexual difference—between women, between men—allows the profoundly *trans*-sexual nature of sexuality to take effect.

Notes

1. See introduction above.
2. In this case one can refer to the writings of F. Jameson and particularly his article entitled 'Postmodernism and Consumer Society' (1982), in H. Foster (ed.), *The Anti-Aesthetic: Essays on Postmodern Culture* (Seattle: Bay Press, 1983), 111–25, in which he analyses two exemplary figures of postmodernism—pastiche and schizophrenia—at the same time that he underlines the importance of the image in its capacity to fix time in a series of presents destined to last forever.

3. Cf. J. Kristeva, *New Maladies of the Soul* (New York: Columbia University Press, 1997), especially the chapter 'The soul and the image'.
4. Translator's note: The italicized terms are all anglicized in the French text.
5. I refer here to R. Krauss's critical article 'Dans cette histoire de point de vue, pouvons-nous compter plus loin que "un"?', in *Feminin/Masculin: Le sexe de l'art* (Paris: Éditions du Centre Georges Pompidou, Gallimard/Electra, 1995), 312–21.
6. Cf. L. Irigaray, *This Sex which is not One* (Ithaca, NY: Cornell University Press, 1985).
7. Translator's note: The italicized terms are anglicized in the French text.
8. C. Owens, 'The Discourse of Others: Feminism and Postmodernism', in H. Forster (ed.) (1983), *The Anti-Aesthetic: Essays on Postmodern Culture* (Seattle: Bay Press, 1983), 61–2.
9. 'The condition of Sherman's work in the Film-Stills—and part of their point, we could say—is the simulacral nature of what they contain, the condition of being a copy without an original' (R. Krauss, *Cindy Sherman: 1975–1993 (with an essay by N. Bryson)* (NY: Rizzoli, 1993), 17).
10. *Untitled Film Stills* (1977–1980), plates 1 to 69, *Cindy Sherman: Retrospective* (Paris: Éditions Thames & Hudson, 1998), 56–95.
11. 'Her images, concatenations of stereotypes, reproduce objects which are already reproductions, that is, stereotyped characters from Hollywood scenes, television melodrama, sentimental novels, and magazine advertising. Furthermore, just as this imitaiton of trashy, two-dimensional characters constitutes the subject of her images, the way in which Cindy Sherman treats them is also determined in advance and controlled by the cultural condition. We constantly find ourselves confronted with formal solutions which are the product of standardised recipes' writes R. Krauss in 'Note sur la photographie et le simulacre' (1983) in R. Krauss; *Le Photographique: Pour une théorie des écarts* (Paris: Editions Macula, 1990), 215–16. Translations are by the translator of this chapter unless otherwise specified.
12. Cf. e.g. *Untitled no. 92* and *Untitled no. 93* (1981), plates 75 and 76, *Cindy Sherman: Retrospective*, 104–5.
13. *Untitled no. 40* (1985), plate 96, ibid. 70.
14. Cf. e.g. *Untitled no. 160* (1986), plate 104, ibid. 138.
15. *Untitled no. 186* and *Untitled no. 187* (1989), plates 111 and 112, ibid. 146–7.
16. *Untitled no. 190* (1989), plate 114, ibid. 149.
17. *Untitled no. 168* and *Untitled no. 175* (1987), plates 106 and 107, ibid. 140–1.
18. J. Lacan, (1978). *Le moi dans la théorie de Freud et dans la technique de la psychanalyse—Le Séminaire, Boch II (1954–1955)* (Paris: Éditions de Seuil, 1978), 186.
19. Cf. e.g. *Untitled no. 263* (1992), plate 130, *Cindy Sherman: Retrospective*, p. 169.
20. 'Sex Pix' (2/2/92), ibid. 202.
21. *Untitled no. 316* (1995), plate 147, ibid. 190.
22. *Untitled* no. 323, *Untitled* no. 324, *Untitled* no. 325 (1995), plates 149, 150, 151, ibid. 192–4.
23. Krauss, *Le Photographique*, 221–2.
24. Translator's note: the English phrase is given in the French text.
25. L. Mulvey, (1991). 'A Phantasmagoria of the Female Body: The Work of Cindy Sherman', *New Left Review*, 188 (July–Aug 1991), 137–50.

26. L. Mulvey, (1975). 'Visual Pleasure and Narrative Cinema' (1975), in *The Sexual Subject: A Screen Reader in Sexuality* (New York: Routledge, 1992), 22–34.

27. 'The image of woman as (passive) raw material for the (active) gaze of man takes the argument a step further into the structure of representation. . . . The argument returns again to the psychoanalytic background in that woman as representation signifies castration, inducing voyeuristic or fetishistic mechanisms to circumvent her threat' (Mulvey, 'Visual Pleasure', 32).

28. Krauss, *Le Photographique*, 93.

29. Cf. J. Lacan, *The Four Fundamental Concepts of Psychoanalysis, The Seminar,* Book XI. (London: Penguin, 1994), 67.

30. R. Krauss, *Le Photographique*, 109.

31. Ibid. 111.

32. P. Fedida, 'Par où commence le corps humain?', in *Les organes. Le fait de l'analyse*, 5 (1998), 287.

33. 'The shapelessness (*mot bataillien*) of the flesh is the form which causes anguish. Better still: anguish has the form of the shapelessness of the organ made of flesh' (ibid. 281).

34. J. Lacan, (1994). *The Four Fundamental Concepts of Psychoanalysis. The Seminar*, Book IV (London: Penguin, 1994), 205.

35. Cf. A. Oppenheimer, 'Le désir d'un changement de sexe: un défi pour la psychanalyse?', in *Psychanalyse à l'Université*, 17/66 (1992), 117–34.

36. 'The concept of gender identity is simply an operating term to designate a certain type of human dilemma relating to the self', notes Stoller, in the preface to the French edition of his book *Sex and Gender*. He confirms here, through the reference to the self, the narcissistic foundation of the notion of gender identity. In R. J. Stoller, *Recherches sur l'identité sexuelle à partir du transsexualisme* (Paris: Gallimard, 1978), 17.

37. Is it necessary to recall Lacan's assertion that 'transference is what manifests in experience the enacting of the reality of the unconscious, in so far as that reality is sexuality'? (J. Lacan, *The Four Fundamental Concepts of Psychoanalysis. The Seminar*, Book IV (London: Penguin, 1994), 174.).

38. Ibid. 83.

39. 'In the disturbing strangeness, it does not escape Freud that the anguish of castration acquires its readability in some way from the feeling of strangeness. This readability is readability of the hermetic and therefore enigmatic power of signification of what ought to have remained *hidden*', writes P. Fédida about the 'anguish of the eyes', or the operation of substitution between the sex organ and the visual organ as a place of anguish, in P. Fédida, 'L'angoisse aux yeux', *Cliniques méditerranéenes*, 51/52 (1996), 93.

40. Lacan, *The Four Fundamental Concepts of Psychoanalysis. The Seminar*, Book IV, 75. [Translator's note]: The importance of 'it' ('ça') in Lacan is great, being roughly equivalent to the Freudian 'id' in the id/ego/superego triangle.

41. Lacan, *Le moi dans la théorie de Freud et dans la technique de la psychanalyse— Le Séminaire*, Book II, 197.

42. J. G. Raymond, *The Transsexual Empire* (London: The Women's Press, 1980), 99.

43. Cf. C. S. Vance, 'More danger, more pleasure: a decade after the Barnard Sexuality Conference', in C. S. Vance (ed.), *Pleasure and Danger—Exploring Female Sexuality* (London: Pandora Press, 1992).

44. 'Because transsexuals have lost their physical "members" does not mean that they have lost their ability to penetrate women—women's mind, women's space, women's sexuality', alleges Janice Raymond. A few lines earlier, she had claimed: 'All transsexuals rape women's bodies by reducing the real female to form to an artefact, appropriating this body for themselves. However, the transsexually constructed lesbian-feminist violates women's sexuality and spirit as well.' (Raymond, *The Transsexual Empire*, 104).

45. Cf. the work of E. Fassain, especially, 'Dans les genres différents: le féminisme au miroir transatlantique', *Esprit*, 196 (Nov. 1993), 99–112, and 'Politique de la critique historique: histories de genre et de sexualité', in 'Pratiques politiques et usages de Michel Foucault', Conference organized by CERI, 13/14 Nov. 1997.

46. 'I believe that what we have come to identify as radical feminism represents such a fundamental departure from its radical feminist roots that it requires renaming. To this end, I will refer to this more recent strain of feminism as cultural feminism, because it equates women's liberation with the nurturance of a female counter culture which it is hoped will supersede the dominant culture' (A. Echoles, 'The Taming of the ID: Feminist Sexual Politics, 1968–83', in C.S. Vance, *Pleasure and Danger*, 51).

47. Cf. the formula of Ti-Grace Atkinson: 'Feminism is the theory, lesbianism the practice', quoted by A. Echols, *Daring to be Bad—Radical Feminism in America 1967–1975* (foreword by E. Willis) (1989) (Minneapolis: University of Minnesota Press, 1997), 238.

48. Translator's note: The English phrase is given in the French text.

49. 'I mean the term lesbian continuum to include a range—through each woman's life and throughout history—of woman-identified experience, not simply the fact that a woman has had or consciously desired genital sexual experience with another woman' (A. Rich, 'Compulsory Heterosexuality and Lesbian Existence' (1980), in H. Abelove, M. A. Barale, D. Halperin (eds.), *The Lesbian and Gay Studies Reader* (New York: Routledge, 1993), 239.

50. Ibid. 240.

51. In order to understand this type of separatism from the masculine sphere, it is necessary to go back further into the history of radical feminism, to the moment at which the difference between women, unacceptable for some, emerges, represented at that time by the *Radicalesbians* whose lesbianism was a political rather than a sexual choice: 'However, in its reincarnation as cultural feminism, lesbian separatism has been modified and refined in such a way as to make it more acceptable to a wider audience. Whereas lesbian separatists advocated separation from men, cultural feminists advocate separation from male values. And rather than promote lesbianism, cultural feminists encourage woman-bonding and thus avoid estranging heterosexual feminists' (explains A. Echols, in 'The Taming of the ID: Feminist Sexual Politics, 1968–83', 56). Equally, we can turn to the analysis suggested by M. Feher in 'Érotisme et féminisme aux États-Unis: les exercices de la liberté', *Esprit*, 196 (Nov. 1993), 113–31.

52. Cf. A. Echols, *Daring to be Bad—Radical Feminism in America 1967–1975*, n. 13, p. 362: A. Echols emphasizes here how difficult it is to distinguish the constructionism of certain 'anti-pornography' feminists from openly essentialist positions, relationships of gender and masculine domination

being seemingly immutable in both. The polemical and transitory character of the denominations which often change according to whether one belongs to a certain camp, like so many hastily borrowed theoretical short cuts, should also be emphasized.

53. Cf. C. S. Vance, *Pleasure and Danger*, pp. xxiii–xxiv. The reader can also refer to *Caught Looking—Feminism, Pornography and Censorship* (1986) (East Haven Conn. LongRiver Books, 1995).

54. Cf. especially G. Rubin, 'The Leather Menace: Comments on Politics and S/M', in Samois (ed.), *Coming to Power: Writings and Graphics on Lesbian S/M* (1981) (Boston, Alyson Publications, 1987), 194–229 and P. Califia, 'A Personal View of the History of the Lesbian S/M Community and Movement in San Fransisco', ibid. 245–83.

55. 'I would suggest as well that drag fully subverts the distinction between inner and outer psychic space and effectively mocks both the expressive model of gender and the notion of a true gender identity', J. Butler, *Gender Trouble—Feminism and the Subversion of Identity* (New York: Routledge, 1990), 137.

56. 'Part of what constitutes sexuality is precisely that which does not appear and that which, to some degree, can never appear. This is perhaps the most fundamental reason why sexuality is to some degree always closeted, especially to the one who would express it through acts of self-disclosure,' writes J. Butler in 'Imitation and Gender Insubordination' (1989), in Abelove et al. (eds.), *Lesbian and Gay Studies Reader*, 315. A few pages later, she adds: 'The unconscious is this excess that enables and contests every performance, and which never fully appears within the performance itself' (ibid. 317).

10   The Prescribed Sex

Sabine Prokhoris*

Sabine Prokhoris trained at the École Normale Supérieure. Currently she is a professor of philosophy, and a practising psychoanalyst in Paris. She is also an editor
of the journal *Les Temps modernes*. She is particularly engaged in the public
debate surrounding the 'Civil Pact of Solidarity' (PACS) working actively
with the Association of Gay and Lesbian Parents and Future Parents. Prokhoris
remarks that her most recent *Le Sexe prescrit: la différence sexuelle en question*
(2000; The Prescribed Sex: Sexual Difference in Question) was born out of a
combination of anger and sadness in the face of the role played by psychoanalysis
in the political debates around PACS generally, but especially with regard to the
regulations concerning the right of same-sex partners to adopt children. In this
contemporary French controversy, Prokhoris applies not only psychological but
especially Foucauldian analyses to current events to argue that far too many psychoanalysts have used their institutional power to intervene in the name of knowledge, science, and truth—all at the expense of real social justice. In these debates,
complex and contested psychoanalytic concepts, as well as the forefathers of
psychoanalysis such as Freud and Lacan, have been invoked only to justify a status
quo that continues to deny same-sex couples the basic right to adopt children. In
this context, Prokhoris reminds us that a primary vocation of psychoanalysis, from
its inception, was not only to analyse and theorize but also, if possible, to heal
psychic suffering (*mald'être*). Prokhoris argues that in order to heal, psychoanalysis must remain open to new theories and events, and renew itself. She
opposes turning psychoanalysis into something it was never supposed to be,
namely, the guardian of the symbolic order.

Analysing basic texts by Freud, Lacan, and Foucault but also drawing on the
history of science (Canguilhem, primarily) as well as modernist world literature
(e.g. Beckett, Colette, Conrad, Henry James, Melville, Musil, Nabokov), Prokhoris
reminds us that psychoanalysis must not have any normative or prescriptive

* 'La Différence des sexes: une formation de l'inconscient' and 'Common singulier', in *Le
Sexe prescrit: La différence sexuelle en question* (Paris: Aubier, 2000), 158–84 and 337–45.
Reprinted by permission of Aubier.

function, but rather an emancipatory one. Specifically Prokhoris criticizes the use made of the concept of sexual difference. In opposition to much current practice and theory, Prokhoris argues that it is a serious mistake to transform this concept into a cornerstone of humanity. In order to question the use and abuse of 'sexual difference' she unfolds anew the original Freudian theory of sexuality, albeit criticizing the normative tendencies already informing it.

Her book is divided into five main parts; the selection here is the two first sections of the third part, 'Le Voisinage des sexes' (the sexual neighbourhood, or sexual neighbouring). This selection begins by reminding us that 'sexual difference' is a formation of the unconscious, at least in significant measure. So is the sexual order itself, in so far as it is the result of the combination of the signifiers 'man', 'woman', and 'child' under the law of the signifier termed 'sexual difference' or, more precisely, 'the difference of the sexes'. In any case, the sexual order is not 'natural', as the term is commonly used, but *sensu stricto* unconscious. It is unconscious, however, not in the sense in which the unconscious would be 'sexed', but instead in the sense that the sexual order is constructed around a set of possibilities or references that itself has its roots in the unconscious. Our sexuation is determined, for the most part, by this complex matrix behind our backs, as it were. In any event, there is no psychic sexuality that would be the expression of an 'always already primary given' (as a—or the—natural sexual difference). Rather, the process of sexuation is that of submission to an aggregate of over-determinations expressed in, or by, the unconscious. For Prokhoris it is precisely this aggregate that needs to be put into question. Accordingly, Prokhoris asks: Is the relation between sex and gender to be determined univocally? If we agree to understand gender as the cultural phenomenon and a consequence of the binary designation, 'masculine' and 'feminine', and thus as an interpretation that bears on sex and sexuality, then the very *difference* between sex and gender cannot itself be considered the expression of a 'natural' sexuation, under the pretext, say, that there are, or happen to be, only two sexes in our particular biological species. Which is to say that we must also continue to interrogate the historicity of the difference between gender and sex—a historicity, however, which must be likewise understood (significantly, if not wholly) as an effect of the unconscious.

Prokhoris rewrites 'sexual difference' as *différencedessexes* in order to emphasize that this concept and practice has currently been turned into a fetish, and as such is above criticism and virtually impossible to circumvent. On Prokhoris's argument, the sexual order regulated by the law of 'sexual difference' determines not only our sexuation but also all basic binary pairs, such as same/other and identity/alterity. Which is to say that this purported law also determines all contrasting oppositions from which we must then 'choose'. It is precisely this stipulation that has defined both 'normality' and what is 'beyond-sex' (*hors-sexe*). Any disruption of such neat binaries is vilified, under the purported law of sexual difference, on the grounds that the human order or essence needs to be safeguarded. Prokhoris argues that the refusal to grant to same-sex couples a status equal to that of heterosexual ones is an example of precisely this entire problematic.

'SEXUALDIFFERENCE': A FORMATION OF THE UNCONSCIOUS

Let us take for granted that the sexual order is not in the slightest bit a natural order—even if it is easy to persuade oneself that it is and so to wash one's hands quietly of the damage it can cause. Rather, it is an unconscious order. Not in the sense that the unconscious is properly speaking sexuated, but in the sense that subjection to the sexual order, which is completely fabricated upon the choice of certain references which interpret the fact of sexuation, thrusts its roots deep into the unconscious. As elsewhere, and we should not forget this in what follows, we are dealing with the superego—that weighty structure of values which are recognized in ourselves nearly always without our knowledge. Admitting to these values makes us part of the human race. They are values not to be ignored: the individual who betrays them suffers the punishment of the pariah condemned to the hell of expulsion from the ordinary world. Conrad's strange heroes, cast onto oceans aboard improbable old rafts, always on the brink of shipwreck, or lost in the heart of the darkest jungles, explore to the limit the dehumanizing effect of this 'betrayal', in the sense that their victims, like Adam and Eve from Paradise, are expelled from the human world. The effect is abominable, devastating, definitively without redemption. Kurtz's last words in his madness in *Heart of Darkness* are: 'The horror'.

Lacan is quite explicit about the proximity that we have begun to perceive between the dimension of the sexual order, the so-called structure of desire, and the dimension of the superego: 'It is here that comes into play the ethical function of eroticism. Freudianism is in brief nothing but a perpetual allusion to the fecundity of eroticism in ethics.'[1] This is, then, an ethics of desire, and one could just as well cite here: 'The only thing one can be guilty of is giving ground relative to one's desire.'[2] Put in other terms, this is stating that the only serious culpability for which we could be condemned without forgiveness is to ignore what gives desire its truth and its value: that is, the subjection of desire to the sexual order. We come back to Kafka's penal colony, but here very precisely in relation to the matter of sex. Except that, as always, Lacan's statement is ambiguous: what might happen when the 'mysteries' of the sexual order are uncovered and as a result threatened with dissolution; when, to put it plainly, the image of its historicity appears, that is, in the last analysis, the mystery of how the sexual order seized power? For, in forging its way into the hidden field of the 'discourse of the other', does not the practice of analysis come to initiate those games which escape us and from which, however, we cannot escape? The only way to avoid this is to claim the right to question and so to transform the rules of the field of the 'discourse of the other', in which a way could be found to formulate an adequate definition of the work and the aims of the psychoanalytic cure, if the work carried out in the course of the cure is analysis, in the proper sense of dissolution, source of new configurations, of 'formations of the unconscious', to use the title of one of Lacan's seminars.[3]

The sexual order, the product of the combination of the signifiers 'man', 'woman', and 'child' under the law of the signifier 'sexualdifference' is *also* a formation of the unconscious. Everything Lacan wrote repeats this idea in a spirit of rivalry. It is not even the least of the formations of the unconscious, even though it claims to be an untouchable principle, an unshakeable foundation of our submissive destinies. On what grounds does this formation bestow its draconian law and its unique meaning upon human existence? It is necessary to try to illuminate this question. What is certain is that Lacan always refuses the most untruthful dimension of the pseudo-psychoanalytic brand of naturalism which is still quite widespread and which harps upon the 'absurd hymn of genital harmony'. This hymn also drones on about the virtues of several 'true' values of 'life', a life which is not 'artificial' for 'a humanity which has not lost its sense of the sacred, nor of sacrifice, nor of procreation'.[4] Thus we read that the future belongs to the 'mothers of families', no doubt promoted to the role of guardians of the political order and the natural order. If we are to believe Kristeva, a committed writer, regarding these matters, then psychoanalysis ought to be able to contribute to this debate, renewing in the process its relevance.

Coming back to the question of the sexes, Lacan makes the radical affirmation that 'men', 'women' and 'children' are *only* 'signifiers'. This affirmation, which is thoroughly psychoanalytic, and resolutely—and in a very Freudian way—refuses to make a concession to any discourse supporting a 'natural' complementariness between the sexes due, of course, to the famous 'sexualdifference', really gives us something to think about. If Freud, in *Three Essays on the Theory of Sexuality*, making a clean break with all naturalist theory, notes that 'from the point of view of psychoanalysis the exclusive sexual interest felt by men for women is also a problem that needs elucidating and is not a self-evident fact based upon an attraction that is ultimately of a chemical nature',[5] Lacan pushes to the furthest limit the Freudian position which established the representation of the determination of 'sexuality' through the games of the unconscious. All things considered, this leads us to posit that what constitutes 'sex', in the sense of belonging to one or the other of the two sexes where this belonging acts as both pedestal and origin of a destiny to be fulfilled, is merely an effect of the 'discourse of the other' which enjoins us to be *sexually* a man or a woman. Hence, within what is openly stated in the Lacanian statement, it is revealed, not unimaginatively, that sex is presumed to constitute a sort of primary given, and an object of the knowledge of psychoanalysis, psychoanalysis possessing a 'certain knowledge of psychic sexuality', as Kristeva puts it in the article mentioned a moment ago. This psychic sexuality expresses natural sexual difference, and the submission which bends sexuality to a set of determining factors articulated in the unconscious, and as such quite capable of being translated as questions—questions as answers which can be unmade as much, and with as much difficulty, as can be unmade the response which any symptom passes itself off as.

A situation such as this is more violent, and much more difficult to unravel than is suggested by the locations of the categories of 'gender', the contents of which can be described and dismantled without excessive danger, the question of sex, as threads play across it through the nets of the unconscious, remaining in the last analysis untouched. This act of location and deconstruction is useful in many respects, but does not allow the question of possible destinies to be emptied of the dimension of the *sexuated*—which touches upon the simple fact that two anatomical sexes exist—in its relation to the dimension of the *sexual*, where the images of the links which bind us with each other become an issue. These images pass through the body-souls capable of sexual pleasure and interpretation—that is, capable of translating certain signs emanating from an other into intense sensory experiences, and inversely, capable of translating fleeting, iridescent sensations into signs. They can do this so well that the bodies, whether they are exultant or suffering, exist as phrases addressed to someone, but incomplete, in suspense, and absolutely never as originary.

We will try to think these relations between the sexuated and the

181

sexual as being unable to be determined unequivocally, even if certain habitual configurations are so commonly anchored in us that they keep us blindly persuaded of their exclusive relevance. To sum up briefly, we could formulate all this in the following way: if what we call 'gender' in effect designates the totality of codes, signs, emblems, and cultural attributes which construct and identify that which is designated by the term 'masculine' or 'feminine', then the very division which allows 'gender' to be created for the sexes—that is, the version of the question of sexuation which interprets that question as the realization of the order of 'difference'—difference being simultaneously fundamental and a founding force—will not have to be considered as a 'natural' expression of sex, on the pretext that there are in effect two sexes in our species, nor as a simple folding of the images of 'gender'. It is in this area particularly that an analysis of the *historicity* of this division occurs, historicity being understood as the effect of the unconscious. In other words, it is the effect of the relations of power knitted by the signifying networks which cross us and which, all the more intransigent since most of the time we are unaware of their journey within us, prune us to fit the trellis of the sexual order. These are highly *material* effects; that is to say, just as they cling so powerfully to the concrete experience of each and every person they seem both to be founded in this experience and to found it, so that they constitute its very substance. In this way they constitute 'reality', under the tender name of the 'Real' in Lacanian language. This is a 'reality' from which we will have a hard time expelling offenders; a 'reality'—or a 'Real'— in the last analysis strangely in collusion with the symbolic order.

SEX AND THE SYMBOLIC

A strange collusion indeed. Thus the division which seals the 'difference' and establishes it will return to determining factors tightly bound to the most implacable decrees of the superego which will prescribe the absolute power of sexuality in terms of an order capable of transcending the contingence and the disturbed disorder of the body. The body is in effect traversed by a polyglot unconscious; for, while the sacred language of the 'sexual order'—a sort of church Latin which cannot be abolished—reigns, it does not necessarily always govern, especially if the insurrection of other dialects—although the ear of the analyst seldom unbends to them—overrides it, and reveals the strength of the force needed for its pre-eminence to remain uncontested. Lacan tells us about the perpetration of just such a show of force when, demystifying the force of the destiny contained in the words 'man' and 'woman', he says: here is what is in the last analysis the motive to act—it is *only* that, a very banal signifying articulation. Not that a signifying articulation, a vice-like grip of the unconscious, is a small thing; on the contrary, it is quite considerable. But at the same time, a signifying articulation is nothing more than the effect of a series of discursive events. We take this effect as something new. This is a mistake, and one which we let ourselves be taken in by. From there, the articulation seems to speak for itself, in a very naturally divided belief. It is the articulation, in a major key, of a dissimilarity in *difference*.

This difference might slip from our fingers if we held on to it at the point of dissimilarity; that is, in the moving, perpetually troubled register of resemblances which are not sufficient to be identical. It is a slippery difference, and, therefore, a difference to be fixed as securely as possible. Then it will be able to constitute a simple, unshakeable bedrock of the order of links, and such that it can also form any universe of thought. Remember the 'impassable buffer of thought' which constitutes the relationship between the sexes, represented essentially in the form of its reduction to this famous difference. However, as soon as the said difference appears, and the Lacanian statement, against all discourse of the supposed observation of anthropologico-natural constants, goes straight to it, not as an original pedestal and a primary or ultimate reference of all representation, here and there, beyond, next to, or outside of which no exercise of thought could be conceived, but as the pure effect of a collage of unconscious representations which link our lives, however powerful this collage undoubtedly is, its efficacy is suspended by the well-maintained permanence of its cogwheels. This permanence is never guaranteed in advance, for cogs often jam. And, across the failures of stories of love and desire, failures to which all of us are some day exposed, there are plenty of opportunities to notice that those cogs in particular are more likely to jam, and that we suffer as a result. The cogs can also fall apart, and not without consequences. Especially if a destructive demon whispers to us to try a different construction. We notice here that inventing, even by error—like the famous story of the *tarte Tatin*[6]—a new disposition is not necessarily or *a priori* bound to fail.

Lacan also emphasizes what Freudian psychoanalysis, as a theory of the unconscious, reveals, and he does this in direct line of descent from Freud and with merciless perception. That is, that our representations, without exception, *a fortiori* those which touch our most intense relations, are crammed with the unconscious, that is with opaque messages, picked up urgently and retranscribed straight into our lives, so that we go wherever they push us, like deep-set watermarks, like nets to cling on to so as not to fall into the void. The void, that is, of the absence of links.

In the course of its explorations, Freudian psychoanalysis also reveals that the knots between these links pass through the question of the erotic. That is to say that the strength of the knots is the result of the tropism, of the irrepressible tendency, thanks to which the links are inscribed in traces of affects, in sensual imprints, through which circulates in a very powerful way that which attracts us to each other. The question of sex and how it is treated are caught up in this, in an at least ambiguous fashion. For if the signifiers of sexuation—'man', 'woman'—which are presupposed to give sexuality its status as law are indeed dependent on the force of attraction which emanates from the knots in the unconscious, that is, from the schemata of links which orient an individual's existence, then the logic from which these schemata profess to be derived as well as the power that they exercise misuse in no small measure the order that they are in part devoted to creating. In other words, between the dimension of the *sexual*, from which derives the strength of the links, and the dimension of the schema of *sexuality*, which is a way of ordering this strength towards the division of the sexes—towards the 'sexualdifference' articulated in terms of the phallic—divergence becomes clear, which divergence relates to the treatment which the question of the *sexuated* will make its object.

The terms of this divergence could be stated in the following way: regarding the sexes in their relation to the unconscious, will we have to encounter the gaps between them as the 'sexualdifference', or in another form, which we might chose to call the 'sexual neighbourhood'? This is not a phrase which I have chosen randomly. I propose to try using it, and to see what results from the perspective it offers, for strictly psychoanalytic motives. In doing so, I am relying as much upon what the exercise of psychoanalysis as upon what certain dimensions of psychoanalytic theory can teach us.

This is in part and most importantly because, if we return to the movements and the reasons which, in the Freudian method of the cure, govern language across the space of the session and throughout the whole cure, we are truly dealing with a process which occurs and extends, step by step, according to a logic of neighbouring, which supposes that signifying fragments become linked and unlinked with each other in successive identifications, at the whim of resemblances which are made and unmade on the basis of differences. The efficacy of the method which emerges in this way will lead to the unravelling of the signifying knots which hold the surging of human existence under their yoke, especially through the hierarchies of values that they dictate. Thus changes will be able to occur which forget destiny. Destiny is how we refer to the inscription, in the history which seems to unfurl a life, of a frighteningly coherent translation of the sequences of signifiers which have seized hold of that life, a translation which comes to function in some way as the only authorized translation. So, not to stray too far from the question we are dealing with here, the question of sexuation and of the imprint it leaves on an existence in the form of necessary images signing a completion, feminine or masculine, so that one does not run the risk of being deceived by it, the Freudian statement which adopts Napolean's famous saying 'anatomy is destiny', says exactly the same thing as Lacan's statement designating men, women, and children as 'signifiers': destiny, to be understood not as something which would lead inescapably and without delay to a primary state of affairs, in this case to the anatomy which nature has given us, but to be understood in the sense of something which insists on occurring as a neurosis of fate. In other words, in the endlessly repeated adherence to the hold of the unconscious, which is maintained at its full strength, otherwise its power would diminish and be repressed.

The recollection that occurs on the occasion of the 'release from repression' is paradoxical: remembering that the signifying knots have a history, and even several histories which are crossed and tangled with each other, is, in the here and now of the dialogue with the analyst, to observe that they are crossroads at which the threads of various messages become entangled, interpreted through our passions, and that the unequivocal status finally accorded to these messages is therefore abusive. It is therefore revocable. Consequently, speaking under the regime of free association bathed in equally floating attention will be proof of the possibilities which rattle at the heart of signifying currents, the fortuitous contacts between them improvising new images, new values, different from the officially recognized ones. The officially recognized images and values are therefore not an original base which can be identified with certainty, the ultimate support and inescapable point of reference of a meaning that transforms a life into a destiny, for better or for worse. Thus the memory of the official images and values which has been crushed by silence will be restored, and this will allow the badges of their power to be lost. This will only be able to happen on condition that analysis *is not* a judgement, where the 'truth' of desire emerges and is established—'truth' itself being subject to the signifier 'sexualdifference'—that analysis is not, then, subjected to an exclusively either/or form of thought: the principle of identity and the principle of the excluded third.

So, to summarize, the schema of analysis is governed by the rules of, we might say, the effects of the neighbouring between signifiers. Here the dimension of the sexual, as a power which pushes us towards contact, excites, awakens, and travels, in waves of intensity, various zones of affinity, becomes mobilized, to put it simply for the moment. These zones of affinity are constituted fortuitously on the basis of what Freud calls the 'polymorphous perverse predisposition' of human sexuality, which is in no way regulated by 'nature', even sexuated nature. The dimension of the sexual is therefore considered to be outside any pre-existing and decisive structure based on 'sexualdifference', that simultaneously orders 'sexuality' and forms the principle of all articulated thought worthy of that name.

Furthermore, regarding the matter of 'neighbouring', and what occurs within it, especially in terms of the neighbouring of the sexes—Beckett's observation that, after all, 'there is so little difference between a man and a woman'[7] is appropriate here—analytic theory—not uniquely the modalities in which its schema functions, but as a theory which is indissolubly a theory of the unconscious *and* a theory of the process of the cure—provides us, through certain conceptualizations, especially those concerning the question of movements of identification, with a way of thinking what is at stake. The stakes concern the conditions of locking and unlocking the norms which define the space of our existences and of their links with other existences. Is it an open space, or on the contrary, a closed space? How can we say 'I'? How can we say 'we'? Can we easily conceive, and if not, why not, that a masculine or feminine other is the same as us?

It is possible to sense that which side one adopts will have important consequences—in any case, consequences which will involve psychoanalysis as it is practised, and as it is theorized; in short, which will involve the politics of psychoanalysis.

We will try to get the measure of the fact that the stakes in this case are quite clearly political, that is to say that a certain version of the theory of sexuality developed by psychoanalysis to establish the sexual order serves as a '*cachesexe*', for a state of power relations which fixes the rules of the game of *inequality*. The extreme violence of certain reactions which have recently enflamed the debate surrounding the changes in the so called 'private' aspects of our lives is a warning of this. This violence demonstrates the extreme rigidity of the obstacles to conceiving of access to a complete equality of rights between same-sex couples and heterosexual couples, an equality which would imply that both types of couple should have the right to have children.

But because this issue has to date raised so many passions, this is a sign that other factors effect it. These factors are tightly interwoven with the configuration of the 'schema of sexuality'. We might suspect, if we more or less explicitly understand that sexual difference, still paired with a 'differential valency' to use Françoise Héritier's[8] expression, constitutes the model on which is built the perception of the totality of relations between things and between beings. Perception here is in terms of 'sameness' and 'difference', the world being constituted of pairs of oppositions. Thus the divisions upon which our communal space is founded, even in their most frighteningly absurd and iniquitous aspects, are deprived of legitimacy based upon 'evidence'. These divisions pivot upon an axis which structures from the very beginning the interface between the 'same' and the 'other' in their various avatars. The knots of the sexual order which prescribe the very narrow access of the individual to the acceptable forms at the heart of which is defined that which stands for subjective 'identity', will at the same time index the ways of being represented and of dealing with questions which do not have a direct relationship with the dimension of sexuality and sexuation, but which might concern, for example, our conception of what is a 'stranger' and its opposite, and more generally the way of envisaging the relationship between 'majority' and minority or minorities. This indexing will occur with staggering efficacy because the threads of the logic which govern it are present in each of us, to the extent that each individual is presupposed to feel, to love, to experience sexual pleasure, to enter into a relationship with the human world, and to reproduce in this way on his or her own account, the regulation of experience in the form of contrasting pairs; a regulation which defines 'normality', realized of course from the point at which the joining of sexuality to sexuation is correctly formulated, and is identically repeated for each individual. This joining of sexuality to sexuation acts as a support for the 'Symbolic'. Except that, fortunately, this joining is, to say the very least, subject to crises.

It is important to grasp the frightening ambiguity with which psychoanalysis, in particularly the Lacanian version—the 'return to

Freud', and let us emphasize again, not *against* Freud—dips into this matter, since this brand of psychoanalysis at once gives very direct access to what the sexual means for the human, and by contributing to the construction of the order of sexuality examined by Michel Foucault, it tends to close the passages which could be outlined between this highly malleable arrangement and more varied schemata than those prescribed in the reduction of psychoanalysis to the measure of 'sexualdifference'.

'Between each of us and our sex, the West has erected an incessant demand for truth. . . . A certain inclination has led us, over several centuries, to put to the question of what we are to the sex,'[9] wrote Michel Foucault, asking himself, as mentioned above, what has led Western man to make of sexuality, or more precisely of the 'schema of sexuality', the 'seismograph' of his subjectivity, and this in relation to a preoccupation with the truth. This question cannot fail to be a troubling one for psychoanalysis. For, as we have begun to perceive, psychoanalysis offers a way of imploding the 'schema of sexuality', but can also contribute in a truly draconian way to locking as tightly as possible the 'schema of sexuality'.

It is a matter of locking in Jacques-Alain Miller's (Lacan's son-in-law and exegete of his work) commentary on Foucault's opposition to the following kind of *fin de non-recevoir*.[10] 'It is not clear that his counter-attack against a schema of sexuality, with psycho-analysis at its heart, did indeed escape all disciplinary and practical frameworks to find its support in the utopia of a body outside sex whose multiple pleasures would no longer be gathered under the unifying thumb of castration? This support, shall we say, was very thin. It was nothing more than a section of perversion to which, in *The Will to Knowledge*, Michel Foucault gave no other consistency than a utopian point which needed to be thought outside psychoanalysis . . .; this utopia was not realized from a happy sexuality, but from a body of plural pleasure, in which the things of love would not form a whole unified by the castrated phallus?'[11]

It is very surprising all the same to read such things, bearing in mind certain lines written by the Freud of the *Three Essays on Sexuality* which are unfortunately able to greatly undermine this magnificent plan. We will take the time to cite some of these extensively so that we are able to perceive from the Freudian position on the question of sexuality *independently* from any transcendent creation of a 'sexual order' without which one would be 'outside sex' according to the words of Jacques-Alain Miller.

In a paragraph which he entitles 'Polymorphous perverse predisposition', after having noted that the child, on contact with that which awakens in him the intensity of sexual feeling, '*can become polymorphously perverse*', which does not show that he is 'outside sex', but 'that an aptitude for them [all possible kinds of sexual irregularities] is innately present in their disposition'. Here Freud continues: 'in this respect children behave in the same kind of way as an average uncultivated woman in whom the same polymorphously perverse disposition persists. Under ordinary conditions she may remain normal sexually, but if she is led on by a clever seducer she will find every sort of perversion to her taste, and will retain them as part of her own sexual activities. Prostitutes exploit the same polymorphous, that is, infantile, disposition for the purposes of their profession; and, considering, the immense number of women who are prostitutes or who must be supposed to have an aptitude for prostitution without becoming engaged in it, it becomes impossible not to recognize that this same disposition to perversions of every kind is a general and fundamental human characteristic.'[12] Admittedly, this is pretty hair-raising stuff, and several comments on it are in order.

First, the affirmation of this 'equal predisposition' clearly indicates that the paths of sexual pleasure and the practices which arouse it are plural and in no case ordered by any transcendence which could be found in the demands of nature and/or of the 'Symbolic'. In the way that it brings to an abrubt close the question of the sexual with the help of the signifier 'sexualdifference', this 'Symbolic' promises a 'happy sexuality', responsible for a healthy hierarchy of practices. Thanks to this hierarchy we can discriminate accurately between what is said to be 'normal, complete' and what is 'outside sex', that is, outside that which is presupposed to be the basis of an authentic humanity. Freud's proposition of an 'equal predisposition' reminds us of the 'equal' attention of listening in analysis: that kind of listening which, when all hierarchies are undone, opens up the psyche to the signifying polymorphism, and sends it back to an 'origin' which it is important that we do not misunderstand. In any case, it is clear that the said 'origin' has nothing to do with what Françoise Héritier, for example, or Sylviane Agacinski, or even Julia Kristeva, although they are aware of what psychoanalysis teaches, do not hesitate to call the 'buffer' of 'sexualdifference', which is first directly encountered in nature. Just in passing, it is this position which allows Sylviane Agacinski to write the following in all good faith, in which she refers to Aristotle and to Freud, associating them haphazardly, and even at

189

times correcting them: 'There are other reasons for which "man and woman cannot exist without each other", other dependencies: erotic dependence for pleasure; biological dependence for procreation; and affective dependence, which shores up all the others. . . . However, in affirming with Aristotle that man and woman cannot exist without each other, we are placing ourselves in the general case of the inter-dependence of the two sexes. No doubt I will be reproached for considering this mutual dependence as *natural*, and thus for admitting that humanity is *naturally* heterosexual. I assume this point of departure as a matter of evidence.'[13]

What Freud talks about could not be further from this, since he situates the sexual 'origin' of the human being not in a presumed 'natural' complementarity of the sexes, the supposed source of any erotic and affective journey, but in the protiform excitability of any body destined to meet with other bodies. Other bodies which, in the relation of being able to feel the erogenous power of contact, and the waves which emanate from it, *intensely resemble* the body. Thus, it is thanks rather to movements of contagion and propagation across sensory zones and to layers vibrating through each other that the sexual 'arrangement' evoked by Freud will take a certain form, even if it is a 'genital' form. This is also a practice as 'adulterous' as all the others, as the Church Fathers were well aware, who, taking the term 'adulterous' in its most widely understood meaning, considered with fear the way in which pleasure could falsify, make unnatural, in a word: adulterate the holy sacrament of marriage, in the very fact of the union of man and woman such as God, distracted perhaps to the point of forgetting the madness of pleasure, had intended it when he created a well-ordered nature composed of two clearly distinct sexes. Which goes to show that One (God in this case) cannot think of everything.

It is therefore the dimension of the encounter and of the distortions effecting the perception of the body in its diverse functions which initiate a geography of pleasure and of pain, the traces of which will transport this body away from paths supposedly predetermined by an anatomy and a physiology dedicated 'naturally'—and for the good of all—to the activity of intercourse for the purpose of procreation. A bodily experience will be created in this way which corresponds to the map outlined by the gestures of an other—for example, according to the sinuous path of a caress—and to nothing else. The result is that the body of a human being, above all an erogenous body, and only subsequently, and on the basis of this, the body of a boy or a girl, will exist literally *outside* 'itself', and therefore outside the limits fixed by some kind of 'identity', even a 'sexual identity'. Boy-body or girl-body, it will always be at the same time more than just that, something else that exceeds indefinitely the assignation of sex, something else which is the erotic itself, overflowing on all sides the sexual determination which will have, in one way or another, put out within it its shifting, very shifting, roots.

This clearly means that the *sexuated* as it is experienced proceeds from the *sexual*, and not the other way around; that it is, therefore, disrupted *from the beginning*. This also means that it is not sexuation which dictates the division of sexuality, but the sexual disposition which Freud calls 'polymorphous perverse'—that is, absolutely malleable and open to any modulations—which determines the images through which the sexuated will enter the schema of sexuality. A schema whose customs and rules will appear as the fruit of an *unnecessary* destiny of this 'origin' open to all four points of the compass. As for the schema outlined by the 'sexual order' theorized by Lacan, subject to 'sexualdifference' articulated in terms of the phallic, and which supports the 'Symbolic order' which is constantly harped on, in order, it would seem, to spare us the horror of being precipitated into the chaos of the 'outside sex', *it is only one among many*. One, however, which claims to dictate the law. How is this state of affairs *created*? How can the stakes be further disentangled from it? How, *psychoanalytically*, can the stakes be appreciated, and what can be deduced from what we learn in the process? We will consider these matters in the remainder of this chapter, along with several points which will allow us to discern more clearly the conditions of the ascendancy of the Symbolic order.

It is, in any case, a strange kind of 'origin' which Freud speaks of, because it is not so much a stable given as a view on the unconscious, we might say, where the unconscious is a space proliferating with links and the vivid traces of links. Thus, to qualify the sexual arrangement as 'perverse' is to say in effect that that which is first—or the 'origin'—immediately becomes second (or third, or nth). It is also to say that the particular texture of the sexual arrangement is nothing other than the distortion with which every individual is endlessly furrowed, and crossed in every sense, through the neighbourings in which unfolds its simple presence in the world. I mean neighbourings in the sense of common walls. There are, if one can so express it, numerous common walls between individuals, and, as we know, while a common wall separates two spaces, it belongs at the same time to one and the other; it is what we call a shared part.

The common walls between humans are not built of stone, brick, or dry mud. They are made of sensitive skin and emotions. They are porous membranes, another name for the 'polymorphous perverse predisposition' which gives to the sexual its 'universally human and original' character, writes Freud. Let us note in passing that the universal in question here is not, as we see, referred to any transcendence of the Symbolic, but appears absolutely immanent to history, indefinitely open, erotic links being possible. As for the lines of common walls which travel across us, undivided lines of division, vivid lines diffusing between individuals, in complicated interlacing patterns, the currents which come and go from one individual to another, propagating links, they are watersheds of identifications, in these confines where the passage from one individual to another occurs in the crossing of one confused zone. It is a zone of confusion because affect and/or sensation, the living tissue of the encounter, exclude from it even space, so that one and the other begin to exist as such, that is to say for themselves, on the basis of the initial experience that they are, in what links them, in this sexual cement, 'polymorphous perverse', *the same*. This is exactly what Freud calls 'sexual community'[14] in *The Interpretation of Dreams*, a community whose identification, at work in the process of subjectifcation is, he says, 'expression'. Lines of the sexual, therefore, and not of the sexuated. Also, of course, lines of all powers, including that of the sexuated—of the signifiers of sexuation—to the extent that the latter passes through the lines of the sexual. They are, however, and by the same power, lines of their possible dissolution.

For power is born in the fixing of fundamentally uncertain confines into borders which are clear and sure of themselves. This is what happens when one inscribes as 'sexualdifference' the experience of sexual neighbouring. By neighbouring is meant the common factor in the sexual element of each individual, which is that chance has bestowed upon them either a male or female constitution. The sexual crosses and exceeds sexuation, but will also constitute sexuation and its destinies. It will constitute sexuation because men and women are, as Lacan wrote, 'signifiers', and because unconscious signifiers, in that they are repressed—that is, cut by the paths that outlined them—are the trace, and even the bodies, of the links which constitute us.

Because they are the unconscious memory of these links, unconscious signifiers, filled with the forgetting which buries them in the material of our lives, function like blind, inflexible, schemata of injunctions. They are inflexible as long as we do not try to deal with them. We will be able to deal with them, however, when it becomes possible to appreciate from what these links, which have become systems, are woven (and to discover this is the very object of the analytic cure)—for they are formed of nothing more than precisely this 'polymorphous perverse predisposition', the matrix of our being in the world. Concerning the question of sexuality and of its import-ance, the problem we are faced with, of which we have undertaken to unfold the difficulties, is that one destiny, and only one, is foreseen by the construction of sexuation as 'sexualdifference', which will certainly be responsible for the 'sexual order', duly governed by the 'iron rule of castration'. But in this construction everything happens as though the skin of which the common walls are made had been transformed into walls of bulletproof glass. Nothing gets through them any more. And the fear is that nothing much breathes any more. We will no longer move. Everyone remains to themselves. Except that it's not that simple, since these rigid, impermeable walls, which are supposed to contain us, actually and in every way cross us right through. It is easy to imagine that this might have the effect of humiliating us, and that it certainly causes several types of suffering. This is what we referred to at the beginning of this work as the 'pain of the norm'. This leads to the question: what should we do with all this? What is, in this case, the task of psychoanalysis?

In any case, it can be seen that 'sexualdifference', the foundation of the 'sexual order', the 'sexualdifference' that designates as 'masculine' or 'feminine' the functions of the man and of the woman in the realization of the said sexual order, is nothing more than a highly hegemonic formation of the unconscious, and as such can be dis-solved. That this is so can be sensed in the Freudian blurring of the categories of sexuation—which, furthermore, renders unstable even the idea of bisexuality—that we meet in *Three Essays on Sexuality*. Freud tells us that 'it is essential to understand clearly that the concepts of "masculine" and "feminine", whose meaning seems so unambiguous to ordinary people, are among the most confused that occur in science.' Holding firm to the masculine-activity relationship, he attempts, nonetheless, a clarification aimed at convincing us that 'the libido is in essence masculine' in both sexes. He tries to lead us down strange and incompatible paths: two models of activity—and therefore of the masculine—intervene. One of them—the corporal—which is not, however, the male organ, is wilful muscular activity, especially of the hand; but the other—the libido—is compared in its activity to a river which spreads and stretches out into adjoining canals

193

if its own bed is not sufficient to hold it. There is, it must be agreed, a world of difference between the river, which lacks muscular power, and a hand which grasps an object. We might even say a whole world to be travelled. But as for some assurance about the 'masculine', we will have to do without. Nothing is very clear except that nothing can be clear, and further—and here we find ourselves in the zones of confines—everything used by Freud to define the indefinable 'masculine' could just as easily be applied to the indefinable 'feminine'. The issue remains unclear.

At this point, the question that remains almost untouched, although it is more and more pressing, is that of the motives of this hegemony, and of the reasons why psychoanalysis sometimes contributes, with worrying efficacy, to its legitimacy. This question touches upon the relationship of the practice of psychoanalysis to the question of norms and of their vital stakes. This is one of the aspects where progress needs to be made. This question also leads us, and a kind of horror of neighbouring can be scented at work in the construction of (sexual) 'difference' which alerts us, to question in greater detail the problematic of our 'own' and the 'stranger', of 'sameness' and 'difference', and everything else which is bubbling away in that particular pot. For, and this is evidently not by chance, one of the most constant, although very vaguely argued, features of the discourses which have aimed to deny same-sex couples an equal status as that of different-sex couples, for the reason that by ruining the 'sexual order' they are ruining the entire human order, has been to maintain, with varying degrees of sophistication, that 'homosexuality' is characterized by the 'love of the same'. That is why the incurable position (*dixit* Lacan) in sexuality, because it was not addressed, was accused not so much of perversion as of incompleteness. Incompleteness thought as the incapacity to assume 'sexual identity', perfectly closed in on itself. This strange perspective also presupposed 'heterosexuality' to be envisaged as 'completeness'. Is it *imperative* that things continue this way?

Let's not complete anything; rather, let's continue ...

COMMUN SINGULIER
BRIEF REMARKS

Joseph Conrad speaks somewhere about a 'feeling of unavoidable solidarity' which, he says, 'binds men together'.[16] Impossible, then, for the individual to escape the links with his or her *equals*. However, this feeling, which is a sort of intimate political feeling, springs up from the most naked part of our own space in that its fundamentally mutual nature—the *extime*, or external intimacy—can be quite unbearable. For it reopens in us like an old wound the perception of the strange and disturbing dimension of our condition: we are from birth deprived, and therefore constrained to find support from the other, the neighbour, in order to survive, and this very movement—the movement that delivers us to the other—will be swallowed up, as through an irresistible magnetic force, in the heart of this zone which intensifies in its own psyche, and renews in welcoming us (a welcome which is impossible unless we are able to allow ourselves to be *touched*), the familiar, sometimes unrecognizable, echo of an experience which is both our own and our neighbour's. So much so that it is in the hollow of the other's weakest, most deprived part that support will be found and the mutual links will become knotted. There is danger in addressing the other. Therefore, we face with horror, or anaesthesia, the proven feeling of '*unavoidable* solidarity' and its unlimited extension in our lives.

There is danger in addressing the other not only because this will hit us where it hurts, at the point where our most intense psychic feelings are mobilized or immobilized—which is not the same thing, even if these two destinies can sometimes form a single unit—but because in addressing the other we will hit upon the calcified gestures which have previously tried to oppose this unbearable deprivation; upon fortified lines, emergency protection, which will allow nothing to be known about them, but through which, and also thanks to which, our call will nonetheless manage to forge itself a passage. How will this happen, though? And at what price? Knowing that, in any case, it will be necessary to wander about in the confusion of signifiers, these paths which can be negotiated but which are covered in brambles, and which link human beings to each other in one way rather than another. Many fairy tales teach us about this course of things which puts safety back to back with anguish, and about its burning line of chance(s). This is fortunate for the attempt to address the other, since a sort of way of using the 'unavoidable solidarity' is given from the beginning, in the unleashing of a universe of translatable signs. Certain translations will then be put into place, on the basis of which will be constituted the structures of norms, the shared grammar of subjectivity. These structures will play upon the sort of mutual condition of identification which is our lot. Furthermore, this will happen in a paradoxical way, since the identification upon which signifying content can have a bearing, content which will say for example 'this is that, and you are this and not that', will simultaneously be able to seal the identification with the obscure distress brought by the situation of initial a-signifying deprivation, which encourages the creation and interpretation of signs, and in which nothing *is* in advance or from the beginning what signifiers claim to write of destiny. But, on the other hand, it is a situation where everyone is the same, that is, in truth, without anything and ready for everything.

Furthermore, this is a situation into which loves plunges us again when it sweeps down upon us; in which Lacan's aphorism that 'love is giving what you don't have to someone who doesn't want it' becomes clear. It remains that, in spite of this, we *can* love. We can be naked. We can, in other words, in the shared and mutual experience of modification to which the free disposition to the love relation is dedicated, allow to come undone what we believe to have and/or to be; these assured 'qualities' or 'identity', like clothes or adornments, which keep us far from the unnamed, which save us from the unnamed through all sorts of gifts which can be listed—and, it is said, are very precious—until one day we are nothing more than clutter, on the verge of suffocation.

However endowed—or crushed—we are, arriving in the world in such a family, in the weave of such a history, in which we are given the responsibility of accurately finding the right place, while at the same time being only anybody, anybody at all and because of this being without anything and ready for everything. So first of all we allow ourselves to be caught in the tightly woven signifying nets, to which we cling so as to stop wandering endlessly. We are ready to hold on to the determining factors which the signifiers arrange, ready to stick to the assignations that they decree. We are exposed to every power, all the more forcefully because the appetite for consent will be more imperious in proportion to the vice of anguish. This appetite for consent is not pure passive submission, but a fixed orientation, which is narrowly channelled from the imaginative resources which preside over the paths of identification, and which is all the more efficient as a result. These paths are more zigzagging, more complex, more fantastic than they seem when we perceive their polished results. For, in its urgency, the aspiration to meaning cobbles together in great haste various verisimilitudes, which are sometimes highly fantastic, and which are also governed by the pure pleasure they bring, the source of their playful creativity. The apprenticeship of language and those incidents where the words which organize the universe exist in a totally different way from the prescribed usage testify clearly to this, hence the strategies of adapting to the rule which are sufficiently subtle that we do not have to renounce them. The famous and truly joyful example of Colette's 'presbytery' opens up in this respect perspectives which are as ingenious as they are poetic. Ah! Well? The 'presbytery' is not the little yellow and black striped snail? Ah! Well? It's the curate's house? Who cares! Since it's *like that*, it won't be over *like that*! After all, the curate only has to behave himself and sleep in a shell to be able to say 'I made myself into a curate on the wall'.[17] It will be agreed that this is a very unorthodox, although apparently very Catholic, 'identity' for a little girl. Furthermore, the signifying universe buzzing with the discourses which circulate in every direction and which cross everyone is potentially so charged with ambiguities and disagreements, and is so extensive, that the bottleneck which rings out and folds back its possibilities in the univocal manner of an injunction, giving free reign in this way to the exorbitant power of the 'discourse of the other' of which only one version will be authorized—the 'sovereignty of the signifier'—could at any moment implode. This is what we have described as the crises which upset the traces of prescribed destinies.

We have seen how this works in relation to the signifiers of sexuation. The way in which the power of the signifiers of sexuation is exercised over everyone could be summarized in the following way. First, offering up the amalgam 'sexualdifference' upon which everything rests, they produce a buffer effect—we remember that this is the term used by Françoise Héritier[18]—which halts, superimposing itself upon it, the disturbing feeling aroused by contact with the other, who is strangely *similar* in his very difference. By similar, I mean capable of identifications, and therefore, potentially polymorphous; knowing the *sexual*—and not from the outset *sexuated*—intensity that this capacity mobilizes. In this way, it has been possible to see through what tortuous paths the signifiers of sexuation control the space of sexuality, which will have to be the very place, and the centre, of order. 'Men, women and children' will thus see their functions assigned on condition that they make this admirable programme work without being thrown into crises of doubt. The price is the confusion that will mean identifications are taken, in their whirl and bustle, for assumptions of 'identity'. The benefit is that the same thing is perpetuated through the game which is closed by the established dominations. For the horror of change, which can be seen unleashed in the arguments inspired by legislation aiming to widen the range of possibilities for sexual and family ties, is really an image of the horror of the *same*, of that which shifts the well known—or what we suppose to be well known— towards that which is as yet undocumented, whose echo suddenly pierces the known and tears it into thousands of fragments from which resurges the fragile and yet so powerful exhilaration which can sometimes spring from our initial deprivation. These fragments can be perfectly recycled by being spun together into new pieces, such as the 'polymorphous perverse sexual disposition' which runs between beings, sexuated just as chance wanted them to be, and which is invincible against any sexual order.

The new power of Freud's discovery, through the theory of the unconscious, which had only one supporter, and the invention of the mechanism of the analytic cure, that melting pot of links, is to have given access to the fabric of power as well as to the means to undo it. The undoing of the powers over us will be based upon the lever which offers the very force which strengthens power—the force stemming from the 'urgency of life', from that which it is necessary to attain at all costs in order to find a way out of deprivation, which in order to attain we will have to invent something. By means of an edge which is some-times terribly burdened and always full of traps. Such is the uncompromising strictness of Freudianism, that the price of emanci-pation will no longer be able to remain hidden. In this sense, psycho-analysis should be thought as a theory of power relations rather than, as it is believed to be due to a naïve blindness, a—*the*—theory of sexuality, even if the latter is understood as a genealogy of sexual prescription. To psychoanalyse, without any innocence, will then cer-tainly separate out representations, following, however, not correct articulations of the 'true', like Socrates the butcher-philosopher, who knew how to conclude, but the lines of crisis, interstices which contest sexual assignations. To psychoanalyse would be to divide and pull free from their foundation the blocks of 'identity' shut up in the prison of the expectations of dictatorial signifiers; signifiers relayed by the vari-ous officials in charge of their transmission, like so many guardians of the temple of the 'symbolic order' and its statues. Preferably Roman statues: 'M. Malraux may rightly say that there is nothing to retain in Roman sculpture from the point of view of the eternal art museum, it remains no less true that the very notion of a human being is linked to the vast diffusion of statues in Roman sites.'[19] We will leave Lacan here to his fantasy. It is, however, a fantasy which governs, under the passion of authority, a certain contemporary modality of the appeal to the guarantee dispensed by a type of psychoanalysis supposed as the expert in ultimate references—in collusion with a brand of anthropology which supposedly possesses the true truth about 'invariants'. This is the *hubris* of orthodoxy—the straight path. It is also, Lacan tells us, the highway, the Roman road which alone can guarantee the eternity of the Empire. It is the highway and not the improbable, although sometimes very clear, paths which are forged, for example, by herds of elephants ...[20]

One might rightfully expect psychoanalysts not to act as obtuse fanatics devoted to this kind of illusion, to this lie to which we owe the supposed sexual 'identities' as well as the exhaustive, hierarchical nomenclature of sexualities: on the right 'heterosexuality', and on the left 'homosexuality'. This is a useless and often deadly lie. It is also a disavowal of the fantasy gestures which invented the image of this lie. It is a denial of the unconscious—which is nonetheless a peak—in view of its seeming manipulation.

Freud, for his part, and he does not deny himself his part, can *dream* of Rome; but the dream, the 'royal path', is not a Roman road, and Freud dreams of himself as Hannibal—again, it is elephants forging the passage ...—and not as Nero. The dream is not a Roman road; on the contrary, it is the totality of the traces of different passages—those of elephants, why not, who, although impressive, do not have a particularly light step.

These gestures of fantasy, which are not, although attempts are made to delude us into believing it, the necessary postures of Roman statues, revealed models of the human, but the effect of the plasticity of the *movements* of identification; we see them ready to bend in a different way, if the game should enter into the cogs of this perfectly regulated matter and jam them. This rarely fails to happen in the course of a life, although far too often, alas!, at an impasse. It is at this point that the work of the psychoanalyst can intervene, allowing the subject to let go of what he is supposed *to have to* be, and working bit by bit, closer and closer, to reveal the horizon, lost in mist, of what one imagines one *can* be. It is demanding work, the daily execution of the cure as well as the critical reflection to which the work constantly adjusts its pace.

One could apply these words of Michel Foucault to this work, which express, in relation to Pierre Boulez, the admiration and the inspiration which gave birth in him to the power of artistic courage, the power of the unheard: 'What is then the role of thought in what one does if thought can be neither simply *savoir-faire* nor pure theory?

Boulez showed the role of thought: to give the strength to break the rules in the act which brings them into play.'[21] This is a great lesson. Others will perhaps denounce it as 'perversion'.

Notes

1. J. Lacan, *The Ethics of Psychoanalysis 1959–1960. The Seminar of Jacques Lacan*, Book VII (London: Routledge, 1992), 152.
2. Ibid. 321.
3. J. Lacan, *Les Formations de l'inconscient 1957–1958. Le Séminaire*, Book V (Paris: Seuil, 1998).
4. J. Kristeva, 'Le Sens de la Parité', *Le Monde*, 23 Mar. 1999.
5. S. Freud, *Three Essays on Sexuality*. The Standard Edition of the Complete Psychological Works of Sigmund Freud, trans. James Strachey, Vol. vii (London: The Hogarth Press and the Institute of Psychoanalysis, 1953), 146.
6. Translator's note: The famous French dessert *tarte Tatin* was invented in the 19th century by a hotel cook, Stéphanie Tatin, who accidentally made a traditional apple tart upside down.
7. S. Beckett, *Malone meurt* (Paris: Minuit, 1995), 10.
8. Editor's note: Cf. Chapter 4, 'Masculine/Feminine: The Thought of Difference'.
9. M. Foucault, *La Volonté de savoir* (Paris: Gallimard, 1998), 102.
10. Translator's note: In French law, a plea that shows in law that the plaintiff had no right to bring it.
11. Text cited above. [Editor's note: but not in this extract.]
12. Freud, *Three Essays on Sexuality*, 191.
13. S. Agacinski, *Politique des sexes* (Paris: Seuil, 1998).
14. S. Freud, *The Interpretation of Dreams*, trans. James Strachey (London: Penguin, 1991).
15. S. Freud, *Three Essays on Sexuality*. The Standard Edition of the Complete Psychological Works of Sigmund Freud, trans. James Strachey Vol. vii (London: The Hogarth Press and the Institute of Psychoanalysis, 1953), 219.
16. J. Conrad, *The Nigger of the Narcissus* (London: Penguin, 1989).
17. Colette, *La Maison de Claudine*, 'Le curé sur le mur' (Robert Laffont, Bouquins, 1997), 220.
18. Editor's note: Cf. Chapter 4: 'Masculine/Feminine: The Thought of Difference'.
19. J. Lacan, *The Psychoses*. Book III *1955–1956*, trans. Russell Grigg (London: Routledge, 1993), 291.
20. 'A highway is not at all the same as the track made by the movement of elephants through an equatorial forest. As important, so it seems, as these tracks are, they are nothing other than the passage of elephants.' Ibid.
21. M. Foucault, *Dits et écrits 1954–1988*, vol. iv: *1980–1988*, (Paris: Gallimard, 1994).

11 Is Love a Place of Sexuated Knowledge?

Alain Badiou*

Philosopher, writer, and social critic Alain Badiou was born in 1937 in Rabat, Morocco. He studied at the École Normale Supérieure and the Université de Paris IV, Sorbonne. He taught philosophy at the Lycée de Reims between 1963 and 1965 and at the Université de Reims from 1965 until 1992. Badiou is currently a professor of philosophy at the École des Arts, Philosophie, et Esthétique (The School of Arts, Philosophy and Aesthetics) at the Université de Paris VIII, Vincennes-Saint-Denis, where he leads a research group on the topic of *Lieux et transformations de la philosophie* (Places and Transformations of Philosophy). He also holds a professorship at the École Normale Supérieure at Paris. From 1989 until 1995 he held the prestigious position of director of the renowned Collège International de Philosophie in Paris. Badiou was the co-director of the philosophical collection entitled *L'Ordre philosophique* (The Philosophical Order) for Éditions du Seuil, one of France's leading publishers.

Although retaining some principles from his earlier affiliation with Maoism, Alain Badiou is critical of any representational politics that appeals to ideological or party identity. Badiou's political militancy instead translates into prescriptions particular for singular social events or conditions. His political life is reflected in his criticism of parliamentary politics and engagement with such issues as the living conditions of *sans papiers* (a term used to refer to unregistered immigrants without residence papers in France) and the status of factories, work, education, and healthcare in general. Together with other militants from the events of May 1968, he co-founded an organization called L'Organisation politique (The Political Organization), which publishes the journal *La Distance politique* (The Political Distance), a journal devoted to leftist political views.

Badiou's numerous publications are diverse in form and subject, ranging from plays, novels, and even an opera libretto, to political and philosophical essays and manifestos. The most important of his philosophical writings is *L'Être et*

---

* L'Amour est-il le lieu d'um savoir sexué?', in *L'Exercise du savoir et la différence des sexes* (Paris: L'Harmattan, 1995), 99–114. Reprinted by permission of L'Harmattan.

l'Événement (Being and Event), which was published in 1988 and marked the real turning point for the development of his thought. Badiou's theory of *the multiple* brings together mathematical set theory, Lacanian psychoanalysis, Maoist politics, and the poetics of Mallarmé, Rimbaud, and Beckett, while remaining true to a Platonist conception of philosophy. A philosopher of immanence, Badiou endorses an ontology in which the concept of multiplicity is central; Truth within his framework is an empty category under which truths produced in different fields can be expected to emerge. Badiou goes back to Plato to retrieve four procedures of truth: politics, science, art, and love. It is within each one of these fields that 'events'—the emergence of the radically new—generate truth.

In 'L'Amour est-il un lieu d'un savoir sexué?' (Is Love a Place of Sexuated Knowledge?) Badiou develops the idea that love is a philosophical category that designates the generation of truth according to a 'Two' that is at play in a particular amorous situation. Designating 'a one and a one' as nominal sexual distinctions between two people whose amorous encounter is the event of love, he argues that love is the paradoxical place where the differential knowledge possessed by 'man' and 'woman' remains united in its absolute disjunction. In other words, Badiou finds in the event of love, the couple's faithfulness to it, and the material marks that result from it (sexuality, cohabitation, children, etc.), a singular sustained place for a generic and multiple truth. Love for Badiou becomes a procedural enquiry into the world from the point of view of the 'Two' and the field of possibility for sexuated knowledge. Moreover, he concludes that of the two forms of sexual knowledge, that of 'woman' grounds the possibility of universality.

The sexes, their difference, and love are risky questions; a certain effect of the comic always hovers over them, we smile at those who act all serious in speaking too often of themselves and their disappointments without knowing it. Guard rail (*Garde-fou*): stick to something with the autonomy and consistency I am able to take on, philosophy.

It has been claimed that philosophy as a systematic will has edified itself by foreclosing sexual difference. I do not believe this at all. Too many signs attest that this is not the case, and we can see every day that contemporary philosophy addresses itself to women. One could even suspect it, and I lay myself open to this, of being partly caught up, as a discourse, in a strategy of seduction.

A more serious objection is in the observation that what has been said about love which is truly real has been said in the world of art, and especially in the art of novelistic prose. The pairing up of love and the novel is essential. Furthermore, it is noticeable that women have excelled in this art, that they have given it a critical impetus: for example, Madame de Lafayette, Jane Austen, Virginia Woolf, Katherine

Mansfield, and many others. And, above all of them, writing in an eleventh century unimaginable to Western barbarians, Lady Murazaki Shikibu, author of the greatest text in which what can be said about love in its masculine dimension is set out, *The Tale of Genji*.

But from where can this pairing up, this junction of love and the novel, be observed? From a place where it is proved that love and art intersect, or that it is possible for them to exist at the same time. This place is philosophy.

The word 'love' will be construed here as a category of philosophy which is inaugural, as we can see in the status of the Platonic Eros. The relation of this category to love as it comes into play in psychoanalysis, for example at the point of transference, will no doubt remain problematic. The latent rule is a rule of internal coherence: 'Make sure that your philosophical category, however particular it is, remains compatible with the analytic concept.' But I will not here verify in detail this compatibility.

Philosophy, or a philosophy, founds its place of thought upon *challenges* and upon *declarations*—in general, upon the challenge of the sophists and upon the declaration that there are truths. In the case which concerns us, there will be:

1. A challenge to the conception of love as fusion. Love does not, from a Two whose structure is a presupposed given, make the One of ecstasy. This challenge is fundamentally the same as the one which dismisses being-for-death. For the ecstatic One only supposes itself to be beyond the Two as a *suppression of the multiple*. Thus it is a metaphor of the night, the idea of the sacred banished from the encounter, the terror exercised by the world. It is Wagner's Tristan and Yseult. In my categories, this is an image of *disaster*, related to the generic procedure of love. This disaster is not that of love itself; it is supported by a philosophical object, the philosophical object of the One.

2. A challenge to the self-sacrificing conception of love. Love is not the laying of the self upon the altar of the Other. I will argue further on that love is not even an experience of the Other. It is an experience *of the world*, or of the situation, on the post-decisive-event condition that there is the Two. I want to distance the Eros from any dialectic of the Heteros.

3. A challenge to the 'superstructural' or illusory conception of love, so dear to the pessimistic tradition of French moralists. By this, I mean the conception stating that love is nothing more than the

ornamental semblance through which the real of sex passes, or that desire and sexual jealousy are the foundation of love. Lacan sometimes touches upon this idea, for example when he says that love is what compensates for the lack of the sexual relation. But he also says the opposite, when he endows love with an onto-logical vocation, that of 'l'abord de l'être' (the approach of being). I believe that love compensates for nothing. It *supplements*, which is totally different. It is only a failure under the fallacious supposition that it is a relation. But it is not a relation. It is a production of truth. Truth about what? About what the Two, and not only the One, brings about in the situation.

I am coming to the declarations, the hypotheses or axioms. My aim is in certain aspects purely logical. Logic is necessary in these matters, which are stuffed with pathetic psychology.

A final precaution: only our historical situation is being addressed. I do not claim to legislate about the state of matters of sex in Papua New Guinea. I state hypotheses relative to the era in which there have been philosophy and its conditions.

The first hypothesis is as follows:

1: *There are two positions of experience*

'Experience' is taken in its most general sense, as a presentation, a situation. There are two positions of presentation, called 'man' and 'woman'. We should acknowledge that the two positions are sexuated. No empirical, objective, or biological logic is acceptable here.

That there are *two* positions only becomes established retroactively. It is, in effect, love and love alone that allows us to state formally the existence of two positions. Why is this? Because of the second, truly fundamental thesis, which is:

2: *The two positions are totally disjointed.*

'Totally' must be taken to the letter: *nothing* in experience is the same for the position man and the position woman. Nothing. That is to say: the positions do not share experience, there is no presentation affected for 'woman' and presentation affected for 'man', and then zones of coincidence or intersections. *Everything* is presented so that no coincidence can be witnessed between what affects one position and what affects another.

We will call this state of affairs *disjunction*. The sexuated positions are disjointed regarding experience in general.

Disjunction cannot be observed, it cannot itself be the object of direct experience or knowledge. For any such experience or knowledge would itself be positioned in disjunction and would encounter *nothing* attesting to the other position.

For there to be knowledge of disjunction—structural knowledge—there must be a third position. This is forbidden by the third thesis:

3: *There is no third position.*

The idea of a third position engages the function of the imaginary: the Angel. The discussion on the sex of Angels is fundamental, for at stake is the *pronunciation of disjunction.* Now this is not possible solely from the point of experience, or of the situation.

What, then, makes it possible for me here to articulate disjunction, without turning to the Angel, without being the Angel? Since the situation is insufficient, it must be being supplemented by something. Not by a third structural position, but by a singular event. This event is what initiates the amorous procedure, and we will agree to call it an *encounter.*

But before we reach this point, it is necessary to go, so to speak, to the other extreme of the problem. This is the fourth thesis:

4: *There is one single humanity.*

What does 'humanity' mean in a non humanist sense? No predicative objective trait can be the basis of this word. It would be ideal or biological, in either case not pertinent. By 'humanity' I understand that which acts as a support for generic procedures, or procedures of truth. You know that I maintain that there are four types of such procedures: science, politics, art, and—of course—love. Humanity is therefore vouched for if and only if there is politics (emancipatory), science (conceptual), art (creative), or love (not reduced to a mixture of sentimentality and sexuality). Humanity is what *supports* the infinite singularity of the truths which are inscribed in these types. Humanity is the historical body of truths.

Let us denote as $H(x)$ the function of humanity. This abbreviation indicates that the term presented as 'x', whatever it is, acts as a support in at least one generic procedure. If we denote the four types of truths as follows: politics by the letter p, science by the letter s, aesthetics or art by the letter a, and love by the letter l, then an *axiom of humanity* can be written thus:

$$s(x) \rightarrow H(x),$$

which means the term presented as x, from being active in a scientific procedure, falls under the function of humanity. Vice versa, we will have:

$$H(x) \rightarrow [s(x) \text{ or } p(x) \text{ or } a(x) \text{ or } l(x)],$$

which means that a presented term falls under the function of humanity if and only if it is active in at least one of the four generic procedures.

From this point on, the term H as such (let's say: the substantive 'humanity') appears as a *potential mixture* of the four types s, p, a, and l. It makes a knot of the four. The presentation of this knot, as we shall see, is at the heart of the disjunction between the positions 'man' and 'woman' *in their relation to truth*.

Now, our fourth thesis, which affirms that there is only one humanity, comes to mean this: every truth applies to *all* of its historical body. A truth, whichever it is, is indifferent to any predicative division of its support.

In particular, a truth as such is removed from any position. A truth is *transpositional*. It is, furthermore, the only thing to be so, and that is why a truth will be called generic. In *L'Être et l'événement*,[1] I attempted to set out an ontology of this adjective.

If we relate the effects of thesis four to the first three theses, we can formulate exactly the problem which will occupy us: How is it possible for a truth to be transpositional, or as good as for our purposes, if at least two positions exist—man and woman—which are radically disjointed in regard to experience in general?

We might expect the following statement to stem from the first three theses: truths are sexuated. There is a feminine science and a masculine science, just as it used to be thought that there was a proletarian science and a bourgeois science. There is a feminine art and a masculine art, a feminine political vision and a masculine political vision, a feminine love (which is strategically homosexual, as certain branches of feminism have vigorously affirmed) and a masculine love. I would add that although this is clearly the case, it is impossible to *know* this.

Now this is not the case in the space of thought that I want to establish. There, it is posited simultaneously that the disjunction is radical, that there is no third position, and that, however, any truth that occurs is generic, removed from any positional disjunction.

In order to understand this, we must come back to the idea of disjunction. To say that the disjunction is total, that there is no neutral observation or third position, is to say that the two positions *cannot be counted as two*. From where could such a count be done? The two is not presented as two except in the three, where it is presented as an element of the three. If there is no three, we need to change the statement of thesis 1, for it is more strictly correct to say:

1b: There is one position and another position.

There is a 'one' and 'one' which do not make two, the one of each 'one' being indiscernible, although totally disjoined from the other. In particular, no position-one includes an experience of the other, which would be an interiorization of the two.

Love is therefore precisely this: the advent of the Two as two, the staging of the Two.

But careful: this staging of the Two is not a *being* of the Two, which would suppose the three. This staging of the Two is a work, a process. It only exists as a journey in the situation, *under the supposition that there is a Two*. The Two is the hypothetical operator, the operator of random seeking, of such a work, or of such a journey.

The occurrence of the supposition of a Two is from the beginning the result of an event. The event is the chance supplementing of the situation we call an encounter. Of course, the event-encounter is only in the form of its disappearance, its eclipse. It is only fixed by being named, and this nomination is a declaration—a declaration of love. The name which declares is pulled from the void of the site from which the encounter draws the little bit of being of its supplementation.

What is the void summoned by the declaration of love? It is the unknown void of disjunction. The declaration of love outs into circulation, in the situation a word pulled from the interval of nothingness which disjoins the positions man and woman. The phrase '*je t'aime*' ('I love you') places two pronouns, 'je' ('I') and 'te' ('you'), next to each other. These pronouns cannot be placed side by side once they return to the idea of disjunction. The declaration fixes the encounter nominally as having the void of disjunction as its being. The Two which operates amorously is actually the name of the disjoined understood in its disjunction.

Love is infinite fidelity to the first nomination. It is a material procedure which re-evaluates the totality of experience, covering fragment by fragment the whole situation, according to its connection or disconnection to the nominal supposition of the Two.

There is a *numeric schema* specific to the amorous procedure. This schema states that the Two fractures the One and experiences the infinity of the situation. One, Two, infinity: this is the numeration of the amorous procedure. It structures the becoming of a generic truth. Truth about what? Truth about the situation *insofar as there exist two disjointed positions*. Love is nothing other than a testing succession of investigations into disjunction, into the Two, so that in the

207

retrospective effect of the encounter, it proves to have always been one of the laws of the situation.

But when *a* truth about the situation as disjointed emerges, it also becomes clear that any truth is addressed to everybody, and guarantees that the function of humanity $H(x)$ is unique in its effects. The point that there is only *one* situation is re-established when we grasp it in truth. One situation, and not two. The situation such that the disjunction is a *law* within it. And truths are all without exception truths about *this* situation.

Love is the place in which it happens that disjunction does not separate the situation in its being. Or that disjunction is not a law, not a substantial delimitation. It is the scientific side of the amorous procedure.

Love fractures the One according to the Two. And it is from this that it can be thought that the situation, although it is worked by disjunction, is such that there is the One, and that it is on the basis of this multiple-One that all truth is assured.

In our world, love is the guardian of the universality of the true. It elucidates the possibility of this because *it makes a truth of disjunction.*

However, at what price?

The Two as a post-decisive-event supposition must be materially *marked.* There must be in it the first referents of its name. These referents, as everyone knows, are bodies marked by sexuation. The differential trait borne by all bodies inscribe the Two under its nomination. The sexual is linked to the amorous procedure as the advent of the Two, in the double occurrence of a name of the void (the declaration of love) and of a material disposition constrained to the bodies as such. Thus the amorous *operator* is composed of a name pulled from the void of disjunction and a differential marking of the body.

From this point of view, and although it is slightly ridiculous to do so, we must assume that the differential sexual characteristics only attest to disjunction under the condition of the declaration of love. Without this condition, *there is no Two,* and the sexual marking is entirely held *in* disjunction, without being able to attest to it. To put it rather crudely: all sexual unveiling of the body which is non-amorous is masturbatory in the strictest sense: it is only concerned with the interiority of a position. This is not a judgement, but a simple delimitation, for masturbatory 'sexual' activity is an activity which is perfectly reasonable in each of the disjointed sexuated positions. Still we are (retroactively) assured that this activity is uncommon when one passes—but can one 'pass'?—from one position to another.

Love alone exhibits the sexual as an image of the Two. It is therefore also the place in which it is stated that there are two sexuated bodies, and not one. The amorous unveiling of bodies is the test of this, that under the unique name of the void of disjunction comes the marking of disjunction itself. Disjunction, which is under its name a loyal procedure of truth, discovers that it has always been radically disjoined.

But this sexuated attestation of disjunction under the post-decisive-event name of its void does not abolish disjunction. It is only a matter of making it a truth. It is therefore quite true that there is no sexual relation, because love founds the Two, not the relation of Ones in the Two. The two bodies do not present the Two—there would have to be a third, the outside-sex—they only mark it.

This is a very delicate point. It must be understood that love makes disjunction a truth under the emblem of the Two, but that it does this *in the indestructible element of disjunction*.

The Two, not being presented, operates in the situation as the complex of a name and a bodily marking. It serves to evaluate the situation through laborious investigations. Cohabitation, social representation, the sexual act, outbursts, language [*la parole*], conflicts, children: all of these are the materiality of the procedure, its journey of truth in the situation. But these operations do not unify the partners. The Two operates *as disjointed*. There *will have been* a sole truth of love for the situation, but the procedure of this unity moves in the disjunction which it makes a truth.

The effects of this tension can be observed on two levels:

1. In the amorous procedure there are *functions* whose positions are redefined by their grouping.
2. What the future of the one-truth authorizes in advance *in know-ledge* is sexuated. Or again: foreclosed by truth, the positions return in knowledge.

Regarding the first point, I will allow myself to return to a text whose support is the work of Samuel Beckett, and whose sub-title is: *L'Écriture du générique et l'amour*. Very briefly put: the becoming of the amorous procedure demands that there is:

A function of *wandering*, of chance, of a risky voyage into the situation, which supports the articulation of the Two and of infinity. A function which exposes the supposition of the Two in the infinite presentation of the world.

A function of *immobility*, which guards, which holds the first nomination, which assures that this nomination of the event-encounter is not swallowed up in the event itself.

A function of the *imperative*: to continue always, even in separation. To believe that absence itself is a mode of continuation.

A function of *narrative*, which inscribes in the process, like a sort of archive, the becoming-truth of the wandering.

Now, one can establish that disjunction is reinscribed in the table of functions. For 'man' is the amorous position which couples the imperative function and the function of immobility, while 'woman' is the position which couples the functions of wandering and narrative. We will not hesitate here to confirm some of those crude and precious common places: 'man' is he (or she) who does nothing, I mean nothing apparent for and in the name of love, because he maintains that that which has been valid once can continue to be valid without proving itself again. 'Woman' is she (or he) who makes love travel, and who desires that her personal language [*parole*] be reiterated and renewed. Or, in the lexicon of conflict, 'man' is secretive, lazy and violent, while 'woman' is gossipy, extremist, and protesting. These are the empirical materials of the labour of the investigations into love in order that there be truth.

The second point is more complex.

First, I will challenge the idea that, in love, each sex can learn *about the other sex*. I do not believe this at all. Love is an investigation into the world from the point of the Two; it is in no way an investigation of each term of the Two into the other. There is a real sense of disjunction, which is precisely that no subject can occupy at the same time and in the same relation both positions. This impossibility lies in the place of love itself. It commands the question of love as a place of knowledge: What, apart from love, is known?

We will distinguish carefully between knowledge and truth. Love *produces* a truth of the situation in which disjunction is a law. This truth is composed infinitely. It is therefore never presented in its entirety. All knowledge *relative to this truth* is arranged as an anticipation: if this truth which can never be complete *will have taken place*, what judgements will there be—not true ones, but truthful ones? Such is the general form of knowledge under the condition of a generic procedure, or procedure of truth. For technical reasons, I call this *forcing*.[2] One can *force* knowledge through a hypothesis about the having-taken-place of a truth *in progress*. In the case of love, the in-process of truth has a bearing upon disjunction. Everyone can force knowledge about sexuated disjunction on the basis of love, under the hypothesis of the having-taken-place.

But this forcing is *in* the situation where love proceeds. If the truth is one, the forcing, and therefore knowledge, are removed from the disjunction of the positions. What 'man' *knows* and what 'woman' knows about love, on the basis of love, remains disjointed. Or again, the truthful judgements made about the Two on the basis of its opening as the result of a decisive event cannot coincide. In particular, knowledge about sex is itself irremediably sexuated. The two sexes are not unaware of each other, they know that they are truthfully disjointed, which is more serious.

Love is the stage on which proceeds a truth about the sexuated positions by means of an inexpiable conflict of knowledges.

Truth is at the point of the un-known. Knowledge is truthful and anticipatory, but disjointed. This disjunction is formally representable in the instance of the Two. The position 'man' supports the division of the Two, this intervening period in which is fixed the void of disjunction. The position 'woman' maintains that the Two endures in wandering. I have had the opportunity to propose the following formula: the knowledge of man organizes its judgements on the *nothing* of the Two; the knowledge of woman on the *nothing but* the Two. One could say: the sexuation of the knowledge of disjointed love:

1. The following truthful masculine statement: 'that which will have been true is that we were two and not at all one';
2. The following feminine statement, just as truthful as the first: 'that which will have been true is that we were two and we were not otherwise'.

The feminine statement aims at being as such. Such is in love its destination, which is ontological. The masculine statement aims at the change of the number, the painful breaking-in of the One through the supposition of the Two. It is essentially logical.

The conflict of knowledge in love exhibits that the One of a truth is always exposed as both logical and ontological. This sends us back to book 3 of Aristotle's *Metaphysics* and to the admirable commentary on it which has recently appeared entitled *La Décision du sens*.[3] The enigma of this text of Aristotle's lies in the passage between the ontological supposition of a science of being as being, and the crucial position of the principle of identity as a pure logical principle. This passage, in general, is no more passing than that which goes from the position woman to the position man. The authors of the commentary show that Aristotle passes 'in force' in the ardour of an intermediary style—the style of the refutation of the Sophists. Between the ontological position and the logical position there is only the medium of refutation. Thus for each position engaged in love, the *other* position only allows itself to be reached as a sophistry which needs to be refuted. Who does not know the exhausting fatigue of these refutations, summarized in the end by the deplorable phrase 'don't you understand me?'? We might say that this is a nervous form of the declaration of love. Someone who loves well understands badly.

I cannot believe that it is by chance that this commentary on Aristotle, which I embellish here in my own way, was written by a woman, Barbara Cassin, and a man, Michel Narcy.

This could be the final word, but I will add a postscript which brings me back to where I started.

The existence of love makes it seem retroactively that in disjunction the position 'woman' is singularly the bearer of the relation of love to humanity. That is, humanity conceived as I conceive it, as the function $H(x)$ which ties an implicative knot with the procedures of truth, either s (science), p (politics), a (art) or l (love).

Still a trivial commonplace, you will say. It is said: 'woman' is such that she only thinks of love, 'woman' is being-for-love.

Let us cross the commonplace with courage.

It will be maintained that the position 'woman' is such that the *subtraction* of love affects it with inhumanity for itself. Or again that the function $H(x)$ only has a value to the extent that the generic amorous procedure exists. The implication is:

$$\text{not } a(x) \rightarrow \text{not } H(x)$$

This implication means that the prescription of humanity only has a *value* to the extent that love exists. Or again: that 'woman' is she (or he) for whom the subtraction of love *devalues* $H(x)$ in all its types, and firstly in the most connected, or crossed, types. Without doubt this explains the excellence of women novelists.

It is not the same for the position 'man': each type of procedure gives through itself value to the function $H(x)$, without taking into account the existence of the others.

If we admit that H is the virtual composition of the four types s, p, a, and l, we can suggest that for the position woman, type l (love) *knots the four types* and that it is only under this condition that H, humanity, *exists* as a general configuration. And that for the position man, each type is a *metaphor of the others*, this metaphor standing for an immanent affirmation, in each type, of humanity (H).

We will then have the two following schemata:

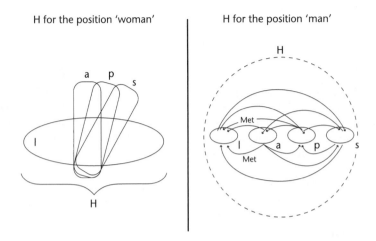

These schemata make clear that the feminine representation of humanity is at the same time conditional and knotted, which allows a more complete perception and if need be a more direct right to inhumanity. However, the masculine representation is at once symbolic and divisive, which can create a lot of indifference, but also a greater capacity to conclude.

Is it a question of a restrained conception of femininity? Does the commonplace, even elaborated, find a scheme of domination which could be summarized thus: the access to the symbolic and the universal is more immediate for men? Or, we could say, less tributary than an encounter.

It could be objected that the encounter is everywhere: *any* generic procedure is a post-decisive-event.

But this is not the essential thing. The essential thing is that love, as I have already said, is the guarantee of the universal, since only it can elucidate the disjunction as a simple law of *a* situation. It can also be said that the value of the function of humanity $H(x)$ is dependent, for the position woman, on the existence of love: the position woman demands for $H(x)$ a guarantee of universality. It only knots the components of H on this condition. The position woman maintains, in its singular relation to love, that it is clear that 'for all x, $H(x)$', whatever the effects of disjunction, or disjunctions (since sexual disjunction is *perhaps* not the only one).

213

Accepting the habitual denoted by ∀ of the universal quantifier, the connection between love and humanity could be reformulated as follows:

$$l(x) \rightarrow \forall\ x)\ H(x),$$

in which we find that the position woman alone *makes all of Humanity*.

Here I am operating a supplementary turn of the screw in regard to the Lacanian formulas of sexuation. Very schematically: Lacan departs from the phallic function $\varphi(x)$. He assigns the universal quantifier to the position man (for every-man), and defines the position woman by a combination of the existential and negation, which comes down to saying that woman is not-all.

This position is in many ways classical. Hegel, saying that woman is the irony of the community, indicated just this existential side effect through which a woman breaks into the all that men strive to consolidate.

But this is in the strict effect of the exercise of the function $\varphi(x)$. The clearest result of what I have just said is that the *function of Humanity $H(x)$ does not coincide with the function $\varphi(x)$*.

Regarding the function $H(x)$, it is in effect the position 'woman' that supports the universal totality, and it is the position 'man' which metaphorically disseminates the virtualities of composition—one of H.

Love is that which, dividing $H(x)$ from $\varphi(x)$, brings back to women, in the entire range of procedures of truth, the universal quantifier.

Notes

1. A. Badiou, *L'Être et l'événement* [*Being and Event*]. (Paris: Seuil, 1988).
2. Translator's Note: The French word used—*le forçage*—refers to the process of artificially maturing plants in greenhouses etc.
3. B. Cassin, *La Décision du sens: le livre gamma de la Métaphysique d'Aristote*. [The Decision of Meaning: Book Gamma of Aristotle's Metaphysics] (Paris: Vrin, 1989).

Is it Necessary to Look for the Universal in the Difference between the Sexes?
The 'Formulae of Sexuation' in Lacan

Monique David-Ménard*

Monique David-Ménard was born in Lyon in 1947. She completed a masters degree in philosophy with Paul Ricœur (Université de Nanterre, 1968), a doctorate in clinical psychopathology and psychoanalysis with Pierre Fédida (Université Paris VII, 1978), and a doctorate in philosophy with Jean-Marie Beysade (Université Paris V, Sorbonne-nouvelle, 1990). She is currently Professeur de Chaire Supérieure and a director of research at the Université Paris VII, Denis Diderot. She is a practising psychoanalyst, and presently serves as the Secretary of the Scientific Commission of the Société de Psychanalyse Freudienne.

David-Ménard's work has focused on the relations between psychoanalysis and philosophy, the status of notions of the universal, and questions of sexual difference. Her revisions of the history of European philosophy proceed by attending to details, issues, and texts considered marginal in traditional interpretations of pre-eminent figures such as Kant (the philosopher with whom she has been most engaged). David-Ménard uses psychoanalysis as a critical lever for revealing the manner in which fantasies, madness, pleasure, and sexuality operate actively in the production of philosophical discourse. She shows how philosophical and scientific concepts are implicated in and transformed by psychoanalysis. In *La Folie dans la raison pure*, she demonstrates that Kant's *Critique of Pure Reason* is traversed by a debate with madness, represented by the writings of the 'spirit-seer' Emmanuel Swedenborg. Her *Hysteria from Freud to Lacan* complicates notions of the biological and the symbolic by interpreting the paradoxical relations between body and psyche in the history of psychoanalytic discourse on hysteria.

In *Les Constructions de l'universel: Psychanalyse, philosophie* (Paris: Presses Universitaires de France, 1997) David-Ménard critiques the exclusionary concept of the universal which has organized much of Western thought. In her reading of

---

* 'Faut-il chercher l'universel dans la différence des sexes: Les "formules de la sexuation" chez Lacan', in *Les Constructions de l'universel: Psychanalyse, philosophie* (Paris: Presses Universitaires de France, 1997), 91–119. Reprinted by permission of Presses Universitaires de France.

Kant with Sade and Lacan, she links dominant constructions of the universal and the hierarchical binaries which inform philosophical problems to the domain of sexual difference, tracing the 'confusion' within constructions of the universal to feelings and phantasms disavowed in the writing of male philosophers. 'Faut-il chercher l'universel dans la différence des sexes? Les "formules de la sexuation" chez Lacan', argues that Lacan develops a conception of the universal in order to think sexual difference and the relation between the sexes. Through her critique of Lacan's recourse to Frege's bivalent logic and his figuration of woman as enigma, David-Ménard elucidates the prestige of the masculine universal in what becomes, in Lacan's thought, an imperative of dividing the world into two sexes, male and female. David-Ménard's writings on sexual difference often turn around questions about the production of knowledge: in *Les Constructions de l'universel* she suggests that it is not coincidental that for the most part, it has been women and sexually dissident men who in their reading and writing have insisted upon the interconnection of drives, phantasms, and concepts in rational thought.

The notion of universality, which since Kant has taken on the modernity of rationalism, is a confused notion, in the Cartesian sense. For Descartes, a confused idea is an idea that becomes confused with another idea: the idea of universality never only designates the universal quantity of the logical subject of a proposition, but, in the systematic nature of Kantian reason, it maintains through its unifying function the memory of Aristotelian logic, which only established a formal logic by binding it to an ontology. In effect, for Aristotle, the serial nature of the universal was linked explicitly to the consideration of the whole: 'I term "commensurately universal" [*katholou*] an attribute which belongs to every instance [*kata pantos*] of its subject, and to every instance essentially [*kath'auto*] and as such [*ê auto*].'[1] In this definition from *Posterior Analytics*, the universal must not be understood only in extension, it is not only that which is common to all individuals of a certain class, nor to all the subjects included in one gender. It is that which belongs to each of them essentially, to each being considered by himself, that is to say, necessarily. This necessity brings the idea of totality into play in two ways: it is through its own internal determination that a notion is universal, and thereby that a notion is inscribed in the consideration of the universe, of the ontologically ordered whole, the hierarchy of which is respected by the valid linkings of our judgements. The Aristotelian syllogism, by working on the positive or negative quality and the universal, particular, or singular quantity of our judgements, allows the linking of the necessary propositions which bring the pluri-vocal nature of the meanings of beings to the analogy by means of which each region of being is related to the others. The universal does not need to free itself from the link between logic and ontology; on the contrary, it bases the fact of their being joined in a logic of attribution, since the function of the liaison of the copula 'to be' which links subject and predicate is so tightly secured in the absolute and analogical sense of to be. All of this is quite well known.

When, with Kant, the absolute loses all ontological determination— the whole as such being unknowable—one should expect the serial or extensive determining of the universal to become autonomous and to lose its previous reference to both the hierarchical order of the universe and to the idea of necessity inherent to a being deployed by the *logos*. Of the Aristotelian whole, the unconditional part remains: the moral law applies to every act and to every man and it presupposes the consideration of a universe of rational will, not a real universe (which would be to return to an ontological hierarchy) but a possible one that Kant names the 'kingdom of ends'. Certainly, the quantity of our judgements when we say 'the law applies to every man' no longer describes man's place in the universe, generically speaking. However, the unconditional nature of the law is well defined by Kant as being that which takes the place of Aristotelian necessity.

We need to say 'the place of' because Kant defines the unconditional by the place he assigns to it on the basis of the articulation of theoretical and practical reason:[2] the world is as a whole unknowable. In particular, one cannot say of the world with any certainty that it is caused by a certain cause, nor that it is not caused, that is to say, that it is free. This closing of all that is that we call world, universe, or cosmos, is no longer a matter of knowing, and we should expect that small word 'whole' to have nothing more to do with *a* whole, a totality. However, in virtue of the fact that the idea of a free cause, although it cannot be established as a reality, is not however, 'impossible in the sense of contradiction',[3] the idea of the whole, unknowable but thinkable, allows the freedom of the will to be inscribed in the place of what was for Aristotle the totality. This totality leaves a space, and this notion of totality changes its name to become known as the unconditional. The unconditional is that which is submitted to no restriction, which applies absolutely, in every case. As the idea of the world, of the whole of phenomena, is an idea not-impossible-in-the-sense-of-contradiction, it can help us to think the freedom of the will: the idea of a free cause, of a cause not caused by anything other than itself, which, in rational cosmology, determines the world without allowing us to know the world, and also determines our relationship to the law. Duty is a determining of our will which is caused only by itself according to practical reason, and it is therefore its absoluteness which established the serial or extensive fact that it applies to every case. With Kant, there is no more universe, but the linking of the logical function of the universal to an absolute persists. That is why we have so often seen the whole return in the philosophy of action or of art—the whole henceforth referred to as the unconditional with the serial. Further, it is in order to make apparent the collusion of the unconditional with the absolute that Sade, in a more radical way than Kant, reduces it to a logical function which could shelter anything—the arbitrariness of sexual pleasure [*jouissance*] as well as the transcendence of the law.

These returns of the whole are not always justified by Kant; a single return of the absolute constitutes the object of a privileged attempt at justification: the attempt through which the idea of freedom is installed in the place of the Aristotelian cosmos in the system. The term 'All Things' remains bound to the idea of totality and to the idea of a world's internal unity because Kant tells us that human action can be analysed like the phenomena of external nature—that is, as a linking of causes and effects—and in such a way, however, that the question arises as to whether our conduct is not also, without contradiction, able to be thought as being determined by nothing in advance, as free, as unconditioned. It is this linking of the cosmological to the practical that Kant himself returns to in saying that the idea of freedom is the keystone of the critical edifice. But if by any chance it were artificial or optional to compare human action to an external phenomenon, if the analogy between external nature and our nature were not the right way in which to tackle the analysis of human action—in particular if this analogy were based upon an overly simple conception of the reality of so-called internal phenomena—then there would no longer be any need to characterize as not impossible either freedom of will, or the absolute reduced to an unconditioned imperative. And, by way of consequence, the serial nature of the universal would be independent from the idea of totality. To say that freedom is the keystone of the critical edifice is thus also to indicate the weak spot of the latter: why is it necessary to trace the analysis of action on to the categories defined for a completely different purpose—that is, the knowledge of external phenomena? Why would it be necessary for reason to be one in all the domains over which it exercises its power? It is obvious that the doctrine of the universal, far from answering this question, actually prevents it from being asked, because it presupposes that the question of the quantity of the judgements that we pronounce concerning a field of our experience is the decisive question which decides the rationality of the thought which apprehends this field. But this choice in never justified. Rather, it is practically brought into play by philosophical rhetoric; and with this practice, the effect of universe returns to the transcendental logic of the universal.

Now, the decision that is made to unify all aspects of reason by insisting upon the quantity of our judgements in every domain is made to the detriment of something else: Kant does not think the process through which a desire is detached from an object. He mentions that this occurs, but the logic of the universal presents the process as complete, at the point where it can be summarized in a table of the functions of the universal, and he ceases to conceive of detachment as an aesthetic process, as a liaison between what he names the faculty of desiring and the faculty of experiencing pleasure and pain.

The notion of universality, far from founding all its uses, sets in motion a strategy which condenses the multiple registers of thought: an anthroplogy which believes it can separate the faculty of desiring and the faculty of experiencing pleasure and pain, a theory of the human before the law, an analogy between external phenomena and our conduct which can supposedly be analysed via the same categories, a doctrine of judgement. In contemporary rather than modern terms, that is to say, Freudian terms, the Kantian universal knots a conception of the indifferentiation of the objects of desire with a conception of the subject of the law. This strategy is summarized in the pseudo-principle according to which 'No one can know *a priori* which representation will be accompanied by pleasure and which by pain', that is to say according to which the order of perceptible desires does not give rise to the *a priori*. Rationally, there is a heavy price to pay, in terms of blind spots and cessations of thought, for the universal to unify the fields of human existence.

HOW LACAN COMES TO THE UNIVERSAL

It is all the more astonishing to note that in contemporary thought, however, the universal, through the bias of the quantification of the judgements which summarize our experiences, continues to be invoked when it is a question of gaining new regions of thought. For example, when Jacques Lacan wanted to demonstrate the impact of the paradoxes constitutive of sexuation, he turned, as we know, to the universal quantifier in order to invent a formal way of writing which might take into account what he called the 'sexual non-relation'.

Let us to begin by considering his formulations as they are first introduced in *Encore*, Book XX of *The Seminar*.[4]

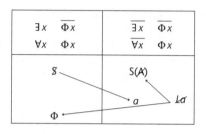

If *PHI* designates the phallic term whose corporal image is the penis subjected to the ordeal of tumescence and detumescence, which makes it an appropriate materialization of the fact that possessing the penis escapes a mastery which wants to be all-powerful, it is possible, according to Lacan, to define the masculine and the feminine through the distinct ways in which the sexes relate to the phallus as signifier of lack.

A man is a being to whom the conjunction of the following two propositions applies: 'For every *x PHI*(*x*)' and 'There exists an *x* such as not *PHI*(*x*)'. This translates into the logic of prepositional functions the Freudian myth of *Totem and Taboo* which says that that which establishes for a man his capacity to be a man is the acceptance of being worried by castration, and this goes hand in hand, in the unconscious, with the certainty that one man at least, the father of the primitive horde, was not castrated, because he derived sexual pleasure from all the women. In the myth, the brothers in league killed the all-powerful father, and their solidarity as men was founded upon the common repression of this murder. Lacan rereads the myth to show that the extraordinary certainty of omnipotence is limited from inside by the repression it suffers: in the unconscious persists the idea that at least one man was not castrated, but that allows the acceptance that real men are castrated, that is to say that that which makes them men is marked by lack. From the logical point of view, a universal propositional function is linked to a particular existential proposition which denies the former. The passage from the omnipotence of the pleasure principle to the limitation of the reality principle is made through this transaction.

Lacan, then, transforms the Aristotelian notion of contradiction, which consisted of excluding from linkings of valid propositions the succession of an affirmative universal proposition and of a negative particular. We do not have at the same time: all men are mortal and Socrates is not mortal. For a logician the criterion of contradiction is invaluable because it permits the exclusion of a sequence of propositions which link by implication an affirmative universal proposition and a negative particular. This kind of policing of language is less easy to establish when it is a matter of the opposition of two contrary qualities: such a man can be at the same time young and old, depending on the way in which and on the moment when the predicate is appointed to the subject. The quantitative criteria of universality or of the particularity of the logical subject will not then be sufficient to constitute valid propositional links. For Aristotle, knowing what to exclude is to know what to admit of as true. Lacan admits of as true two contradictory propositions, in so far as they describe most accurately the compromise which is established in the subject and which divides him between a residue of belief and the recognition of his castration. He adds, moreover, that popular wisdom sees more clearly than the logician in this matter, when it states that the exception confirms the rule. Therefore he proposes that the solidarity fixed up between an affirmative universal and the negative particular which contradicts it takes into account what thought owes to the process of castration. From this point of view, we can see Sade as a highly competent logician; since, as we have seen, he sets up the exception of the sexual pleasure of one man as that which brings into play the universality of the rule by breaking it. Therefore, for Lacan, it is not simply a matter of demonstrating that castration, in so far as it determines sexual identity, can be expressed in terms of a logical formula; it is also a question of showing that logic bears the mark of the paradoxes of sexuation. The relationships that Lacan established between logic and psychoanalysis are mutual. On the other hand, from the clinical point of view, it is a question of showing that all realization of desire for a man belongs to that which 'exceptionally' violates a law, the only way of assuring its general validity ...

As for women, the same establishing of the reality principle is summarized by the following formula: 'There exists no x such that is not $PHI(x)$', coupled with 'it is not the case that for all x $PHI(x)$'. This formula is read as 'There exists no woman who does not have a relation to the phallic function'. This proposition is joined with the following: 'It is not all of a woman that is linked to this function.' This

221

also corresponds to the idea that women are not marked in every respect by castration; something in that which makes them women is played out in the excess in relation to this determination which, however, concerns them as well. So be it: a woman is 'not all' in the phallic function. This usage of negation modifying the universal quantifier is a move away from Frege[5] on Lacan's part, since the latter proposed to only hold in logic the negations effecting the functional proposition itself and not those effecting a term. At the same time, Lacan adds a remark which has inspired many contentious or admiring debates depending on the case: the formulas which summarize the feminine position do not make any universal quantifier positively intervene, and this implies that *Woman does not exist, Woman* in general is a formula deprived of meaning, which means both that for a man, such as *Don Juan*, even if women are *mille e tre*, they do not form a class, and that women do not inscribe in the universal what is, however, the very modality of thought. Women are never capable of saying of what consists, universally, their position as woman; they are excluded from the nature of things which is the nature of words,[6] excessive in relation to the Symbolic which presupposes the usage of propositional functions endowed with the universal quantifier. Whether one praises this excess which establishes the feminine as being close to a mythical position or whether one deplores it, since it implies that women cannot think themselves by themselves, it nonetheless remains that between women and the universal Lacan establishes a non-relation. These affirmations follow those of Freud, who came to write that women's capabilities of sublimation are limited, for at 30 years old the mobility of the displacements of the sex drive and object substitution is fixed for women in a supposedly immutable and quasi natural sequence: faeces, the father's penis, a child ... The advocates of the 'formulas of sexuation' comment that it is not at all a matter of discrediting women, that, besides, the formulas concerning the feminine bring into play existential propositions which have many other logical properties than shutting in the subjects concerned in the enclosure of the universal, and that, furthermore, women are partially inscribed in the phallic function, and that, what is more, a biological man can be inscribed in a feminine position and a biological woman in a masculine position, without any problem. Lacan, in a way which could not be indifferent to the theme of this essay, separates woman and universality. The question is now to discover if and how the critique that I am presenting of the notion of the universal is inscribed in this debate.

To this end, it is first of all necessary to understand in what sense, for Lacan, sexuation is a matter of logic. For, if it is only a question of describing an asymmetry in relation to the phallic issue, it was perhaps unnecessary to return to the different positions of men and of a woman to the universal. While returning to logic, Lacan proposes first of all in *L'Étourdit*,[7] in effect, to describe the paradox of which sexuated existence consists through the resources of grammatical and rhetorical subtleties: 'Man is not without having it, woman is without having it.' This is the brilliant and complex formula through which Lacan defines sexuation. This phrase brings asymmetry into play through a subtle dialectic of 'to be' and 'to have' which turns around an already general term, as the being of *PHI* would want it, but reduced here to an allusive and elided personal pronoun. On the other hand, 'not being without', this expression questions the logic of attribution through a negation which alleviates the ontological weight of the verb 'to be', indicating in this way that that which defines sexuation escapes all ontological determination, and thus without doubt escapes Aristotelian logic. But we can see how the expression remains dissatisfying: for, from the feminine side, sexuation still appears to be linked to being and this whiff of naturalism could not satisfy the Lacanian thesis according to which sexuation subverts the ontology on which Western thought has relied since the Ancient Greeks. The recourse to logic, and more particularly to the logic of Frege, who broke from the Aristotelian onto-logic allows Lacan to radicalize his contention.

THE NUMBER IN FREGE AND THE UNARY TRAIT (*EINIGER ZUG*) IN FREUD

Lacan borrowed from the logician Frege at two separate times: in 1961–62, the still unpublished seminar *L'Identification* made it apparent that, in order to think the subject of the unconscious which is formed through a series of identifications with characteristics of the Other, which Freud named the unary trait, *eineger Zug*,[8] it was useful to refer to Frege's philosophy of the number. In *The Foundations of Arithmetic*,[9] Frege examines 'Views on unity and one'. In this text, he puts an end to a confusion which has affected the notion of number from Euclid up to and including Liebniz, and consists of not distinguishing between two meanings of unity: we wrongly presuppose that 1 is both the first of the whole numbers and a unity which plays a part in the formation of every number in the series of whole numbers. Now, this confusion in arithmetic between the first of the whole numbers and the law of composition of any number makes of the number an internal unity based on the model of a logical subject endowed with properties which are its attributes: in this case, writes Frege, 'we are . . . taking "one city" in the same way as "wise man" '. The lack of rigour in the definition of the number is the result of what mathematicians pledge to the logic of predication. 'Being isolated, being undivided, being incapable of dissection—none of these can serve as a criterion for what we express by the word 'one'.'[10]

These famous examples are decisive, for it is a matter of nothing less than breaking away from the idea that language could say 'being' thanks to the liaison function of the verb 'to be'. It is not only a question of pointing out that a number is not a property like any other; it is a question of rethinking, by isolating the number and redefining it, as one sees it, all the pretensions of our language: in the logical description of valid inferences, the verbs 'to be' and 'to have'— the bearers of an ontological illusion—are made to disappear. From then on, two types of propositions can be distinguished that will be treated differently, according to whether they are endowed with the truth value *True* or the truth value *False*. This is why Frege only retains as negation that which has a bearing upon the entire proposition, which means that these two sorts of propositions can be distinguished, negations having a bearing upon terms which confer upon the negative a deceptive significance. It will no longer even be necessary to say: 'it is true that or it is false that . . .'. A written sign will suffice to mark this difference and to dispel the illusions linked to the usage of the verb 'to be' and of negation.

In the first instance, then, Lacan, while citing Frege's thought in its coherence as a whole, is mainly interested in the thought on the number and on unity. For in identification in psychoanalysis, there is a phenomenon whereby the subject is counted, which implies a loss of the subject's 'being': the subject is counted as one by a decisive trait which comes to him from the Other. The trait results from the fact that the subject has had to lose his first objects of incestuous love, and that he becomes what remains of these objects, or again, that which, of the constituting Other, has marked him; he becomes identical to this or that trait of the Other. In the same way that Frege does not conceive of the number as an internal unity, Lacan does not conceive of the subject as a being, but as traits which inscribe that which comes to him from outside of him in what he believes to be the most 'himself'. The subject is not a 'self', if he is constituted by identifications; the unary is not the one. It prohibits the whole, the unified. On the other hand, it appears in the repetitions which punctuate the life of a subject as what he has that is 'unlike any other', that is *einzig*, as Freud said. The recourse to Frege's theory of the number allows Lacan in 1961–62 to assert more convincingly than could the theory of the signifier on its own that the subject formed in the relationship between the unconscious and the conscious is a function and not a being. Furthermore, in 1961–62, Lacan insists upon writing: in identification, the subject of the unconscious touches upon the foundation of logic, for with the unary trait is a question of an inscription logically anterior to any effect of significance.

SEXUATION AS PROPOSITIONAL FUNCTION, QUANTIFICATION, EXISTENCE

Secondly, the reference to Frege serves to think not only identification, but also 'that which supplements that which never ceases to not be written in the sexual relationship'. The sexual relationship determines nothing by itself, but the writing of the relationship of the sexes to the phallus supplements the theoretical impossibility constituted by the effect, in thought, of the misunderstanding which constitutes human sexuality. Thought *takes into account* this experience of inadequacy through which the relationship of the sexes to the phallus can be written. It really is a question of 'taking into account', in effect, because this transformation of logic, which writes existence instead of speaking being, far from dismissing the criteria of quantity in judgements, reinforces and redefines its importance. When Frege replaces the subject and predicate of the old logic through another elementary cutting up of the propositions which distinguish function and argument, everything about the proposition changes: even if the subject and the predicate could be general, variable terms, in a propositional function the terms are general in another sense. The function is the position of a relation; the argument, which contains a variable, completes the function and to the function becomes joined the concept which is defined as the function which has, for every argument, a value of truth. For example, $2x + 1$ is a function, and $2x + 1 = 0$ is a concept which receives, for every value of the variable, a value of truth. In mathematics, the latter is called the solution to an equation. But, in the logic which relies upon mathematics in order to redefine natural language, the solution becomes the value of truth. Even if everything changes, from a predicative proposition to a propositional function, in both cases the logician assigns an important role to the category of quantity. Aristotle distinguished the quantity of the subject from a judgement; Frege defines the quantifier of propositional functions in the new logic. A consideration of quantity occurs three times in this logic: first, the arguments bring into play variables which represent universal terms; secondly, the notion of the extension of a concept introduces the number into the differentiation between True and False, since there are two values of truth, and only two, for a concept which is defined on the basis of a function. Finally, as we saw with the examples '0 moon' and 'four noble horses',[11] Frege no longer speaks of existence except through quantification: 'Affirmation of existence is in fact nothing but the denial of the number nought'.[12] The referential function of language in Frege bends itself to the principle of only admitting of a relationship between words and things through the expedient of quantification (except for proper nouns, which are logical constants).

What could interest Lacan in this project? This attempt to redefine existence drastically seemed to him appropriate to the dissolution of the ontological illusions which are no longer only attached to identification, but also to the encounter of the sexes in so far as it does not create a relation, if it is not through what the sexuated positions which take the phallus as function can write about it, since a real relation between the sexes is lacking.

In the still unpublished seminar *La Logique du fantasme*, and especially in the sessions of 12 and 19 April 1967, Lacan situates the sexual act in the following way: he states first of all that there is no sexual relation. This means that the subject, in the sexual act, does not meet the object of his desire that the other seemed to him to harbour. This object can never be the instrument of a completeness which, thanks to the other, would be experienced through sex, for it represents the part of the subject which is inadmissible to himself and which the sexual encounter confirms as inadmissible through the element of dissatisfaction which is always part of it and which is symbolized for both sexes by the tumescence and detumescence of the penis. This object confronts the subject with that part of himself which escapes him at the same time as it constitutes him, the object called '*a*'.[13] That the object is the cause of desire implies that it is internal to the structure of the subject. No other would strictly speaking be able to give it, even if the sexual act maintains the illusion that this is possible. It is here that the question of the 'sexual non-relation' unites with that of identification: Lacan affirms that the object '*a*' is not only linked to the sexual act, but to another act, directly linked to the unconscious, and which is radicalized through transference, that is, through repetition. Now, the object which causes desire and stimulates the repetitions whereby the subject acts that which he cannot say, creates a return back to the unary trait, that is to say, to the traumatic mark left by the other in the structure of the subject's desire. This object, while determining *a priori* the sexual encounters of a subject—for an other is only real if he seems to contain this object—is, according to Lacan, covered up by the illusion of union and of being borne by the sexual act. On the contrary, it can appear as such in the sublimatory destinies of the sex drive [*pulsion*] which renounce direct sexual satisfaction and allow to emerge in the productions of the subject the blueprint of the object, constitutive and inadmissible. In Lacanian thought, sexual dissatisfaction—the act never totally satisfies the desire—is the phenomenon understood by the theory of repetition and the sexual non-relation. This also implies, metapsychologically, that one cannot say that the sex speaks: the unconscious speaks about the sex, but the sex itself is not the unconscious. In the meeting of sexuated bodies, the sexual identity of each partner is only found through what fails and what sends each one back to his desire: 'If the sexual relation existed, that is what it would want to say: that the subject of either sex can touch something in the other on the level of the signifier, I mean that this would allow for, in the other, neither conscious nor even unconscious, simply agreement.'[14] Lacan takes it upon himself to undo this illusion: the term of sexuality signifies that indeed the sex does not speak, even if the signifying material of the unconscious is sexual. And, from the point of view of the relation between the sexes, this implies that the referent of the sexes cannot be found, that there is no essence of the masculine and the feminine that the sexual act could fulfil. We could discuss certain aspects of the Lacanian theory of the sexual non-relation,[15] but, for our present purposes, it is necessary to grasp the point at which in a theory of clinical psychoanalysis the critique of ontology and, more precisely, the recourse to quantification in the writing of the formulas of sexuation come into play.

In the unpublished seminar of 1971–72 entitled '... Ou pire ...', but also in published texts such as *L'Étourdit* or the *Seminar* Book XX: *Encore*, Lacan attempts to expose how a writing which captures the masculine and the feminine in the net of quantification can take account of 'that which never ceases to not be written' in the relationship between the sexes.

The first thing that interests Lacan, as we have seen, is that dealing with the relationship between the sexes in terms of function and argument allows a universal judgement and an opposing existential judgement to be joined in order to describe the male position. The same function, modified by a negation which bears first of all upon the existential quantifier and the function, and then upon the universal quantifier ('not all'), allows the female position to be described. One can grasp through these formulas that the two sexes do not enter into a relation with each other in a mode of complementarity, although they are both determined in relation to the same function, the so-called phallic function. But it is also decisive that, in their conjunction which is not a relation, the masculine and the feminine are here functions; there is man and there is woman, or rather, there is a woman (since *Woman* does not exist) without there being any question of essence. Here Lacan plays on the harmonics of the word 'function', in particular in the description relating to man: the existential judgement, which has no guarantee in being, whereby a man detaches himself from the universality of men, describes the risky, exceptional aspect of the act through which a man presents himself as a man. It is thanks to the exception which formalizes the existential, he says, that 'There is such a thing as One'—to be said '*Y a d'l'un*'—or still yet '*Unien*',[16] that will then be distinguished from the unary of the identifying trait... It is by always taking himself to a greater or lesser degree for the father of the horde, whilst at the same time knowing that all men are castrated that a man is man. Furthermore, the polysemy of the formulas, in the reading of them proposed by Lacan, allows us to understand that the problematic of the object-cause of desire, which allows at least one man to escape from the universality of men taken as a totality, and the myth of the father, that is, he of the at-least-one who was not castrated, are joined. The existential judgement corresponds, then, to the particularizing function of the object which is the only element which might make man escape from the tautology of the universal. This tautology refers back to the narcissism of the phallic function which reunites men. (It should be noticed that in Lacan the expression of the phallic function has a contradictory meaning depending on the context, as though it referred back to the two propositions of the 'man' position at the same time.) The interpretation of the formulas from the man side is then as follows: only the particularizing adventures of his desire for women which incarnate that which, in himself, cannot be thought in the symbolic, make of man a man. Thus, what the negative existential judgement formalizes would be the only woman to have escaped the universal which defines a man as an element of a whole; *a* man exists by being an exception in relation to that which shuts him up in the universal of the masculine, that is to say, which shuts him up in the narcissism of the love which leaves no transcendence to the other.

In order to put forward this theory, Lacan uses a remark from Frege which he reinterprets to his own ends. According to Frege, universal judgements are pure possibilities: 'It is true that at first sight the proposition "All whales are mammals" seems to be not about concepts but about animals; but if we ask which animal that we are speaking of, we are unable to point to any one in particular.'[17] In an existential proposition, on the contrary, it is said that one has at hand a man and that he is such and such. On this point, Frege 'corrects' Aristotle, for whom the universal proposition, characterizing beings capable of internal intelligibility, had a greater dignity than the particular. With the logic of functions, one can no longer speak of ontology but rather of reference,[18] and universals are conditionals, implying nothing referential. In Lacan, the privilege of the existential 'which says no to the phallic function' is linked to his attempt to conceive the male position as an act, with no guarantee in being but establishing an existence.

A contrario, when Lacan says 'Woman does not exist', he is not only expressing that she is not defined as universal in what is feminine about her, but also that her sexuated position is not an act which could be written as an exception to a rule. Certainly she is in excess in relation to the universality of a symbolic determination, but this excess does not bring her into existence; the negation 'not all' does not refer to an act, rather, it refers back to an enigma which Lacan affirms as necessary... Woman is an enigma for herself and for men.

It will certainly be necessary to overturn things in saying that it is because men need to put the feminine in the place of the enigma that they are led to say, in a mirror image in relation to themselves, that women find themselves in a position of excess in relation to the symbolic, incapable of saying from what their sexual pleasure is made. Women's sexual pleasure only seems so mysterious to men because it does not have as a lever the only kind of orgasm representable for them, and of which their sex organ is the emblem. We will soon have to consider the formulas of sexuation as the formalization of a masculine fantasy, which is not without interest, but which does not take us much further than Kant's idea that women have no sense of duty, and that they do not experience guilt, that they are only moral when morality seems beautiful to them. By writing that which supplements the sexual non-relation, Lacan thought he would find a formulation of the non-relation which would be unscathed by what he was describing, that is, sexuation. Without doubt he failed in this. But it is not vital to criticize Lacan if we want to understand from what the prestiges and the virtues of the universal are made, and the reasons for his admiring recourse to Frege.

TO WHAT EXTENT CAN A PSYCHOANALYST BE A LOGICIAN?

Let us note first that the interpretation that Lacan gives of his ideography of sexuation does not comply with the strict requisites of the determination of a model in logic. Rather, he superimposes in an approximate way a theory of the symbolic and the object upon the notations of his formal language. But this is not in itself a criticism which renders his work invalid, because this kind of formalism is thought-provoking.

On the other hand, in the usage of the term universality, an ambiguity subsists in the holistic or totalizing character of the 'all men' to which 'for every (x)' refers. On the one hand, this description of the non-relation between man and woman always centres on a single term, the phallus; on the other hand, this description is not completely liberated from the prestige of totalization, even though this prestige has been denounced. In the seminar '... Ou pire ...', 17 May 1972, Lacan insists first of all upon the difference between the One of attribution and what he names the One of difference, showing how propositional functions avoid the idealism of philosophy linked to attribution: in effect, a proposition such as 'man is good' questions the capacity of the subject to truly live up to this attribute. This is the departure of Platonic philosophy: 'One always finds, moreover, enough reasons to show that he is capable of not living up to this attribute, of experiencing a failure to fulfil it'. Greek grammar encourages, through attribution, the confrontation of what is sensed with its conceptual and from then on ideal model. The truth of something that can be sensed is in its imperfect participation with the intelligible thing which founds it. On the contrary, in a propositional function, the concept is constructed in such a way that it is by the number that one responds to the question of truth: 'When it is a matter of articulating its consequence, this One of difference has as such to be counted in what is stated about what it founds, which is whole and is made up of parts. The One of difference is not only countable but must be counted among the parts of the whole.' Thus Lacan senses that the concept and the propositional function bring the number not only into the quantification of the argument, but also into the relation of the functions to the value of truth. And that, in this very measure, the sets which define the functions do not have to be conceived as totalities which would be unified by an essential attribute. The One which appears with the existential quantifier—there is one existential quantifier which says that $PHI(x)$ is not the truth—is a One of difference exactly because it counts itself and because the fact of which the judgement consists has the truth value True. This is why Lacan adds: 'For, of course, it remains nonetheless that the relation *for every man* is what defines man, attributively as *every man*; What is every or all, what are *all men* in so far as they establish one side of this articulation of substitution, this is the point we take up again...?' Curiously, in this moment of reflection, only the One of the existential proposition is called the One of difference, the universal quantifier of the second judgement which characterizes the masculine seems less strictly subject to Frege's principles and to rejoin a whole which is more classic in construction. Is this a hapax? No: in the famous text of the following year, *L'Étourdit*, Lacan, insisting on the fact that in human reproduction life reproduces the question of what is sex, he adds, 'It's from there that it becomes necessary for us to obtain two universals, two *wholes* sufficiently consistent to separate in speaking beings—who, being beings, believe themselves to be beings—two halves so that they do not become too muddled in coiteration when the speaking beings manage it.'[19]

This text, more accomplished in its formulation than the seminar '... Ou pire ...', is quite remarkable. In it, one can grasp what motivates the return of a conception of the pre-Frege and pre-holistic universal in Lacanian thought on sexuation. In its imperative nature, this sentence of Lacan's indicates how two aspects of sexuation which are perhaps less interdependent than he states, are linked. For in the end, analysing the non-complementarity of sexual relations could form the object of a theory of the misunderstanding without the sexes being theoretically separated into two wholes. Everything that Lacan proposes about the exception to the law of castration in order to define the male position, and everything he proposes about the 'not all' to define the female position, rests on the idea that the analysis of an essential failure in the sexual relation presupposes that two halves which are wholes are constituted in advance. But why is it necessary to think the non-relation only by presupposing that the sexes are wholes? In what way does the fact that there are two ways of ruining the sexual relation, according to the formulation in *Encore*,[20] imply a consideration of totalization of each of these ways, which is from then on supposed to form a half which is a whole? The question which Lacan evokes, of knowing whether there are in fact, in any society, as many men as women, and the theoretical consideration of the number of humans to be divided between these two ways of ruining the sexual relation—are these questions really indispensable, as Lacan says, to the analysis of the non-relation? And do they take into account the importance of quantification in Frege, when a psychoanalytic model of Frege's logic is presented? In fact, in the quoted sentence from *L'Étourdit*, the 'it is necessary' introduces not a division, but also an unconditional which develops, as in Kant and without any more justification in Lacan than in Kant, into a serial universal which is presupposed to form a totality. More precisely, the imperative 'it is necessary' has here a double meaning: it is a theoretical possibility, a hypothetical imperative, in the Kantian sense, in that the quantification of the functions permits us to better think sexuation as a division between two terms. But there is something else in this 'it is necessary': the categorical imperative for human beings to be determined as man or woman; this imperative is categorical in that one cannot escape such an obligation, which is practical in nature, in the Kantian sense, since it takes over from a theoretical impossibility in the determining of an essence of the sexes. Secondary to this, the division can be treated as a necessity in the framework of a bivalent logic; there is no possible third sex, even if infantile sexuality forges all sorts of fantasy representations of the sexes and their relation to children's existence.

LACAN WITH KANT

There is here, in effect, a configuration analogous to that of the Kantian categorical imperative: it is because there is no essence of the moral

Good preceding its determination by the law that the law obliges us unconditionally; and Kant comments upon this unconditionality by 'installing' the unconditional of liberty in the place of this thinkable but unknowable totality that is the idea of the world. The theoretical effect produced by this metaphor is the representation of the moral world as a whole formed by the rational will that Kant names the 'kingdom of ends'. Lacan carries out an analogous construction: it is because there is no essential determination of sex in human beings— the biological and cultural givens always leaving a remainder which our fantasies build upon—that these fantasies, far from being left to the indeterminacy of the imaginary, are framed by the obligation to chose between two sexes. For Lacan, sexuation demands, to the extent that it obliges us to choose between two sexes and that it only disposes of one signifer, the phallus, to compensate for the uninscribable part of this difference, the return to Frege's bivalent logic which, further, makes it possible to take account of the a-ontological character of this obligatory choice. But, because of its double meaning, this obligation is still thought by Lacan in Kantian terms, as though the two halves which it evokes were taking the place of an essential determination of sex which cannot be found in psychoanalysis, in the same way that knowledge of the world could not be found in Kantian cosmology. The analogy which persists in Lacan between the unconditional of the moral law and the unconditional of sexuation has the effect of impos- ing the representation of the sexes as 'two halves which are wholes', a representation which doubtless has the same metaphorical status as the kingdom of ends in Kant... As a result, the reform it is hoped for in returning to Frege in order to think sexuation as a function is arrested, since a pre-Fregian notion of the totality 'works' under quantification.

The ideography of sexuation is, in fact, at the bridge of two philo- sophical—or anti-philosophical, as Lacan likes to say—gestures: the appeal to Frege is joined with the memory of the reading of Kant. The phrase 'it becomes necessary for us to obtain two universals, two *wholes* sufficiently consistent . . .' only makes explicit one of these components, the appeal that Lacan makes to Frege: for there is a homology between the bivalence of truth values and the bivalence of the sexuated positions between which human beings are divided.

The fact that there is no third term in the matter of sex, that the choice must be made between masculine and feminine, resembles the notion of the bivalence of the concepts in logic: a concept is a function whose value is always a truth value, that is, either True or False. But, for

Frege, it does not follow that True and False are halves which can be analysed as wholes. When the logician encounters this question, which is implied in effect by one of the uses he makes of quantification, Frege hesitates; in fact he is less affirmative than Lacan: 'One could also say that to judge is to distinguish from the different parts at the heart of the value of truth ... To each meaning to which a value of truth corresponds, one could associate a certain way of dividing the value of truth. But it must be said that I use the term "part" in a very particular way. I have transposed the relation of the part to the whole, from a proposition in its denotation, and I call the denotation of a word part of the denotation of a proposition when the word is itself part of the proposition. This form of expression could be contested, however ... It would be appropriate to invent a more appropriate expression.'[21] Frege makes explicit the problems presented by the fact that he makes of the value of truth the denotation of an expression and that this implies the consideration of the proposition as of a whole which is made up of parts, a determination which he does not think from the beginning according to the rules that he is in the process of defining. The traps of totality await the logician who wishes to retranslate natural language into propositional functions, and he says so. But Lacan is less prudent: the theme of the division of human beings into two denotations of propositions—man or woman, like true or false—is transformed in writing into an imperative; the theoretical necessity of the division is supposed to note the unconditional imperative of the choice without the nature of this correspondence being questioned. But, as a result, the sexes are called without any justification 'two halves which are wholes'.

On another important point, the return to Frege finds, at the same time as a real interest, a limit which Lacan does not make explicit: the conception of the relationships between words and things cannot be the same for a logician and a psychoanalyst. This is true in general, but in particular when the logician is someone who thinks the logical content of a thought by discrediting on principle all consideration of the subject who conceives. Frege is exclusively interested in 'thoughts with no bearer'; and his polemic against any form of psychologism, even that of Husserl, is well known. Even if it is not a matter of confronting logic and psychoanalysis with each other, it seems initially that this would not be problematic: the subject of psychoanalysis, writes Lacan, is the subject of science, understood as the subject who falls from the formation of modern sciences, at the same time produced by them and discarded... until psychoanalysis picks him up again, one might say. And it is instructive to notice that Freud and Frege, who were contemporaries, exclude themselves from this epistemological process even though they are part of it. For example, they each published an article on negation in the 1920s. But it is one point on which this concordatory epistemology, according to the expression Georges Canguilhem applied to Bachelard, does not hold: for a psychoanalyst a language [*langage*], provided that it respects the syntax and the semantics of a well-constructed language [*langue*], does not open out onto reality. This question arises when Lacan again takes up Frege's discussion of universal propositions, which are only conditional, and of particulars, which have a reference. If the reality principle is defined as an internal modification of the pleasure principle, can we trust in psychoanalysis the sole particular proposition—the negative existential proposition—to assure that it has a real subject as reference, different from a universal pure possibility? In psychoanalysis, one never takes as evidence the relationship of a proposition to a reality. One examines how, in this proposition, a desire is organized, and how the omnipotence of this desire is limited. Only this limitation, which realizes itself through the resources of discourses, ensures a relation of the fantasy to reality. In psychoanalysis, the relationship to reality is gained through a process; it is not the simple correlation of a referential power of language which is supposedly a spontaneous virtue. In other words, multiple resources can be put into place—resources that might constitute a subject's relationship to that which is other than the all-powerfulness of his desires. The logical organization of discourse is not in itself a sufficient guarantee of a being released from the hallucinatory character of the desire which is realized in the dream but also in other forms of thought. This release is on condition that the 'fact' that certain objects which are represented as having previously procured satisfaction have been lost is inscribed in the work and the rules of the formation of dreams, of symptoms, and in the rhetoric and style of discourses. Perhaps psychoanalytic theory can rejoin logic in a timely fashion by showing what the existential proposition can do theoretically to describe the masculine. But the divergence between the analysis of discourses generally carried out by the logician and the psychoanalyst is what makes the interest of their agreement on certain points valuable.

WHAT A WOMAN CANNOT NOT KNOW CONCERNING THE PHALLIC FUNCTION

The formulas of sexuation are of great interest when it comes to suggesting paths for research in the paradoxical question of sexual difference: the masculine, says Lacan, only escapes from the tautology of the phallic by posing itself as an exception, which corresponds, in the clinic of the sex life, to the only way out of the narcissism of this love which is determination by an object, the cause of desire, but encountered in a male or female other. A woman, on the contrary, is not in a position of exception to a rule, even if, as a woman, she is only determined in part by the object and only partially caught up in the phallic problematic. Lacan maintains that she is in relation to what is lacking in the Symbolic, but in such a way that she can say nothing about it, since precisely her affinity with this weak point of the Symbolic as Other places her outside discourse.

Now it could well be that a woman is not outside discourse, but is difficult to inscribe in the formulas of sexuation which are seemingly cut to measure in order to formalize certain aspects of masculine sexuality. That sexuated love is the experience of an asymmetry and of an impossibility of defining sexual identities in terms of essence, that this dimension of experience crosses not only existence but also thought, even the most formal or conceptual thought: on these fundamental points Lacan dared, following Freud, to put forward a great deal. But, concerning the description of the point of impossibility which polarizes the encounter between the sexes, he without doubt failed to make of the feminine anything but the internal limit of the masculine. The formulas of sexuation themselves suffer from this tautology which Lacan describes as characteristic of the masculine position in the universal affirmation of phallicism, with its contradictory addition. And the consequence of this is that the expression 'not all in the phallic function' does not open in Lacan onto any different position.[22] A feminine position, instead of standing out on the horizon as a beyond of the phallic with only a negative determination, cannot be thought as a sexual position, that is to say, relative to the address that it seeks in the fantasy, which has the condition of concerning the opposite sexuated position, of being defined by this relation, but without being the negative reflection of this relation. The 'not all in the phallic function' is rather an otherwise than a beyond; and this otherwise does not leave intact this phallic function 'itself', that is as it is thought

236

in the enclosure of the universal from which the only conceivable exit is a point of flight which cannot be determined. What defines a woman, or women as such—whether existential or universal is of little importance here, the important thing is that it is not a question of the indefinite *Woman*—what defines a woman, then, is that during sexual pleasure [*jouissance*] she cannot not know that the penis is not the phallus. A woman cannot share the certainty of the unity of the penis and the phallus which characterizes both the men it relates to and Lacan's theoretical position in the formulas of sexuation. And this is not because there could be a beyond the phallus, whether it could be said or not, but because the very experience of a sexual relation which, in effect, is not a relation, implies, for a woman, the experience of the disjunction of the penis and the phallus. She is dependent upon the penis as an erotic object, but the very experience of her dependence in the register of the object means that she cannot take the penis as the emblem of the symbolic. The covering over of the phallus with the penis upon which Lacanian thought is constructed in the formulas of sexuation falls in this very same way. Besides, the dependence of a woman on the object-penis is itself very specific: to the extent that phallus and penis coincide, that is, to the extent that she remains in love with her father in an incestuous way, the object is not for a woman what falls from the symbolic, still less the relic of the symbolic, as is the case for the Lacanian object *a*. And when she distances herself from incest, the penis of a man to whom she is linked is no longer raised to the status of representing the symbolic order. This is why, as I said, in sexual pleasure [*jouissance*] a woman discovers that the penis is not the phallus.

The formulas of sexuation are interesting in that their formalism makes it possible to give a different interpretation of the 'not all' to that imagined by Lacan—since the meaning relates to the imaginary—when he situates the feminine at the edge of that which he conceived for the masculine. The 'not all' can also be understood in the following way: a woman, precisely because she does not not know phallic *jouissance*, cannot not know that the penis of a man who makes her come [*jouir*] is not the phallus. Certainly, it makes her dream and desire, but it is not for her endowed with all the symbolizing powers lent to it by this man upon whom she depends. The symbolizing of what there is to be represented as being potentially lost follows different substitutive paths, which, in the course of an analysis or in our love life, do not have the status of enigma lent to them by Lacan. When it is a matter of being able to experience sexual pleasure or being able to lose, symbolization does not necessarily put a woman in relation to the weak point of the Other which, at the same time, would situate her outside discourse. The mystical position for a woman is doubtless only one of the symbolizing strategies, that which responds as a mirror image to what certain, but not all..., men expect of her. This is of some consequence, because it is a matter of recognizing that the phallus is not the emblem of all access to the symbolization of desire.

If one accepts the idea that a written formula can have several interpretations, it will be noticed at the same time that the new interpretation of the 'not all', through the simple fact that it exists, contests that the Lacanian interpretation of the feminine as an enigma is a truth independent from a sexuated position of its author. A woman is not an enigma for herself, even if she can only be imagined as such from the point of view of man; and ideography does not put an end to the fact that there are two versions of the non-sexual relation: by confusing, as is perhaps inevitable for a man, penis and phallus, Lacan inscribes a dependence of women in relation to the Symbolic which consists in the fact that as women they would be undefinable in the symbolic. But if there is dependence, on the feminine side, this concerns rather the relation to the penis as object than the relation to the phallus. In effect, in describing the paths particular to the experiences of loss, of perdition, and of substitution of objects on the woman's part, one does not make of feminine sexuality an entity independent of its relationship to the masculine. Lacan is right to say that the feminine is not a nature, but neither is it a beyond of the masculine, nor a sexuated position less marked by the object 'a' and directly in relation with what the Other is lacking. It is rather that the relation to the object and to the Symbolic, for a woman, is more distinct than for a man, to the extent that a part of what she has to be represented as lost only secondarily concerns her relation to the masculine; to the extent also that, in the register of the object, the dependence whereby she finds herself in relation to the penis colours differently the function of the object: for Lacan, the object of the drive is what unmakes and renders destitute the idealization of the figures of the Other in love. As such, even if this object is phenomenologically approached in an encounter, following the example of the fascinating objects which captivate Alcibiades in Socrates, the essential thing is that it divides the subject and causes his desire. Equally in feminine sexuality the object divides the subject; what makes a woman come [*jouir*] appears as having been encountered in an other but corresponding to what is the most inadmissible and yet constituent part of herself. But the penis of a man comes to represent the object slightly differently than, for example, the object 'breast' for a man: the identity of the penis and the phallus corresponds to the preservation of incestuous investments for a woman, and, in this register, the Symbolic remains eroticized, an eroticization that the phallic position of masculine partners perpetuates. On the other hand, if there is an access for the feminine to the Symbolic, it is from the dissociation of the object—penis and the phallus and from the transformation of the 'experiences of the worst' linked to the feminine by the maternal intermediary.

It is, then, the whole mechanism of the relations between objects and the collision of the subject with the symbolic, the modalities of the distinction between love and desire as well, which differ in the feminine from the masculine or the theory of the masculine.

If one sticks to the various interpretations which can be made of the 'not all in the phallic function', one will be led to dissociate this Lacanian idea from that according to which Woman does not exist: women exist from the experience that, in *jouissance*, a woman cannot not know that the penis is not the phallus. For a man, the confusion of the penis and the phallus is systematic, and the experience of the object does not undermine this postulated identity. On the contrary, for a woman, it is the very relation to the object which invalidates this equivalence; she postulates it only from the point of view of the incestuous investments which link her to a father and of her concern not to disturb the postulates by means of which men support themselves, as if they were universal truths, untouched by fantasy. In the register of the object, the eroticization of dependence is presented differently, even if it is true, in both sexes, that the object is what causes desire and what, in doing so, confronts the subject with that which divides him. This is only otherwise accentuated for a woman, since the penis of a man represents for her what she depends upon: it is never that which makes her come [*jouir*] without condensing some decisive aspects of what makes her desire. But this dependence upon the penis does not cover up the symbolizing virtue lent to the phallus in order to attain to loss. Here, the paths of the erotic and the symbolic do not become confused.

To affirm that there is no sexual relation—that is, that love is not the *parousia* of the Other,[23] nor the experience of a completeness and a complementariness of the sexes—does not have the same meaning for a woman and a man. Through this affirmation a man comments upon his relation to the object which brings him out of phallic narcissism. Through this formula a woman comments upon the experience of the dissociation of the penis and the phallus. She cannot not know that what she expects from the man in the phallic problematic will be disappointed, since the penis is not the phallus, and it will return in any case, even in a happy experience, to symbolize alone, or through other paths, the part of her sexual life to which the phallus cannot give form.

In interpreting differently to Lacan the 'not all in the phallic function' which figures in the formulas of sexuation, it has happened that I have made no more reference to the question of the universal, either to characterize two halves which are supposed to be wholes, or to evoke the serial nature of objects of desire. At the same time, I have made reference to processes of substitution of objects through which human beings of both sexes represent to themselves what it is to be man or woman in the experience of having to seek, to abandon, to lose, and to find again that which could make them come [*jouir*]. This correlation is not hazardous: for a woman, in the moment of thought which is ours, thought is not first defined by the universality of what it states or writes, but by the process of detachment from a statement in relation to the subjective position of the individual who makes the statement—the universality of the thought which is produced in this way being merely a consequence of this process. There is also a relation between the fact that, in sexual *jouissance*, a woman cannot not know that the penis is not the phallus and the theoretical processes which revaluate the concept of universality. In effect, as we have seen, the symbolization of that which can be lost does not coincide with the problematic of the object, while the formulas of sexuation presuppose their coincidence by the covering over of the phallus and the penis. The recourse to the universal quantifier and the idea that it is necessary to obtain two wholes distinctly situated in relation to the universal quantifier are in solidarity with this unification.

It appears, then, that the present work is complicit in the problem it presents, and could not be untouched by it: no theoretical formulation which thinks the paradoxes of sexuation could overhang the problem which it elaborates, not even thanks to ideography. And this is because the concept of the universal itself as well as its diverse manifestations is not untouched by this articulation. In theory, taking this fact into account makes it possible to situate a thought, which defines itself as universal, as a thought which detaches itself, by means of a specific textual work, from that which demands it in the order of the drive. What differentiates a philosophical text from a literary text or the narrative of a dream is the way in which philosophical statements go to great lengths to ignore this detachment at work. What characterizes philosophy is this challenge, which sometimes succeeds, to the always active link between drive and thought. The challenge succeeds in the conceptual order which is rewarded with violence[24]—perhaps with a murder of self—carried out by the passage to the concept. But the murder of self does not cancel the conceptual success. It is not necessary to recoil in horror from philosophical systems by highlighting the extent to which they are based upon a challenge to the self. It is true that such a refusal is at work in the exposition of their systematic nature. But that does not invalidate the order of conceptual truth that they produce, for, in virtue of the eminently substitutable nature of objects of the sex drive, the objects of a thought can be other than sexual in the strict sense. Sexuality invests a great deal into what is not sexuality. The paradox of philosophy is that this investment can work as an exclusion of the active link between drive and thought. But the fantasy process, when it is made readable, does not suppress the heterogeneity of the conceptual work which it helps to produce.

Notes

1. Aristotle, *Posterior Analytics* [Online], trans. G. R. G. Mure. Available at **http://classics.mit.edu/Aristotle/posterior.1.i.html**
   Translator's note: the Greek terms are included in the French text.
2. Emmanuel Kant, *The Critique of Pure Reason* (London: Palgrave Macmillan, 2003).
3. See Monique David-Ménard on this idea, in *La Folie de la raison pure: Kant lecteur de Swedenbourg* (Paris: Vrin, 1989), chs. 1 and 5. Since the appearance of this work, an American philosopher has also related the Kantian notion of antinomy of pure reason to the paradoxes of the relationship between the sexes. Cf. Joan Copjec, 'Sex and the Euthanasia of Reason', in *Read my Desire: Lacan against the Historicists* (Cambridge, Mass.: MIT Press, 1994).
4. J. Lacan, *On Feminine Sexuality: The Limits of Love and Knowledge*. Book XX. *Encore 1972–1973*, trans. Bruce Fink (New York: W.W. Norton, 1998).
5. G. Frege, 'Negation', in *Logical Investigations*, trans. P. T. Geach and R. H. Stoothoff (Oxford: Blackwell, 1970).
6. J. Lacan, *On Feminine Sexuality: The Limits of Love and Knowledge*.
7. J. Lacan, *L'Étourdit*, in *Scilicet* (Paris: Seuil, 1973).
8. S. Freud, *Psychologie des foules et l'analyse du moi* (Paris: Petit Bibliothèque Payot, 1981), ch. VII: 'L'identification'.
9. G. Frege, *The Foundations of Arithmetic: A logico-mathematical enquiry into the concept of number*, trans. J. L. Austin (Evanston, Ill.: Northwestern University Press, 1996).
10. Ibid. 58.

11. Not included in this extract.
12. Ibid. 65. On the importance of this text for philosophy and psychoanalysis, see C. Imbert, 'Pour une structure de la croyance', in *Nouvelle Revue de Psychanalyse: La Croyance*, 18 (1978), 143.
13. Translator's note: the '*a*' stands for *autre*, meaning 'other'.
14. From an unpublished seminar of Lacan entitled *La Logique du fantasme* [The Logic of the Fantasy].
15. See Monique David-Ménard 'Ce que la psychanalyse change à l'acte. Le lit de l'amour et le lit de l'analyse', in *L'Acte sexual, Revue international de psychopathologie*, 19 (1995), 358 (Paris: PUF).
16. Translator's Note: Lacan plays here with the aural similarity between the French for 'There is such a thing as One' ('*Y a d'l'un*') and the word '*Unien*' which sounds similar to 'union'.
17. Frege, *The Foundations of Arithmetic*, 60.
18. On the possible readings of Frege, see A. Benmakhlouf, *Gotleb Frege: logicien, philosophe* (Paris: PUF, 1997).
19. *L'Étourdit*, 12.
20. Lacan, *On Feminine Sexuality: The Limits of Love and Knowledge*.
21. By going a bit further into the thought on the feminine, one can avoid renewing completed theories on the supposedly obvious relationship of the maternal to the feminine, which Lacan does not question: 'She finds the cork for this *jouissance* [based on the fact] that she is not-whole—in other words that makes her absent from herself somewhere, absent as subject—in the *a* constituted by her child' (Ibid. 35).
22. M. David-Ménard, 'L'identification hystérique', in *Les Identifications* (Paris: Denoël, 1987).
23. Lacan, *On Feminine Sexuality: The Limits of Love and Knowledge*.
24. When Monique Schneider shows that the passage from universal theory to the Œdipus complex in Freud is in solidarity with a challenge of certain decisive elements of his childhood, she is convincing. Without doubt, in the field of psychoanalysis where theory is more directly in relation to the subjective position of its author, one can conclude that the Œdipus theory is false. But that is not sufficient to conclude that any universal theory is false, cf. 'L'Universel et ses humeurs', in *La Raison et ses raisons, Io, Revue International de Psychanalyse*, Erès (1993).

Further Reading

Introduction

JUDITH BUTLER, *Gender Trouble: Feminism and the Subversion of Identity* (New York: Routledge, 1991).

SIMONE DE BEAUVOIR, *The Second Sex*, trans. H. M. Parshley (New York: Random House, 1989).

TINA CHANTER, *The Ethics of Eros* (New York: Routledge, 1994).

HÉLÈNE CIXOUS, 'The Laugh of the Medusa', in *French Feminism Reader*, ed. Kelly Oliver (New York: Rowman & Litlefield), 257–75.

CHRISTINE DELPHY, 'Rethinking Sex and Gender', in *French Feminism Reader*, ed. Kelly Oliver (New York: Rowman & Littlefield, 2000), 63–76.

JACQUES DERRIDA, *Of Grammatology*, trans. Gayatri Spivak (Baltimore: Johns Hopkins University Press, 1976).

MOIRA GATENS, *Feminism and Philosophy: Perspectives on Equality and Difference* (Bloomington: Indiana University Press, 1991).

ANN ROSALIND JONES, 'Writing the Body: Toward an Understanding of *L'Écriture Féminine*', in *Feminist Studies* (Summer 1981).

JACQUES LACAN, *Écrits: A Selection*, trans. Bruce Fink (New York: Norton, 2004).

DOROTHY LELAND, 'Lacanian Psychoananlysis and French Feminism: Toward an Adequate Political Psychology', *Hypatia* (Winter 1989).

TORIL MOI, *Sexual/Textual Politics: Feminist Literary Theory* (London: Methuen, 1985).

KELLY OLIVER, *Reading Kristeva: Unraveling the Double-Bind* (Bloomington: Indiana University Press, 1993).

MONIQUE PLAZA, ' "Phallomorphic Power" and the Psychology of "Woman" ', in *Ideology and Consciousness* (1978).

DOMNA STANTON, 'Difference on Trial: A Critique of the Maternal Metaphor in Cixous, Irigaray, and Kristeva', in *The Thinking Muse: Feminism and Modern French Philosophy*, ed. Heffner Allen and Iris M. Young (Bloomington: Indiana University Press, 1989).

SUSAN SULEIMAN, 'Writing and Motherhood', in *The (M)other Tongue: Essays in Feminist Psychoanalytic Interpretation*, ed. Shirley Nelson Garner (Ithaca: Cornell University Press, 1985).

Chapter 1. Difference/Indifference between the Sexes

FRANÇOISE COLLIN

Maurice Blanchot et la question de l'éscriture (Paris: Gallimard, 1971).

'Comme si un livre de philosophie avait quelque chose à voir avec écrire',
   Revue des sciences humaines, 1 (1982), 185, 7–11.
Le Rendez-vous (Paris: Tierce, 1988).
Emmanuel Levinas (Paris: Cahiers de L'Herne, 1990).
Le Sexe des sciences (Paris: Autrement, 1992).
Sarah Kofman, ed. Françoise Collin (Paris: Broché, 1997).
Le différend des sexes, de Platon à la parité (Paris: Pleins Feux, 1999).
L'Homme est-il devenu superflu? Hannah Arendt (Paris: Odile Jacob, 1999).
Je partirais d' un mot: le champ symbolique (Paris: Fus art, 2000).
L'Imagination politique des femmes (Paris: L'Harmattan, 2000).
Les Femmes de Platon à Derrida: Anthologie critique (Paris: Plon, 2000).

Chapter 2. A Deceptive Universalism

GISÈLE HALIMI

With Simone de Beauvoir, *Djamila Boupacha* (Paris: Gallimard, 1962); trans.
   Peter Green as *Djamila Boupacha, the Story of the Torture of a Young
   Algerian Girl which Shocked Liberal French Opinion* (New York: Macmillan,
   1962).
Le Procès de Burgos (Paris: Gallimard, 1971).
With Marie Cardinal, *La Cause des femmes* (Paris: Grasset, 1973); trans.
   Rosemary Morgan as *The Right to Choose* (St Lucia: University of
   Queensland Press, 1977).
Le Programme commun des femmes (Paris: Grasset, 1978).
Viol: le Procès d'Aix-en-Provence (Paris: Gallimard, 1978).
Le Lait de l'oranger (Paris: Gallimard, 1988); trans. Dorothy S. Blair as *Milk of
   the Orange Tree* (London: Quartet Books, 1990).
Embellie perdue (Paris: Gallimard, 1995).
La Nouvelle Cause des femmes (Paris: Éditions du Seuil, 1997).
Fritna (Paris: Plon, 1999).
L'Autre Moitié de l'humanité (Brussels: Liège, 1999).

Chapter 3. Versions of Difference

SYLVIANNE AGACINSKI

Philosophie et politique de l'architecture (Paris: Galilée, 1992).
Critique de l'égocentrisme: l'événement de l'autre (Paris: Galilée, 1996).
Politique des sexes (Paris: Seuil, 1998); trans. Lisa Walsh as *Parity of the Sexes*
   (New York: Colombia University Press, 2000).
Le Passeur de Temps: Modernité et nostalgie (Paris: Seuil, 2000).
Parity of the Sexes, trans. Lisa Walsh (New York: Columbia University Press,
   2000).

Chapter 4. Masculine/Feminine: The Thought of the Difference

FRANÇOISE HÉRITIER

L'Exercice de la parenté (Paris: Éditions du Seuil-Gallimard, 1981).

'Semen and Blood: Some Ancient Theories Concerning their Genesis and Relationship' and 'Older-Women, Stout-hearted Women, Women of Substance', in Michel Feher *et al.* (eds.), *Zone 5: Fragments for a History of the Human Body* (New York: Zone Books, 1989), 159–75, 281–99.

Les Deux Sœurs et leur mere: Anthropologie de l'inceste (Paris: Éditions Odile Jacob, 1994); *Two Sisters and their Mother: The Anthropoligy of Incest*, trans. Jeanine Herman (New York: Zone Books, 1999).

De la violence: Séminaire de Françoise Héritier (Paris: Éditions Odile Jacob, 1996).

Contraception: Contrainte ou Liberté?, ed. With Étienne-Émile Baulieu and Henri Leridon (Paris: Éditions Odile Jacob).

Chapter 5. A Little Learning: Women and (Intellectual) Work

MICHÈLE LE DŒUF

'A Woman Divided', *Cornell Review*, Ithaca (1978).

'Simone de Beauvoir et l'existentialism', *Le Magazine*, trans. as 'Operative Philosophy: Simone de Beauvoir and Existentialism', *Ideology and Consciousness*, 6 (1979), 47–54.

L'Imaginaire philosophique (Paris: Payot, 1980); trans. Colin Gordon as *The Philosophical Imaginary* (Stanford, Calif.: Stanford University Press, 1989).

L'Étude et le rouet. Des femmes, de la philosophie, etc. (Paris: Éditions Du Seuil, 1989); trans. Trista Selous as *Hipparchia's Choice: An Essay Concerning Women, Philosophy, etc.* (Oxford: Blackwell, 1991).

'Women, Reason, etc.', *Differences*, 2/3 (1990), 1–13.

'Gens de Science bis: Le Mauvais Genre dans l'éprouvette', *Nouvelles questions féministes*, 15/2 (1994).

'Problèmes d'investiture (de la parité, etc.)', *Nouvelles questions féministes*, 16/2 (1995).

Le Sexe du savoir (Paris: Aubier, 1998; 2nd edn., Paris: Champs Flammarion, 2000).

'Pas toutes les mêmes', *Forum Diderot sur 'De la différence des sexes entre les femmes'*, (Paris: PUF, 2000).

Chapter 6. The Meaning of Equality

JULIA KRISTEVA

La Révolution du langage poétique (Paris: Seuil, 1974); trans. Margaret Waller as *Revolution in Poetic Language* (New York: Columbia University Press, 1984).

Pouvoirs de l'horreur (Paris: Éditions du Seuil, 1980); trans. Leon Roudiez as *Powers of Horror* (New York: Columbia University Press, 1982).

'Interview with Julia Kristeva', in *Women Analyze Women*, ed. Elaine Baruch and Lucienne Serrano (New York: New York University Press, 1988).

Histoires d'amour (Paris: Éditions Denoël, 1983); trans. Leon Roudiez as *Tales of Love* (New York: Columbia University Press, 1987).

'Julia Kristeva in Conversation with Rosalind Coward', *Desire, ICA Documents* (1984), 22–7.

Soleil Noir: Dépression et mélancolie (Paris: Gallimard, 1987); trans. Leon Roudiez as *Black Sun: Depression and Melancholy* (New York: Columbia University Press, 1989).

Les Nouvelles Maladies de l'âme (Paris: Libraire Arthème Fayard, 1993); trans. Ross Guberman as *New Maladies of the Soul* (New York: Columbia University Press, 1995).

Sens et non-sens de la révolte: Pouvoirs et limites de la psychanalyse I (Paris: Fayard, 1996); trans. Jeanine Herman as *The Sense and Nonsense of Revolt* (New York: Columbia University Press, 2000).

La Révolte intime: Pouvoirs et limites de la psychanalyse II (Paris: Fayard, 1997).

The Portable Kristeva, ed. Kelly Oliver (New York: Columbia University Press).

Le Génie feminine, vol. i: *Hannah Arendt* (Paris: Fayard, 1999).

The Crisis of the European Subject, trans. Susan Fairfield (New York: The Other Press, 2000).

Chapter 7. The Difference between the Sexes, a Historical Difference

GENEVIÈVE FRAISSE

Clémence Royer, philosophe et femme de sciences (Paris: La Découverte, 1984).

Muse de la raison: démocratie et exclusion des femmes en France (Aix-en-Provence: Éditions Alinéa, 1989); trans. Jane Marie Todd as *Reason's Muse: Sexual Difference and the Birth of Democracy* (Chicago: University of Chicago Press, 1994).

Opinions des femmes: de la veille au lendemain de la Révolution française (Paris: Côté-Femmes, 1989).

L'Exercice du savoir et la différence des sexes (Paris: Éditions L'Harmattan, 1991).

La Raison des femmes (Paris: Plon, 1992).

Edited with Georges Duby and Michèle Perrot, *A History of Women in the West*, vol. iv: *Emerging Feminism from Revolution to World War* (Cambridge, Mass.: Belknap Press of Harvard University Press, 1993), trans. from *L'Ottocento, Sotria delle donne in Occidente* (Rome: Bari, Laterza, 1991).

With Jean Borreil and Christine Buci-Guicksmann, *La Raison nomade* (Paris: Payot, 1993).

La Différence des sexes (Paris: Presses universitaires de France, 1996).

Les Femmes et leur histoire (Paris: Gallimard, 1998).

La Controverse des sexes (Paris: Presses universitaires de France, 2001).

Chapter 8. Genealogy of Masculinity

MONIQUE SCHNEIDER

De l'exorcisme à la psychanalyse: le feminin expurgé (Paris: Retz, 1979).

Freud et le plaisir (Paris: Denoël, 1980).

La Parole et l'inceste: de l'enclos linguistique à la liturgie psychanalytique (Paris: Aubier Montaigne, 1980).

'*Père, ne vois-tu pas ...?*' *Le Père, le maître, le spectre*, in L'Interpretation des rêves (Paris: Denoël, 1985).

'Interview with Monique Schneider', in Elaine Hoffman Baruch and Lucienne J. Serrano (eds.), *Women Analyze Women* (New York: New York University Press, 1988).

Le Trauma et la filiation paradoxale. De Freud à Ferenczi (Paris: Ramsay, 1988).

La Part de l'ombre. Approche d'un trauma féminin (Paris: Aubier, 1992).

Don Juan et le procès de la séduction (Paris: Aubier, 1994).

Généalogie du masculin (Paris: Aubier, 2000).

Chapter 9. The Excess Visibility of an Invisible Sex or the Privileges of the Formless

CLAIRE NAHON

'Granoff, le freudisme et la puissance animique', *L'Inactuel*, NS 6 (Spring 2001), 117–29.

'Les Transsexuels: d'une certaine vision de la différence', *Cahiers de psychologie clinique* (forthcoming).

'L'envers du miroir ou la psychanalyse à l'épreuve de l'homosexualité', *Cliniques méditerranéennes* (forthcoming).

Chapter 10. The Prescribed Sex

SABINE PROKHORIS

'Le Drame de Faust dans l'œuvre de Freud: Travail de la citation et élaboration métapsychologique', Thesis, 3ᵉ cycle, Psychanal. (University of Paris VII, 1987).

La Cuisine de la sorcière (Paris: Aubier, 1988).

'Psychanalyse, Littérature: Quelle Rencontre', *Les Cahiers Charles V* (University of Paris), 7/11 (1989).

The Witch's Kitchen: Freud, 'Faust', and the Transference, trans. G. M. Goshgarian (Ithaca, NY: Cornell University Press, 1995).

Le Sexe préscrit: la différence sexuelle en question (Paris: Aubier, 2000).

Chapter 11. Is Love a Place of Sexuated Knowledge?

ALAIN BADIOU

L'Être et l'événement (Paris: Seuil, 1988), in *L'Ordre philosophique* series.

Manifeste pour la philosophie (Paris: Seuil, 1989), in *L'Ordre philosophique* series; trans. Norman Madarasz as *Manifesto for Philosophy* (Albany, NY: SUNY Press, 1999).

Le Nombre et les nombres (Paris: Seuil, 1990), in *Des travaux* series.

D'un désastre obscure (Paris: Éditions de l'Aube, 1991).

L'Éthique (Paris: Hatier, 1993); trans. Peter Hallward as *Ethics: An Essay on the Understanding of Evil* (New York: Verso, 2001).

Deleuze (Paris: Hachette, 1997); trans. Louise Burchill as *Deleuze: The Clamor of Being* (Minneapolis: University of Minnesota Press, 2000).

Saint Paul. La Fondation de l'universalisme (Paris: PUF, 1997).

Court traité d'ontologie transitoire (Paris: Seuil, 1998).

Abrégé de métapolitique (Paris: Seuil, 1998).

Petit Manuel d'inesthétique (Paris: Seuil, 1998).

Chapter 12. Is it Necessary to Look for the Universal in the Difference between the Sexes?

Monique David-Ménard

L'Hystérique entre Freud et Lacan: Corps et langage en psychanalyse (Paris: Éditions Universitaires, 1983); trans. Catherine Porter as *Hysteria from Freud to Lacan: Body and Language in Psychoanalysis* (Ithaca, NY: Cornell University Press, 1989).

La Folie dans la raison pure: Kant lecteur de Swedenborg (Paris: Vrin, 1990).

Tout le plaisir est pour moi (Paris: Hachette Littératures, 2000).

Index